Human Rights

Rhetorics and Practices

Books by B. N. Ray

Tradition and Innovation in Indian Political Thought

Political Theory : Interrogations and Interventions

Critical Theory : The Marx-Marcuse Encounter

Liberalism and the Communitarian Challenge

John Rawls and the Agenda of Social Justice

C.B. Macpherson and Liberalism

Contemporary Political Thinking

Nietzsche After Hundred Years

Citizenship in a Globalising World

Gandhigiri

Reading Gandhi

Political Theory and Thought

Indian Political Thought

Foundations of Western Political Thought

Political Philosophy

The Radical Monk: Social and Political Philosophy of Swami Vivekanand

Reading Marx

Human Rights
Rhetorics and Practices

B. N. Ray

R. K. Mahana

Kaveri Books
New Delhi - 110 002

First Published in 2018

ISBN: 978-81-7479-217-4

Published by

Kaveri Books

4832/24, Ansari Road

New Delhi-110002 (India)

Tel: 011-23288140, 23245799

E-mail : kaveribooks@vsnl.com

kaveribooks@gmail.com

Website: www.kaveribooks.com

Typeset at

Delta Book World, New Delhi - 110 002.

PRINTED IN INDIA

Dedicated to

Dr. Achyuta Samanta

Founder of KISS and KIIT

a vigorous human rights activist
who has been protecting, defending and promoting
human rights of the poor, marginalized and voiceless people.

Preface

Much has been written about human rights, too much in all probability. The concept is now so well established in the popular imagination that school children are oblivious too if pop stars include it in their lyrics and wide range of people from politicians to poets variously hail or blame it for all manner of changes in the contemporary world. Human rights has become so pervasively known that it is becoming taken for granted and few people question what it really means or even why it is important. And in terms of the academic study of human rights, the literature is so vast, diverse and imperishable that to read every thought written on the topic would require a life time in a library. In such a situation given the sheer number and range of academic social sciences books published on the subject, the publication of getting one more such as this might appear superfluous. One might be forgiven for thinking that all there is to write about human rights has been written already.

The promise of the book is that this is not so and that – what is more – there is a need to stern the deluge of ideas about human rights with a broad stocktaking intervention that both reassesses the stock of the debate and makes a series of evaluative arguments about which ideas have greater or lesser value. The further promise for writing this book, therefore, is that much which has been written about human rights is lacking in important aspects – analytically, theoretically and empirically – and that the so-called human rights debate has some considerable degree fractured into multiple confused and inconsistent strands.

The book neither claims nor sought to provide a central guide to the human rights literature but it does confine its critical engagement to identification of potential strengths and weaknesses with concepts and thinkers. As it is appropriate for those kinds of texts, it does not adopt a certain overarching position nor develop an overarching argument.

The content of the book, mostly compiled from various sources, guides the reader through the key arguments of leading thinkers, explaining their place in the wider human rights debate and evaluating their critical reception. The book ends with a concluding chapter that examines how thinking about human rights is likely to develop in future.

Contents

Introduction

The principle that human rights must be defended, protected and promoted has become one of the commonplaces of our age. In recent years, as political commitment to human rights has grown, philosophical commitment has waned. Since 1945, political commitment has been expressed in numerous Charter and Declarations of which the 1948 Universal Declaration of Human Rights and the European Convention for the Protection of Human Rights are only the most familiar. Simultaneously, membership of organizations such as Amnesty International has burgeoned, and human rights legislation has increased at both national and international level. Even though, as Lukes points out, human rights are violated virtually everywhere, the principle that they should be defended is asserted virtually everywhere. 'Virtually no one actually rejects the principle of defending human rights'.

For in the same post-war period, the philosophical credentials of human rights have been subjected to considerable scrutiny, and have regularly been found wanting. There is, of course, nothing new in philosophical skepticism about human rights: every undergraduate student is familiar with Bentham's assertion that Natural rights is simple nonsense: natural and imprescriptible rights, rhetorical nonsense nonsense upon stilts. And with Karl Marx's allegation that none of the so-called rights of man goes beyond egoistic man, man as he is in civil society, namely an individual withdrawn behind his private interests and whims and separated from the community. But what is troubling is that these philosophical reservations have increased rather than diminished against a political background almost wholly hospitable to the defence of human rights. Influential strands within political theory thus run directly counter to influential strands within political practice and generate not only a question about the status of human rights in political theory, but also a question about the status of political theory itself. For something, surely, has gone wrong if political theory persists in rejecting as indefensible precisely those concepts which political practice endorses as indispensable?

Our aim in this chapter is to suggest a possible approach between theory and practice: if it is true, as Maclntyre claims, that belief in human rights is a mere superstition, akin to belief in unicorns and witches, then that has worrying implications for practical policies which invoke human rights. If, on the other hand, appeal to human rights is indispensable in practical politics, then that has alarming implications for the direction and self-understanding of a great deal of contemporary political theory. What is needed, therefore, is a clearer understanding of what rights claims actually imply in practice, together with a clearer understanding of the proper role of political theory in informing political practice.

The reference to Bentham and Marx draw our attention to two familiar theoretical problems associated with human rights. Bentham, like Maclntyre after him, is concerned about the ontological status of rights: the invocation of human rights in political argument may appear no more than an appeal to unjustified intuition unless and until evidence is provided for the existence of the rights invoked. And Maclntyre and Bentham are at one in thinking that no such evidence is available. Thus Maclntyre scathingly concludes that the best reason for asserting so bluntly that there are no such rights is indeed of precisely the same type as the best reason we possess for asserting that there are no witches, and the best reason which we possess for asserting that there are no unicorns: every attempt to give good reasons for believing that there are such rights has failed.

Maclntyre's language is, perhaps, unhelpfully provocative: for one thing, claims about what does or does not count as a 'good reason' for the existence of human rights will be every bit as controversial as claims about whether there are such rights. Unlike unicorns and witches, human rights are not thought of as spatio-temporal objects and, for that reason alone, claims about their existence are not controverted by physical and biological science. In this context, therefore, what counts as a 'good reason' will itself be disputable. Nevertheless, Maclntyre's criticism does indicate a genuine difficulty inherent in appeal to human rights. This is that such appeal is naturally interpreted as foundationalist either in the sense that it invokes rights as a basic category, or in the sense that it implies a background which is essentially theological. But appeal to intuition is unduly optimistic and, in the modern world at any rate, theological premises are of limited persuasive power. Either way, theories of human rights purpose to provide a foundation for moral and political thinking, but the foundation is elusive and precarious.

Moreover, it is important to note that these concerns about human rights spring, in part, from a particular conception of what philosophy in general, and political philosophy in particular, can do. Maclntyre's attack on human rights is in fact an attack on a much more general understanding of the nature and purpose of philosophy a conception which arose in the Enlightenment period and which, in Maclntyre's view, has infected philosophy ever since. The aim is to provide foundations for political beliefs and practices and to base those foundations in reason itself. Philosophy aims to justify, and it can justify by showing how the political and moral practices in which we engage are ones which spring from and are sanctioned by reason. But Maclntyre contends that there is no such thing as human reason tout court and consequently no distinctively human rights. All rationality must be embedded in a tradition and therefore foundationalist accounts must hope to find their foundations, not in reason itself, but in the specific conceptions of reason which spring from within specific traditions. But, of course, an understanding of human rights as merely manifestations of a particular tradition is entirely at odds with the universalism implicit in the language of rights.

Other recent writers have gone yet further, arguing not simply that Enlightenment philosophy looks for foundations in the wrong place, but that it is a mistake to look for foundations at all. Thus, Richard Rorty insists that foundationalist theories of human rights are 'outmoded': they represent an understanding of the philosophic enterprise which cannot be sustained and instead of seeking foundations, we should instead look merely for the articulation and extension of our practices through the medium of sentimental story telling.

Though divided in their diagnosis of the problem, both Rorty and MacIntyre are agreed that foundationalist understandings of human rights are doomed to fail. This may be because there is no such thing as distinctively human reason in which human rights can be grounded, or it may be because the search for foundations is intrinsically misguided. Either way, human rights are the product of a confused understanding of the possibilities available to philosophy.

A second, and more specific set of concerns about human rights, as indicated by Marx, is that appeal to human rights presupposes a specific, and contentious, political ideology; the ideology of possessive individualism. Where human rights are asserted, they are asserted as claims by individuals and against the power of the state, or against other individuals. But to assume that rights are needed against the state is to assume that there must always be antagonism between the interests of the state and the interests of individuals, and this is a denial of the kind of ideal society envisaged by socialists and communitarians alike. Furthermore, to suppose that rights are needed against other individuals is, apparently, to endorse an egoistic or selfish understanding of human nature and human flourishing. As Jeremy Waldron asks whether self-respect and human dignity really depend upon being in a position to make strident, querulous, adversarial claims against other people? Is that what it really boils down to? This indeed would be a theory which not only leads to see in others the limitation of my freedom: it would be a theory that leads me to see that my fulfilment, my freedom and my self- realization depend upon my muscular and self-assertive capacity to place limits on yours.

This view of human fulfillment, if indeed it is that which is implicit in human rights, is starkly at odds with socialist or communitarian conceptions of the good society, and for that reason socialists have traditionally had a somewhat ambivalent attitude towards the language of human rights. Some have been anxious to re-interpret human rights in a way which avoids the 'muscular and self-assertive' implications referred to by Waldron. They have argued for the extension of rights to include social and economic rights in addition to the more familiar 'liberty' rights, and in doing so they evince their concern that rights should be more than a means of protecting individuals against the incursions of others; they should also be the socially provided mechanisms whereby people are enabled to realize their potential.

Others, however, have argued that rights are, at root, individualistic and, for that reason, inhospitable to socialist ideals. Moreover, and most troublingly, when rights are extended beyond the traditional rights of forbearance to include rights to the provision of goods necessary for individual flourishing, it becomes difficult to determine exactly which rights may properly be claimed, and exactly what action a commitment to rights demands of others. The point is eloquently expressed by Milan Kundera that the more the fight for human rights gains in popularity, the more it loses any concrete content, becoming a kind of universal stance of everyone towards everything, a kind of energy that turns all human desires into rights. The world has become man's right and everything in it has become a right: the desire for love a right to love, the desire for rest a right to rest, the desire for friendship a right to friendship, the desire to exceed the speed limit the right to exceed the speed limit, the desire for happiness the right to happiness, the desire to publish a book the right to publish a book, the desire to shout in the street in the middle of the night the right to shout in the street.

The anxiety which is implicit in Kundera is that whilst the traditional rights, rights of forbearance, appear to make negligible demands on others, these more extensive rights, rights to provision, result in almost unlimited demands on others. It seems, then, that we are faced with a dilemma: if rights are simply rights of forbearance, then they may be satisfied but, so understood, they are vulnerable to Marx's criticism and do indeed imply egoism and individualism. They imply that we owe to others no more than forbearance and that showing care and compassion, of obligatory at all, is a much less pressing, or 'strict' obligation. But if we extend rights beyond rights of forbearance in an attempt to avoid the Marxist criticism, the consequence is that the list of rights grows uncontrollably, as does the list of demands made on others by the rights holder.

Moreover, these two kinds of anxiety about rights are connected: Raymond Plant refers to human rights as "providing foundationalist political philosophy with what is probably its greatest intellectual challenge" (1991: 291) and we are now in a position to see why this is so. Without foundations a theological background, or stipulative metaphysics human rights seem ontologically precarious and there is a danger that appeal to them will simply degenerate into Kundera's universal stance of everyone toward everything'. Yet the metaphysical or theological foundations which rights require are unavailable to us in the modern world: we eschew the metaphysical assumptions which would make rights talk legitimate. However, once the search for foundations has been abandoned, there appears to be no constraint on the list of rights which may be claimed: rights become merely an alternative way of referring to needs, interests or desires.

Constructions of Rights

In response to these anxieties about human rights, some modern political philosophers have abandoned the foundationalist approach in favour of what is known as a 'constructivist' account of human rights. This strategy attempts to renounce both foundationalism and appeal to raw intuition. One of its most familiar incarnations is in the early work of John Rawls, who aims to derive rights from assumptions about rationality without appealing either to a theological background or to implausibly rich metaphysical assumptions. Of course, in doing this, Rawls asserts what Maclntyre denies, namely that there is such a thing as human rationality independent of a tradition, and that the human capacity for rationality can provide the starting point, if not the foundation, of a defense of human rights. By expounding his theory in this way Rawls aims to avoid the charge of metaphysical extravagance often leveled at rights theories. Equally, however, he also aims to avoid relativism, and to do so by emphasizing a conception of rationality which is thin enough to be plausibly asserted of all human beings. In this way, it aims to tread a path between realism and relativism: by renouncing the search for foundations, whether metaphysical or theological, it aims to avoid realism, and by insisting upon a conception of human reason which can be asserted of all human beings, it aims to avoid relativism. As Waldron argues that the human rights must be characterised by the scope of the claims being made rather than hint at anything about their justification. The term refers to universality and a commitment to equality and non-discrimination, particularly across races and peoples. Particularly, it leaves open the question of justification.

Thus, this understanding of human rights carries with it an understanding of the proper aspirations of political philosophy which is significantly different from that criticized by Maclntyre. It does not construe rights as justificatory entities, but as universal commitments, and in consequences it sees philosophy as being, in some part, a matter of articulating rather than justifying practical political policies: what is articulated is a universal rationality.

There are, however, serious problems associated with this understanding of human rights, and with the conception of philosophy which it implies. There are only two such problems here. Firstly, and as has already been indicated, we may have reservations about whether there can be a conception of rationality thin enough to be attributable to all human beings, yet simultaneously rich enough to generate a theory of human rights. Put more directly, we may wonder whether there is, in fact, any space between realism and relativism which Rawlsian theory can inhabit. Critics like Maclntyre argue that Rawls's conception of rationality is no more nor less than an account of what we in modern Western liberal democracies deem rational and that therefore while Rawls' account may appeal to 'people like us', it can and should carry no weight with people who inhabit entirely different kinds of community. 'What' we may ask is the point of saying to a person quite unlike ourselves who has lived and whose ancestors have lived quite happily with some practice or other for generations? This practice violates your human rights. Indeed, Rawls himself appears to have been moved by considerations of this sort, but the difficulty for him is that the more he is persuaded by these considerations, the more relativist his final position becomes, and the less compelling will his theory be as a justification of intervention in societies where human rights are, or appear to be, under threat. In order to justify intervention in alleged cases of rights violation, we need something stronger than an account of human rights premised on a conception of rationality which applies only to 'people like us'.

The second problem which confronts a constructivist account of rights is that of specifying exactly which rights there are. Just as the socialist attempt to extend rights beyond the traditional rights of forbearance generated a difficulty about proliferation of rights claims, so here there is a comparable problem of specifying the set of rights implied by a constructivist theory. For example, Rawls' theory aims to identify a set of rights which secures maximal liberty for each compatible with equal liberty for all, but it is not clear that maximal liberty can be uniquely and uncontentiously identified nor, for that reason, that a set of rights which secures maximal liberty can be specified that there is no unique way of accommodating different rights. There are indefinitely many ways of describing possible actions and hence indefinitely many ways of picking out sets of copossible, equal rights. Again, the rejection of the metaphysical and theological premises originally associated with rights theories renders problematic any attempt to specify exactly which rights there are and why.

What conclusions are then to be drawn from this rather dispiriting parade of anxieties and reservations about human rights in political theory? As an attempt to justify political practice, human rights do indeed seem at best 'outmoded': we lack, or reject, the metaphysical and theological premises which made a justificatory account of rights plausible, and the aspiration of political philosophy to provide a foundation from which political practice could be entirely justified to all people at all times has been fatally damaged by that lack, or loss, of faith. But this conclusion is primarily a conclusion about the pretensions of a certain sort of political philosophy, not a conclusion about the political practice of appealing to human rights: it tells us that insofar as philosophy ever aspired to provide a complete justification of or foundation for political practice, and aimed to fulfill that aspiration through a theory of human rights, it was doomed to fail. Or at least that, in the conditions of modernity, it can no longer serve that purpose.

In response, writers such as Rawls and Gewirth have argued for a constructivist account of human rights, one which eschews metaphysical and theological baggage, but which nevertheless aims to go beyond the purely stipulative. Such an account begins from human reason, or agency, and attempts, not so much to justify as to articulate what reason implies in the realm of political practice. However, this project too is flawed, since it is not clear that there is the requisite space between realism and relativism. Again, this conclusion is a conclusion about the aspirations of political theory, but it is more worrying than the previous one, for it suggests that human rights are problematic on either understanding of what philosophy can do. Understood as a set of claims about the foundations of political practice, philosophy reveals that we no longer have, and maybe never did have, such foundations; but understood as an attempt to articulate what we believe, philosophy reveals that human rights are just that they are what we in Western liberal democracies believe. They are not, as they purport to be, universal and timeless, nor do they justify intervention in the practices of others. Either way, political theory appears to lead to the conclusion that we are not entitled to the conception of human rights which political practice requires.

Reconstructing Rights

In *Modern Political Thought*, Raymond Plant states that human rights express our conviction that the boundaries of nations are not the boundaries of moral concern. And so they do. This, indeed, is one reason why human rights present foundationalist political philosophy with its greatest intellectual challenge. In asserting that there are human rights, we aspire to transcend political and cultural boundaries and to declare some things right (or wrong) irrespective of what is required by specific cultures or within specific nations. Now if we begin from political theory, the task which faces us is to explain exactly how we can be entitled to transcend those boundaries and that task appears Herculean. However, if we begin from politics if, that is, we emphasize the facts of the political world the very nature of the boundaries between nations, or between cultures, is itself problematic, and this fact is significant for theories of human rights.

In political theory, it is often assumed that there are boundaries between nations and cultures and that our task is to explain how moral claims may transcend them. But in the political world, the boundaries between nations and cultures are not always clear or given. Sometimes they are the subject of acrimonious dispute, but often they are fluid and indeterminate: the cases of Israel, Ireland, and the former Yugoslavia bear testimony to the contentiousness of boundaries, while the case of modern Europe bears testimony to their fluidity. In both cases, the philosophical aspiration to transcend boundaries assumes a clarity which is contradicted by the political facts.

In partial response to this problem, it is sometimes suggested that national boundaries reflect cultural distinctions. The basic idea behind a cultural justification of political boundaries is the thought that cultural identities are deep, singular and permanent in a way that political structures are not. But even this thought is contentious: identities are frequently multiple and fluid. At some times different aspects of identity are easier to harmonize than at others, and even in those contexts where identity is assumed to be single and fixed, that assumption may be more a convenient philosophic fiction than a reflection of the realities of people's lives. Onora O'Neill refers to the first point in noting that "once upon a time it was easy to be German and Jewish; once upon another time it became impossible. Once upon a time it was easy to be Irish and British; latterly it has been easy only for those of Irish origin living in Britain". Similarly, Amy Gutmann notes the potentially deceptive nature of assumptions about the fixity and homogeneity of identity within a specific culture. Taking the example of the Mormons, who are characteristically understood as having 'a total system of belief and behaviour, dedicated to particular hopes, dreams and interpretation', she notes that this characteristic understanding is false to the reality of Mormon life and teaching. Gutmann writes that in 1890, twelve years following the Supreme Court decision in Reynolds v. United States that upheld state prohibition of polygamy, the Mormon Church officially reversed course and prohibited polygamy, again on doctrinal grounds. Yet approximately 30,000 Mormons today, so called Mormon fundamentalists, still believe in polygamy and practice it despite plenty of pressure to the contrary...none of these views represents the Mormon understanding of kinship because there is no single such social understanding endemic to Mormonism, either today or for any significant period of Mormon history, despite the fact that Mormonism has long been seen by outsiders as a nonpluralistic, monolithic culture.

What these social and historical facts suggest is that criticisms of rights theories often depend for their force upon a simplistic understanding of the political. It is argued that appeal to human rights reflects our desire to transcend boundaries, but that that desire requires allegiance to a transcendentalism which is no longer available to us. However, on inspection, the belief that there are boundaries to be transcended is itself suspect. Partly because we all now live in 'global village', the sheer ability to retain monolithic cultures has become more difficult. But Gutmann's reference to the history of Mormonism suggests that the assumption of homogeneity never was true to the reality of Mormon life: even within the most monolithic of cultures there always was, and remains, a high degree of pluralism in interpretation of scripture and in understandings of the way to live. In some sense, therefore, it is misleading to refer to human rights as reflecting an aspiration to transcend national or cultural boundaries. Moral concerns do indeed transcend such boundaries, but the boundaries themselves are fluid and indeterminate even when they are premised on assumptions about cultural identity.

Rights begin from the political and social realities of all our lives, and address problems about the forms which negotiation may take in circumstances where such boundaries are disputed, or identities fragmented. Put differently, they set limits to the ways in which one identity, or set of identities, may be reconciled with others, and they raise doubts about the optimism implicit in questions such as what is the point of saying to a person quite unlike ourselves who has lived and whose ancestors have lived quite happily with some practice or other for generations, this practice violates your human rights? For while it is not impossible that there are such people, attention to the fluidity of national boundaries, and the fragmentation of cultural identities suggests that they will be the exception rather than the rule. The harsh realities of political life show us, not that boundaries are fixed and identities determinate, but rather that boundaries are at best fluid, at worst disputed, and identities fragmented and often conflictual.

The second, and connected, suggestion takes its cue from the interesting fact that defenses of human rights in political theory tend to take the form of story-telling, or imaginative hypotheses. When we begin with a question about what the philosophic enterprise can achieve, human rights appear doomed. Foundationalist, intuitionist, stipulative and constructivist accounts all lead to the general conclusion that human rights cannot bear the philosophical weight which is put on them. In that sense, it is perhaps unsurprising that defenders of human rights begin, not with the theoretical aspects of political theory, but with its political dimension. They ask what would a society without human rights look like, or what kind of society is envisaged by the proponents and opponents of human rights respectively.

Sometimes, as with Lukes and Feinberg, these stories take the form of imaginative hypotheses, but often they take the form of discussions of actual history. In one way, as has been said, this is unsurprising. But in another way, it is very surprising indeed: defenders of human rights are regularly accused of operating with concepts which are abstract and distant from the realities of life. And rights themselves have come under attack as strange, quasi-metaphysical entities, abstractions from the real world. Against this background, we may wonder why those who seek to defend human rights should begin, if not with the real world, then with detailed story-telling about possible worlds.

Richard Rorty has argued that there are, in the end, two kinds of thinkers: those who believe that beneath the contingent clutter of the world there is something called 'Truth' or 'Geist' or 'the Good' (the philosophers); and those who believe that the contingent clutter of the world is all that there is (the poets). Advocates of human rights have traditionally been associated with the former kind of thinker, but inspection of some of the most prominent literature on human rights suggests that it is precisely in the contingent clutter of the real world that people find appeal to human rights most necessary. Pace Rorty, it is not the philosophical desire for Truth which motivates appeal to rights, but rather reflection on the practicalities of actual political and moral life. Rorty's distinction between philosophers and poets thus suggests a different, but connected distinction: the distinction between optimism and pessimism, or between what Stuart Hampshire calls innocence and experience. Hampshire writes that if one follows the liberal tradition of Mill, Sidgwick, G.E. Moore, and John Rawls, one is liable to think of great public evils as a failing away from the pursuit of justice or of the good, whether it be happiness, or good states of mind, or the realization of primary goods, such as liberty: as if we had to understand those actions and policies which we consider purely evil as being the loss of those things which we consider just or good. But it is equally possible to interpret, and to understand, the things we consider primary goods as being the prevention of great evils, liberal moralists, and particularly the greatest of them. Machiavelli and Hobbes, still retain their hold on us, because they convey a vivid sense of the forces of destruction which are always at large and which have to be diverted and controlled if any kind of decent civilized life is to continue.

Nowadays, to say that we are clever animals is not to say something philosophical and pessimistic but something political and hopeful, namely: If we can work together, we can make ourselves into whatever we are clever and courageous enough to imagine ourselves becoming. This sets aside Kant's question: What is Man? and substitutes the question: What sort of world can we prepare for our great-grandchildren?

In addition to being anti-foundationalist, Rorty's account is also fundamentally optimistic and forward looking: it emphasizes the good which we may do for the future via our cleverness and courage. It is this optimism, or what Hampshire terms 'innocence' and it may be emphasized by contrasting Rorty and Lukes.

Lukes's discussion takes the form of five 'fables' about possible societies (Utilitaria, Proletaria. Communitaria, Libertaria and Egalitaria) and their attitudes to human rights. Of these five, only two (Libertaria and Egalitaria) allow room for human rights, and only Egalitaria, in Lukes's view, takes human rights sufficiently seriously. Even Egalitaria is defective, however, because ultimately it is unattainable and unmaintainable a mirage, built upon the implausible hope that the inhabitants can view anyone, including themselves, impartially, seeing everyone's life as of equal worth and everyone's well-being and freedom as equally valuable. As Lukes points out, a casual glance around the world tells us that this is not the way people are in fact inclined to view one another. Virtually overnight, Yugoslavs turned into Croats and Serbs, it matters deeply to some Canadians that they are Quebecois, and to some Czechoslovaks that they are Slovaks. Contemporary politics is, for Lukes, the ground of pessimism rather than optimism, and it is in the philosophical doctrine of human rights that we may find such comfort as there is. Since for Lukes it is futile to expect people actually to take the impartial view of each other, to see everyone's life as of equal worth, hope for the future lies in adherence to a philosophical theory of rights which can serve as a bulwark against the worst deliverances of practical politics: to defend human rights is to defend a kind of egalitarian plateau on which political conflicts and arguments can take place. It is to allow cultural identity without committing oneself to cultural superiority or, worse, to cultural cleansing. In this context, philosophical theory is a nice thought prompted by a demonstrably nasty world.

For Rorty, by contrast, the hope must lie in an attempt, via story-telling, to enlarge the sympathies of people for one another, to encourage people to see the differences between themselves and others as fewer, and less important, than the similarities. Lukes, we may say, is a pessimist and Rorty an optimist. Or, rather differently, Lukes takes the side of experience, in Hampshire's sense, and Rorty the side of innocence. What are the costs attached to an adherence to innocence, and what view of political philosophy is encapsulated in a commitment to human rights borne of an acknowledgement of experience?

The contrasts between Lukes and Rorty may be traced through three each of which is instructive in the context of a discussion of human rights and which, when taken together, may provide a new perspective on the role of human rights in political theory. Firstly, we may contrast Rorty's emphasis on the future with Lukes' awareness of the past. Where Rorty enjoins us to consider what we may become, if we can work together, Lukes emphasizes the fact that what we may become is always circumscribed by our understanding of who we are. And who we are is, in part, a retrospective not a prospective matter. Thus, he writes to consider the idea of fraternity. Unlike liberty and equality, which are conditions to be achieved, who your brothers are is determined by the past. You and they form a collective in contradistinction to the rest of mankind, and in particular to that portion of it that you and they see as sources of envy of resentment.

More generally, in looking forward, we must always look from where we now are, and where we now are is a matter which is 'given' or partly determined by the past.

Secondly, and connectedly, this emphasis on the past will influence our ability and willingness to follow Rorty's injunction to 'see others as like ourselves'. Without a theory of human nature, or an answer to Kant's question 'What is man'?, the optimism inherent in Rorty's account appears ungrounded, and the cultural and social importance of history, or of what is 'given' will serve to undermine attempts to see differences as fewer and less important. We need to ask, by what criterion are the differences fewer and less important?, and again, without implicit appeal to a theory of human nature, that question lacks an obvious answer.

These two sets of considerations lead to a third, which is that appeal to human rights might best be understood as a set of rules, prompted by political considerations, for the accommodation of difference, rather than justifications for the assertion of similarity. Rorty implies that, since we cannot answer Kant's question, we must simply attempt, through sentimental story-telling, to diminish the number and significance of differences between ourselves and others. But perhaps there is a more important task to perform that of setting limits to the ways in which we may treat others, whilst acknowledging the differences between ourselves and them. Gutmann's discussion of the Mormons, and O'Neill's discussion of boundaries, both suggest that these differences may be less permanent and more fluid than is often supposed. These considerations are the grounds of optimism. At the same time, however, Lukes' discussion suggests that, where such differences occur, they are likely to be accorded great significance in the lives of individuals, and indeed to be partly constitutive of people's own self-understanding. These considerations, therefore, are the grounds of pessimism. The role of human rights is not to promote a false optimism by implying that there is a single human nature which underlies the differences between people, but rather to temper pessimism both by acknowledging the fluidity of boundaries, and by using the facts of fluidity to construct rules which will guide attempts to see others as like ourselves.

Since boundaries between nations are less clear and fixed than is often supposed, and since the boundaries between different cultures are less complete and rigid than is often supposed, we may be led in the direction of hypostatizing human rights as a kind of universal grammer, a statement of what is common to all the different and diverse nations and cultures. Or, following Rorty, we may be led to an optimistic assumption about the possibility of generating solidarity between otherwise different people via a prospective account of what we might become. Attention to the fluidity of boundaries, or to a prospective philosophy inspire optimism. But attention to the past to the significance of culture in people's lives generates pessimism: if we are to create solidarity and minimize differences, then that must be done in a way which does not drive out local allegiance and loyalties. And this, in turn, seems to thwart attempts to appeal to human rights. Our suggestion therefore is that human rights should be construed as an attempt to specify the conditions under which prospective optimism can legitimately be pursued in political theory.

In the literature, theories of human rights are commonly thought to betray one or both of the following beliefs: that there is a single human nature, common to all people, however different they may appear; and that that human nature may serve as the justifying ground for a political theory which dictates what is right or wrong across the boundaries of nations and cultures. Thus construed, human rights theories are expressions of philosophical optimism, even arrogance, and this is true both of traditional theories and of Rorty's anti-foundationalist account. By contrast, human rights should be seen as an expression, not of philosophical optimism, but of political pessimism: they imply no commitment to a thick theory of human nature, but serve rather as a warning against overenthusiastic attempts to create solidarity. It may be said that the specification of those constraints will, in itself, imply a theory of human nature, and perhaps that is so. However, such a theory will be very 'thin' and will require only minimal agreement about what is evil, not any agreement about what constitutes 'the good for man', nor any commitment to the possibility of creating similarity or solidarity amongst diverse people. On this understanding, human rights are bulwarks against evil, borne of an acknowledgement of difference, not harbingers of goods consequent upon a commitment to similarity, whether created or discovered.

What, finally, does this suggestion imply for the role of human rights in political theory, and for the aspirations of political theory itself? It implies that human rights should be seen not as appeals to universal and timeless goods, but as acknowledgements of the diverse and fluid. As such, they do not reflect an understanding of philosophy as the pursuit of Truth, or the discovery of similarity, but neither do they subscribe to an understanding of philosophy as a matter of creating similarity. Rather, the philosophical task is to acknowledge both the fact and the fluidity of difference: both the fact that there are boundaries between nations and the fact that those boundaries are subject to change. So understood, philosophy neither creates nor discovers similarity. On the contrary, it acknowledges the ineliminability of difference, couples that with a recognition that specific differences may change from time to time and from place to place, and then proposes human rights as regulatory devices for the accommodation of difference, not justifications for the assertion of similarity.

All this, however, must be read against a political background, for the world contains not merely difference, but also evil, and the political impetus for human rights comes from the recognition of evil as a permanent threat in the world. Therefore, when philosophy is skeptical about a common human nature it must be careful not to allow that skepticism to render it impotent in the face of real and palpable evil. Where philosophy sees difference to be accommodated, politics sees evil to be eliminated. The real trick lies in showing how we can do both simultaneously: how in the political world we may act against evil without becoming tyrannical, and how in the philosophical realm we may accommodate difference without denying that some differences are manifestations of evil. Philosophers often tell us that in this area there is no Truth to be discovered, but politics reminds us that we cannot afford to believe that that is so.

1

What Are Human Rights?

All human beings are born free and equal in dignity and rights.

– *Universal Declaration of Human Rights*, 1948.

The central tension of human rights is that they became politically significant precisely at the moment when it was no longer possible to justify them.

– Serena Parekh, 2008:1.

Human rights are moral principles or norms, which describe certain standards of human behaviour, and are regularly protected as legal rights in national and international law. They are commonly understood as inalienable fundamental rights to which a person is inherently entitled simply because she or he is a human being, and which are inherent in all human beings regardless of their nation, location, language, religion, ethnic origin or any other status. They are applicable everywhere and at every time in the sense of being universal, and they are egalitarian in the sense of being the same for everyone. They require empathy and the rule of law and impose an obligation on persons to respect the human rights of others. They should not be taken away except as a result of due process based on specific circumstances; for example, human rights may include freedom from unlawful imprisonment, torture, and execution.

The strong claims made by the doctrine of human rights continue to provoke considerable skepticism and debates about the content, nature and justifications of human rights to this day. The precise meaning of the term *right* is controversial and is the subject of continued philosophical debate. While there is consensus that human rights encompasses a wide variety of rights such as the right to a fair trial, protection against enslavement, prohibition of genocide, free speech, or a right to education, there is disagreement about which of these particular rights should be included within the general framework of human rights. Some thinkers suggest that human rights should be a minimum requirement to avoid the worst-case abuses, while others see it as a higher standard.

Human rights are rights inherent to all human beings, whatever our nationality, place of residence, sex, national or ethnic origin, colour, religion, language, or any other status. We are all equally entitled to our human rights without discrimination. These rights are all interrelated, interdependent and indivisible. Universal human rights are often expressed and guaranteed by law, in the forms of treaties, customary international law, general principles and other sources of international law. International human rights law lays down obligations of Governments to act in certain ways or to refrain from certain acts, in order to promote and protect human rights and fundamental freedoms of individuals or groups.

HISTORY OF HUMAN RIGHTS

Although ideas of rights and liberty have existed in some form for much of human history, there is agreement that the earlier conceptions do not closely resemble the modern conceptions of human rights. According to Jack Donnelly, in the ancient world, "traditional societies typically have had elaborate systems of duties... conceptions of justice, political legitimacy, and human flourishing that sought to realize human dignity, flourishing, or well-being entirely independent of human rights. These institutions and practices are alternative to, rather than different formulations of, human rights" (Donnelly 2003:71). The history of human rights can be traced to past documents, particularly Constitution of Medina (622), Al-Risalah al-Huquq (659-713), Magna Carta (1215), the Twelve Articles of Memmingen (1525), the English Bill of Rights (1689), the French Declaration of the Rights of Man and of the Citizen (1789), and the Bill of Rights in the United States Constitution (1791).

The modern sense of human rights can be traced to Renaissance Europe and the Protestant Reformation, alongside the disappearance of the feudal authoritarianism and religious conservativism that dominated the Middle Ages. One theory is that human rights were developed during the early Modern period, alongside the European secularization of Judeo-Christian ethics. The most commonly held view is that the concept of human rights evolved in the West, and that while earlier cultures had important ethical concepts, they generally lacked a concept of human rights. For example, McIntyre argues there is no word for "right" in any language before 1400 (Freeman 2002: 15-17). Medieval charters of liberty such as the English Magna Carta were not charters of human rights, rather they were the foundation and constituted a form of limited political and legal agreement to address specific political circumstances, in the case of Magna Carta later being recognized in the course of early modern debates about rights. One of the oldest records of human rights is the statute of Kalisz (1264), giving privileges to the Jewish minority in the Kingdom of Poland such as protection from discrimination and hate speech. Samuel Moyn suggests that the concept of human rights is intertwined with the modern sense of citizenship, which did not emerge until the past few hundred years (Moyn 2010).

16th–18th Century

The earliest conceptualization of human rights is credited to ideas about natural rights emanating from natural law. In particular, the issue of universal rights was introduced by the examination of extending rights to indigenous peoples by Spanish clerics, such as Francisco de Vitoria and Bartolomé de Las Casas. In the Valladolid debate, Juan Ginés de Sepúlveda, who maintained an Aristotelian view of humanity as divided into classes of different worth, argued with Las Casas, who argued in favour of equal rights to freedom from slavery for all humans regardless of race or religion.

John Locke, the 17th-century English philosopher, discussed natural rights in his work, identifying them as being "life, liberty, and estate (property)", and argued that such fundamental rights could not be surrendered in the social contract. In Britain in 1689, the English Bill of Rights and the Scottish Claim of Right each made illegal a range of oppressive governmental actions. Two major revolutions occurred during the 18th century, in the United States (1776) and in France (1789), leading to the United States Declaration of Independence and the French Declaration of the Rights of Man and of the Citizen respectively, both of which articulated certain human rights. Additionally, the Virginia Declaration of Rights of 1776 encoded into law a number of fundamental civil rights and civil freedoms;

> "We hold these truths to be self-evident, that all men are created equal, that they are endowed by their Creator with certain unalienable Rights, that among these are Life, Liberty and the pursuit of Happiness".
>
> – United States Declaration of Independence, 1776

These were followed by developments in philosophy of human rights by philosophers such as Thomas Paine, John Stuart Mill and G.W.F. Hegel during the 18th and 19th centuries. The term human rights probably came into use sometime between Paine's The Rights of Man and William Lloyd Garrison's 1831 writings in The Liberator, in which he stated that he was trying to enlist his readers in "the great cause of human rights". Although the term had been used by at least one author as early as 1742 (Turnbull 1742).

19th Century

In the 19th century, human rights became a central concern over the issue of slavery. A number of reformers, notably British Member of Parliament William Wilberforce, worked towards the abolition of the Atlantic slave trade and abolition of slavery. This was achieved across the British Empire by the Slave Trade Act 1807, which was enforced internationally by the Royal Navy under treaties Britain negotiated with other nations, and the Slavery Abolition Act 1833. In the United States, all the northern states had abolished the institution of slavery between 1777 and 1804, although southern states clung tightly to the "peculiar institution". Conflict and debates over the expansion of slavery to new territories constituted one of the reasons for the southern states' secession and the American Civil War. During the the reconstruction period immediately following the war, several amendments to the United States Constitution were made. These included the 13th amendment, banning slavery, the 14th amendment, assuring full citizenship and civil rights to all people born in the United States, and the 15th amendment, guaranteeing African Americans the right to vote. In Russia, the reformer Tsar Alexander II ended serfdom in 1861, although the freed serfs often faced restrictions of their mobility within the nation.

Many groups and movements have achieved profound social changes over the course of the 20th century in the name of human rights. In Europe and North America, labour unions brought about laws granting workers the right to strike, establishing minimum work conditions and forbidding or regulating child labour. The women's rights movement succeeded in gaining for many women the right to vote. National liberation movements in many countries succeeded in driving out colonial powers. One of the most influential was Mahatma Gandhi's movement to free his native India from British rule. Movements by long-oppressed racial and religious minorities succeeded in many parts of the world, among them the African American Civil Rights Movement, and more recent diverse identity politics movements, on behalf of women and minorities in the United States.

The establishment of the International Committee of the Red Cross, the 1864 Lieber Code and the first of the Geneva Conventions in 1864 laid the foundations of International humanitarian law, to be further developed following the two World Wars.

20th Century

The World Wars, and the huge losses of life and gross abuses of human rights that took place during them, were a driving force behind the development of modern human rights instruments. The League of Nations was established in 1919 at the negotiations over the Treaty of Versailles following the end of World War I. The League's goals included disarmament, preventing war through collective security, settling disputes between countries through negotiation and diplomacy, and improving global welfare. Enshrined in its charter was a mandate to promote many of the rights later included in the Universal Declaration of Human Rights.

At the 1945 Yalta Conference, the Allied Powers agreed to create a new body to supplant the League's role; this was to be the United Nations.

The United Nations has played an important role in international human-rights law since its creation. Following the World Wars, the United Nations and its members developed much of the discourse and the bodies of law that now make up international humanitarian law and international human rights law. Analyst Belinda Cooper argued that human rights organizations flourished in the 1990s, possibly as a result of the dissolution of the western and eastern Cold War blocs. Ludwig Hoffmann argues that human rights became more widely emphasized in the latter half of the twentieth century because it "provided a language for political claim making and counter-claims, liberal-democratic, but also socialist and post colonialist (Hoffmann 2010: 2).

Cairo Declaration of Human Rights in Islam

The CDHR was signed by member states of the OIC in 1990 at the 19th Conference of Foreign Ministers held in Cairo, Egypt. It was seen as the answer to the UDHR. In fact, the CDHR was "patterned after the UN-sponsored UDHR of 1948". The object of the CDHR was to "serve as a guide for member states on human rights issues. CDHR translated the Qur'anic teachings as follows: "All men are equal in terms of basic human dignity and basic obligations and responsibilities, without any discrimination on the basis of race, colour, language, belief, sex, religion, political affiliation, social status or other considerations. True religion is the guarantee for enhancing such dignity along the path to human integrity (al-Ahsan 2009: 571). On top of references to the Qur'an, the CDHR also referenced prophetic teachings and Islamic legal tradition.

NATURAL RIGHTS, LEGAL RIGHTS AND HUMAN RIGHTS

Natural and legal rights are two types of rights. Natural rights are those that are not dependent on the laws or customs of any particular culture or government, and therefore universal and inalienable (i.e., rights that cannot be repealed or restrained by human laws). Legal rights are those bestowed onto a person by a given legal system (i.e., rights that can be modified, repealed, and restrained by human laws).

The concept of natural law is closely related to the concept of natural rights. During the Age of Enlightenment, the concept of natural laws was used to challenge the divine right of kings, and became an alternative justification for the establishment of a social contract, positive law, and government – and thus legal rights – in the form of classical republicanism. Conversely, the concept of natural rights is used by others to challenge the legitimacy of all such establishments.

The idea of human rights is also closely related to that of natural rights: some acknowledge no difference between the two, regarding them as synonymous, while others choose to keep the terms separate to eliminate association with some features traditionally associated with natural rights (Jones 1994: 73). Natural rights, in particular, are considered beyond the authority of any government or international body to dismiss. The 1948 United Nations Universal Declaration of Human Rights is an important legal instrument enshrining one conception of natural rights into international soft law. Natural rights were traditionally viewed as exclusively negative rights, whereas human rights also comprise positive rights. Even on a natural rights conception of human rights, the two terms may not be synonymous.

The proposition that animals have natural rights is one that gained the interest of philosophers and legal scholars in the 20th century and into the 21st century.

The legal philosophy known as Declarationism seeks to incorporate the natural rights philosophy of the United States Declaration of Independence into the body of American case law on a level with the United States Constitution, since the unanimously agreed upon Doctrines of the Declaration of Independence is the foundational authority upon which the People and the Continental Congress of the 13 British Colonies of America based their power to legitimately separate from Britain and establish its own government (i.e. the Constitution of the United States). Declarationism philosophy, therefore, insists that if the United States rejects the natural rights philosophy of the Declaration of Independence upon which it was founded, it of necessity becomes, retro-actively, an illegitimate government in treasonous rebellion against its rightful government of Crown and Parliament in London; and therefore, the Declaration and Constitution must be held as legally inseparable throughout the entire United States of America (both Federal and State) and its territories.

History

The idea that certain rights are natural or inalienable also has a history dating back at least to the Stoics of late Antiquity and Catholic law of the early Middle Ages, and descending through the Protestant Reformation and the Age of Enlightenment to today.

The existence of natural rights has been asserted by different individuals on different premises, such as a priori philosophical reasoning or religious principles. For example, Immanuel Kant claimed to derive natural rights through reason alone. The United States Declaration of Independence, meanwhile, is based upon the "self-evident" truth that "all men are ... endowed by their Creator with certain unalienable Rights".

Likewise, different philosophers and statesmen have designed different lists of what they believe to be natural rights; almost all include the right to life and liberty as the two highest priorities. H. L. A. Hart argued that if there are any rights at all, there must be the right to liberty, for all the others would depend upon this. T. H. Green argued that "if there are such things as rights at all, then, there must be a right to life and liberty, or, to put it more properly to free life" (Green 1895:114). John Locke emphasized "life, liberty and property" as primary. However, despite Locke's influential defense of the right of revolution, Thomas Jefferson substituted "pursuit of happiness" in place of "property" in the United States Declaration of Independence.

Ancient

Stephen Kinzer, a veteran journalist for The New York Times and the author of the book *All The Shah's Men*, writes in the latter that:

The Zoroastrian religion taught Iranians that citizens have an inalienable right to enlightened leadership and that the duty of subjects is not simply to obey wise kings but also to rise up against those who are wicked. Leaders are seen as representative of God on earth, but they deserve allegiance only as long as they have *farr*, a kind of divine blessing that they must earn by moral behavior.

The Stoics held that no one was a slave by nature; slavery was an external condition juxtaposed to the internal freedom of the soul (*sui juris*). Seneca the Younger wrote:

> It is a mistake to imagine that slavery pervades a man's whole being; the better part of him is exempt from it: the body indeed is subjected and in the power of a master, but the mind is independent, and indeed is so free and wild, that it cannot be restrained even by this prison of the body, wherein it is confined.

Of fundamental importance to the development of the idea of natural rights was the emergence of the idea of natural human equality. As the historian A.J. Carlyle notes: "There is no change in political theory so startling in its completeness as the change from the theory of Aristotle to the later philosophical view represented by Cicero and Seneca.... We think that this cannot be better exemplified than with regard to the theory of the equality of human nature" (Carlyle 1903: 8,9). Charles H. McIlwain likewise observes that "the idea of the equality of men is the profoundest contribution of the Stoics to political thought" and that "its greatest influence is in the changed conception of law that in part resulted from it." (McIlwain 1932:14-15). Cicero argues in De Legibus that "we are born for Justice, and that right is based, not upon's opinions, but upon Nature." (book 1, section 28).

Modern

Centuries later, the Stoic doctrine that the "inner part cannot be delivered into bondage" re-emerged in the Reformation doctrine of liberty of conscience. Martin Luther (1523) wrote:

> Furthermore, every man is responsible for his own faith, and he must see it for himself that he believes rightly. As little as another can go to hell or heaven for me, so little can he believe or disbelieve for me; and as little as he can open or shut heaven or hell for me, so little can he drive me to faith or unbelief. Since, then, belief or unbelief is a matter of every one's conscience, and since this is no lessening of the secular power, the latter should be content and attend to its own affairs and permit men to believe one thing or another, as they are able and willing, and constrain no one by force.

John Locke, the 17th-century English philosopher, discussed natural rights in his work, identifying them as being "life, liberty, and estate (property)", and argued that such fundamental rights could not be surrendered in the social contract. Preservation of the natural rights to life, liberty, and property was claimed as justification for the rebellion of the American colonies. As George Mason stated in his draft for the Virginia Declaration of Rights, "all men are born equally free," and hold "certain inherent natural rights, of which they cannot, by any compact, deprive or divest their posterity"(Maier 1993:134). Another 17th-century Englishman, John Lilburne (known as Freeborn John), who came into conflict with both the monarchy of King Charles I and the military dictatorship of Oliver Cromwell governed republic, argued for level human basic rights he called "freeborn rights" which he defined as being rights that every human being is born with, as opposed to rights bestowed by government or by human law.

The distinction between alienable and unalienable rights was introduced by Francis Hutcheson. In his Inquiry into the Original of Our Ideas of Beauty and Virtue (1725), Hutcheson foreshadowed the Declaration of Independence, stating: "For wherever any Invasion is made upon unalienable Rights, there must arise either a perfect, or external Right to Resistance ... Unalienable Rights are essential Limitations in all Governments." Hutcheson, however, placed clear limits on his notion of unalienable rights, declaring that "there can be no Right, or Limitation of Right, inconsistent with, or opposite to the greatest public Good."(Hutcheson 2004: 192). Hutcheson elaborated on this idea of unalienable rights in his *A System of Moral Philosophy* (1755), based on the Reformation principle of the liberty of conscience. One could not in fact give up the capacity for private judgment (e.g., about religious questions) regardless of any external contracts or oaths to religious or secular authorities so that right is "unalienable." Hutcheson wrote: "Thus no man can really change his sentiments, judgments, and inward affections, at the pleasure of another; nor can it tend to any good to make him profess what is contrary to his heart. The right of private judgment is therefore unalienable" (1755: 261-2).

In the German Enlightenment, Hegel gave a highly developed treatment of this inalienability argument. Like Hutcheson, Hegel based the theory of inalienable rights on the de facto inalienability of those aspects of personhood that distinguish persons from things. A thing, like a piece of property, can in fact be transferred from one person to another. According to Hegel, the same would not apply to those aspects that make one a person:

> The right to what is in essence inalienable is imprescriptible, since the act whereby I take possession of my personality, of my substantive essence, and make myself a responsible being, capable of possessing rights and with a moral and religious life, takes away from these characteristics of mine just that externality which alone made them capable of passing into the possession of someone else. When I have thus annulled their externality, I cannot lose them through lapse of time or from any other reason drawn from my prior consent or willingness to alienate them.(Hegel 1967, section 66).

In discussion of social contract theory, "inalienable rights" were said to be those rights that could not be surrendered by citizens to the sovereign. Such rights were thought to be natural rights, independent of positive law. Some social contract theorists reasoned, however, that in the natural state only the strongest could benefit from their rights. Thus, people form an implicit social contract, ceding their natural rights to the authority to protect the people from abuse, and living henceforth under the legal rights of that authority.

Many historical apologies for slavery and illiberal government were based on explicit or implicit voluntary contracts to alienate any "natural rights" to freedom and self-determination. The de facto inalienability arguments of Hutcheson and his predecessors provided the basis for the anti-slavery movement to argue not simply against involuntary slavery but against any explicit or implied contractual forms of slavery. Any contract that tried to legally alienate such a right would be inherently invalid. Similarly, the argument was used by the democratic movement to argue against any explicit or implied social contracts of subjection (*pactum subjectionis*) by which a people would supposedly alienate their right of self-government to a sovereign as, for example, in Leviathan by Thomas Hobbes. According to Ernst Cassirer,

> There is, at least, one right that cannot be ceded or abandoned: the right to personality...They charged the great logician [Hobbes] with a contradiction in terms. If a man could give up his personality he would cease being a moral being. ... There is no pactum subjectionis, no act of submission by which man can give up the state of free agent and enslave himself. For by such an act of renunciation he would

> give up that very character which constitutes his nature and essence: he would lose his humanity (Cassirer 1963: 175).

These themes converged in the debate about American Independence. While Jefferson was writing the Declaration of Independence, Richard Price in England sided with the Americans' claim "that Great Britain is attempting to rob them of that liberty to which every member of society and all civil communities have a natural and unalienable title"(Price 1979: 67). Price again based the argument on the de facto inalienability of "that principle of spontaneity or self-determination which constitutes us agents or which gives us a command over our actions, rendering them properly ours, and not effects of the operation of any foreign cause." (Price 1979:67–68) Any social contract or compact allegedly alienating these rights would be non-binding and void, wrote Price:

> Neither can any state acquire such an authority over other states in virtue of any compacts or cessions. This is a case in which compacts are not binding. Civil liberty is, in this respect, on the same footing with religious liberty. As no people can lawfully surrender their religious liberty by giving up their right of judging for themselves in religion, or by allowing any human beings to prescribe to them what faith they shall embrace, or what mode of worship they shall practise, so neither can any civil societies lawfully surrender their civil liberty by giving up to any extraneous jurisdiction their power of legislating for themselves and disposing their property. (Price 1979: 78–79).

Price raised a furor of opposition so in 1777 he wrote another tract that clarified his position and again restated the de facto basis for the argument that the "liberty of men as agents is that power of self-determination which all agents, as such, possess" (Price 1979: 136). In Intellectual Origins of American Radicalism, Staughton Lynd pulled together these themes and related them to the slavery debate:

> Then it turned out to make considerable difference whether one said slavery was wrong because every man has a natural right to the possession of his own body, or because every man has a natural right freely to determine his own destiny. The first kind of right was alienable: thus Locke neatly derived slavery from capture in war, whereby a man forfeited his labor to the conqueror who might lawfully have killed him; and thus Dred Scott was judged

> permanently to have given up his freedom. But the second kind of right, what Price called "that power of self-determination which all agents, as such, possess," was inalienable as long man remained man. Like the mind's quest for religious truth from which it was derived, self-determination was not a claim to ownership which might be both acquired and surrendered, but an inextricable aspect of the activity of being human (Lynd 1969: 56-57).

Meanwhile, in America, Thomas Jefferson "took his division of rights into alienable and unalienable from Hutcheson, who made the distinction popular and important" (Wills 1979: 213) and in the 1776 United States Declaration of Independence, famously condensed this to:

> We hold these truths to be self-evident, that all men are created equal, that they are endowed by their Creator with certain unalienable Rights...

In the 19th century, the movement to abolish slavery seized this passage as a statement of constitutional principle, although the U.S. constitution recognized and protected slavery. As a lawyer, future Chief Justice Salmon P. Chase argued before the Supreme Court in the case of John Van Zandt, who had been charged with violating the Fugitive Slave Act, that:

> The law of the Creator, which invests every human being with an inalienable title to freedom, cannot be repealed by any interior law which asserts that man is property.

The concept of inalienable rights was criticized by Jeremy Bentham and Edmund Burke as groundless. Bentham and Burke, writing in 18th century Britain, claimed that rights arise from the actions of government, or evolve from tradition, and that neither of these can provide anything inalienable. (See Bentham's "Critique of the Doctrine of Inalienable, Natural Rights", and Burke's Reflections on the Revolution in France). Presaging the shift in thinking in the 19th century, Bentham famously dismissed the idea of natural rights as "nonsense on stilts". By way of contrast to the views of British nationals Burke and Bentham, the leading American revolutionary scholar James Wilson condemned Burke's view as "tyranny."

The signers of the Declaration of Independence deemed it a "self-evident truth" that all men are "endowed by their Creator with certain unalienable Rights". In *The Social Contract*, Jean-Jacques Rousseau claims that the existence of inalienable rights is unnecessary for the existence of a constitution or a set of laws and rights. This idea of a social contract – that rights and responsibilities are derived from a consensual contract between the government and the people – is the most widely recognized alternative.

One criticism of natural rights theory is that one cannot draw norms from facts. This objection is variously expressed as the is-ought problem, the naturalistic fallacy, or the appeal to nature. G.E. Moore, for example, said that ethical naturalism falls prey to the naturalistic fallacy. Some defenders of natural rights theory, however, counter that the term "natural" in "natural rights" is contrasted with "artificial" rather than referring to nature. John Finnis, for example, contends that natural law and natural rights are derived from self-evident principles, not from speculative principles or from facts (Finnis 2011: 23-58).

There is also debate as to whether all rights are either natural or legal. Fourth president of the United States James Madison, while representing Virginia in the House of Representatives, believed that there are rights, such as trial by jury, that are social rights, arising neither from natural law nor from positive law (which are the basis of natural and legal rights respectively) but from the social contract from which a government derives its authority.

Thomas Hobbes

Thomas Hobbes (1588–1679) included a discussion of natural rights in his moral and political philosophy. Hobbes' conception of natural rights extended from his conception of man in a "state of nature". Thus he argued that the essential natural (human) right was "to use his own power, as he will himself, for the preservation of his own Nature; that is to say, of his own Life; and consequently, of doing anything, which in his own judgement, and Reason, he shall conceive to be the aptest means thereunto." (Leviathan. 1, XIV)

Hobbes sharply distinguished this natural "liberty", from natural "laws", described generally as "a precept, or general rule, found out by reason, by which a man is forbidden to do, that, which is destructive of his life, or taketh away the means of preserving his life; and to omit, that, by which he thinketh it may best be preserved." (Leviathan. 1, XIV)

In his natural state, according to Hobbes, man's life consisted entirely of liberties and not at all of laws – "It followeth, that in such a condition, every man has the right to everything; even to one another's body. And therefore, as long as this natural Right of every man to everything endureth, there can be no security to any man... of living out the time, which Nature ordinarily allow men to live." (Leviathan. 1, XIV)

This would lead inevitably to a situation known as the "war of all against all", in which human beings kill, steal and enslave others in order to stay alive, and due to their natural lust for "Gain", "Safety" and "Reputation". Hobbes reasoned that this world of chaos created by unlimited rights was highly undesirable, since it would cause human life to be "solitary, poor, nasty, brutish, and short". As such, if humans wish to live peacefully they must give up most of their natural rights and create moral obligations in order to establish political and civil society. This is one of the earliest formulations of the theory of government known as the social contract.

Hobbes objected to the attempt to derive rights from "natural law," arguing that law ("lex") and right ("jus") though often confused, signify opposites, with law referring to obligations, while rights refer to the absence of obligations. Since by our human nature, we seek to maximize our well being, rights are prior to law, natural or institutional, and people will not follow the laws of nature without first being subjected to a sovereign power, without which all ideas of right and wrong are meaningless – "Therefore before the names of Just and Unjust can have place, there must be some coercive Power, to compel men equally to the performance of their Covenants..., to make good that Propriety, which by mutual contract men acquire, in recompense of the universal Right they abandon: and such power there is none before the erection of the Commonwealth." (Leviathan. 1, XV)

This marked an important departure from medieval natural law theories which gave precedence to obligations over rights.

John Locke

John Locke (1632–1704) was another prominent Western philosopher who conceptualized rights as natural and inalienable. Like Hobbes, Locke believed in a natural right to life, liberty, and property. It was once conventional wisdom that Locke greatly influenced the American

Revolutionary War with his writings of natural rights, but this claim has been the subject of protracted dispute in recent decades. For example, the historian Ray Forrest Harvey declared that Jefferson and Locke were at "two opposite poles" in their political philosophy, as evidenced by Jefferson's use in the Declaration of Independence of the phrase "pursuit of happiness" instead of "property"(Harvey 1937: 120). More recently, the eminent legal historian John Phillip Reid has deplored contemporary scholars' "misplaced emphasis on John Locke," arguing that American revolutionary leaders saw Locke as a commentator on established constitutional principles (Reid 1987, 1986). Thomas Pangle has defended Locke's influence on the Founding, claiming that historians who argue to the contrary either misrepresent the classical republican alternative to which they say the revolutionary leaders adhered, do not understand Locke, or point to someone else who was decisively influenced by Locke (Pangle 1988). This position has also been sustained by Michael Zuckert (1998, 2002).

According to Locke there are three natural rights:

- Life: everyone is entitled to live.
- Liberty: everyone is entitled to do anything they want to so long as it doesn't conflict with the first right.
- Estate: everyone is entitled to own all they create or gain through gift or trade so long as it doesn't conflict with the first two rights.

The social contract is an agreement between members of a country to live within a shared system of laws. Specific forms of government are the result of the decisions made by these persons acting in their collective capacity. Government is instituted to make laws that protect these three natural rights. If a government does not properly protect these rights, it can be overthrown.

Thomas Paine

Thomas Paine (1731–1809) further elaborated on natural rights in his influential work Rights of Man (1791), emphasizing that rights cannot be granted by any charter because this would legally imply they can also be revoked and under such circumstances they would be reduced to privileges:

It is a perversion of terms to say that a charter gives rights. It operates by a contrary effect – that of taking rights away. Rights are inherently in all the inhabitants; but charters, by annulling those rights, in the majority, leave the right, by exclusion, in the hands of a few... They consequently are instruments of injustice.

The fact therefore must be that the individuals themselves, each in his own personal and sovereign right, entered into a compact with each other to produce a government: and this is the only mode in which governments have a right to arise, and the only principle on which they have a right to exist.

American Individualist Anarchists

While at first American individualist anarchists adhered to natural rights positions, later in this era led by Benjamin Tucker, some abandoned natural rights positions and converted to Max Stirner's Egoist anarchism. Rejecting the idea of moral rights, Tucker said that there were only two rights: "the right of might" and "the right of contract". He also said, after converting to Egoist individualism, "In times past... it was my habit to talk glibly of the right of man to land. It was a bad habit, and I long ago sloughed it off.... Man's only right to land is his might over it." (Tucker 1897: 350).

According to Wendy McElroy (1981):

> In adopting Stirnerite egoism (1886), Tucker rejected natural rights which had long been considered the foundation of libertarianism. This rejection galvanized the movement into fierce debates, with the natural rights proponents accusing the egoists of destroying libertarianism itself. So bitter was the conflict that a number of natural rights proponents withdrew from the pages of Liberty in protest even though they had hitherto been among its frequent contributors. Thereafter, Liberty championed egoism although its general content did not change significantly.

Several periodicals were "undoubtedly influenced by Liberty's presentation of egoism; The Ego and The Egoist, both of which were edited by Edward H. Fulton. Among the egoist papers that Tucker followed were the German Der Eigene, edited by Adolf Brand, and The Eagle and The Serpent, issued from London. The latter, the most prominent English-language egoist journal, was published from 1898 to 1900 with the subtitle '*A Journal of Egoistic Philosophy and Sociology*'. Among those American anarchists who adhered to egoism include Benjamin Tucker, John Beverley Robinson, Steven T. Byington, Hutchins Hapgood, James L. Walker, Victor Yarros and E.H. Fulton.

Contemporary

Many documents now echo the phrase used in the United States Declaration of Independence. The preamble to the 1948 United Nations Universal Declaration of Human Rights asserts that rights are inalienable: "recognition of the inherent dignity and of the equal and inalienable rights of all members of the human family is the foundation of freedom, justice and peace in the world." Article 1 of the California Constitution recognizes inalienable rights, and articulated some (not all) of those rights as "defending life and liberty, acquiring, possessing, and protecting property, and pursuing and obtaining safety, happiness, and privacy." However, there is still much dispute over which "rights" are truly natural rights and which are not, and the concept of natural or inalienable rights is still controversial to some.

Erich Fromm argued that some powers over human beings could be wielded only by God, and that if there were no God, no human beings could wield these powers (1973).

Contemporary political philosophies continuing the liberal tradition of natural rights include libertarianism, anarcho-capitalism and Objectivism, and include amongst their canon the works of authors such as Robert Nozick, Ludwig von Mises, Ayn Rand, and Murray Rothbard. A libertarian view of inalienable rights is laid out in Morris and Linda Tannehill's *The Market for Liberty*, which claims that a man has a right to ownership over his life and therefore also his property, because he has invested time (i.e. part of his life) in it and thereby made it an extension of his life. However, if he initiates force against and to the detriment of another man, he alienates himself from the right to that part of his life which is required to pay his debt: "Rights are not inalienable, but only the possessor of a right can alienate himself from that right – no one else can take a man's rights from him." (Tannehill and Tannehill 1970: 11).

Various definitions of inalienability include non-relinquishability, non-salability, and non-transferability. This concept has been recognized by libertarians as being central to the question of voluntary slavery, which Murray Rothbard dismissed as illegitimate and even self-contradictory. Stephan Kinsella argues that "viewing rights as alienable is perfectly consistent with – indeed, implied by – the libertarian non-aggression principle. Under this principle, only the initiation of force is prohibited; defensive, restitutive, or retaliatory force is not."

Samuel P. Huntington, an American political scientist, wrote that the "inalienable rights" argument from the Declaration of Independence was necessary because "The British were white, Anglo, and Protestant, just as we were. (Advocates for the Declaration's adoption) had to have some other basis on which to justify independence".

Different philosophers have created different lists of rights they consider to be natural. Proponents of natural rights, in particular Hesselberg and Rothbard, have responded that reason can be applied to separate truly axiomatic rights from supposed rights, stating that any principle that requires itself to be disproved is an axiom. Critics have pointed to the lack of agreement between the proponents as evidence for the claim that the idea of natural rights is merely a political tool.

Hugh Gibbons has proposed a descriptive argument based on human biology. His contention is that Human Beings were other-regarding as a matter of necessity, in order to avoid the costs of conflict. Over time they developed expectations that individuals would act in certain ways which were then prescribed by society (duties of care etc.) and that eventually crystallized into actionable rights.

FEATURES OF HUMAN RIGHTS

Human rights have the following features.

1. Universal and Inalienable

The principle of universality of human rights is the cornerstone of international human rights law. This principle, as first emphasized in the Universal Declaration on Human Rights in 1948, has been reiterated in numerous international human rights conventions, declarations, and resolutions. The 1993 Vienna World Conference on Human Rights, for example, noted that it is the duty of States to promote and protect all human rights and fundamental freedoms, regardless of their political, economic and cultural systems.

All States have ratified at least one, and 80% of States have ratified four or more, of the core human rights treaties, reflecting consent of States which creates legal obligations for them and giving concrete expression to universality. Some fundamental human rights norms enjoy universal protection by customary international law across all boundaries and civilizations.

Human rights are inalienable. They should not be taken away, except in specific situations and according to due process. For example, the right to liberty may be restricted if a person is found guilty of a crime by a court of law.

2. Interdependent and Indivisible

All human rights are indivisible, whether they are civil and political rights, such as the right to life, equality before the law and freedom of expression; economic, social and cultural rights, such as the rights to work, social security and education, or collective rights, such as the rights to development and self-determination, are indivisible, interrelated and interdependent. The improvement of one right facilitates advancement of the others. Likewise, the deprivation of one right adversely affects the others.

3. Equal and Non-discriminatory

Non-discrimination is a cross-cutting principle in international human rights law. The principle is present in all the major human rights treaties and provides the central theme of some of international human rights conventions such as the International Convention on the Elimination of All Forms of Racial Discrimination and the Convention on the Elimination of All Forms of Discrimination against Women.

The principle applies to everyone in relation to all human rights and freedoms and it prohibits discrimination on the basis of a list of non-exhaustive categories such as sex, race, colour and so on. The principle of non-discrimination is complemented by the principle of equality, as stated in Article-1 of the Universal Declaration of Human Rights: "All human beings are born free and equal in dignity and rights."

4. Both Rights and Obligations

Human rights entail both rights and obligations. States assume obligations and duties under international law to respect, to protect and to fulfil human rights. The obligation to respect means that States must refrain from interfering with or curtailing the enjoyment of human rights. The obligation to protect requires States to protect individuals and groups against human rights abuses. The obligation to fulfil means that States must take positive action to facilitate the enjoyment of basic human rights. At the individual level, while we are entitled our human rights, we should also respect the human rights of others.

However, particular kinds of human rights will have additional features as discussed below:

5. Human Rights are Rights

Lest we miss the obvious, human rights are rights. Most if not all human rights are claim rights that impose duties or responsibilities on their addressees or dutybearers. Rights focus on a freedom, protection, status, or benefit for the right holders. The duties associated with human rights often require actions involving respect, protection, facilitation, and provision. Rights are usually mandatory in the sense of imposing duties on their addressees, but some legal human rights seem to do little more than declare high-priority goals and assign responsibility for their progressive realization. One can argue, of course, that goal-like rights are not real rights, but it may be better to recognize that they comprise a weak but useful notion of a right (See Beitz 2009 for a defense of the view that not all human rights are rights in a strong sense. And see Feinberg 1973 for the idea of "manifesto rights"). A human rights norm might exist as (a) a shared norm of actual human moralities, (b) a justified moral norm supported by strong reasons, (c) a legal right at the national level (where it might be referred to as a "civil" or "constitutional" right), or (d) a legal right within international law. A human rights advocate might wish to see human rights exist in all four ways.

6. Human Rights are Plural

If someone accepted that there are human rights but held that there is only one of them, this might make sense if she meant that there is one abstract underlying right that generates a list of specific rights. But if this person meant that there is just one such specific right such as the right to peaceful assembly this would be a highly revisionary view. Human rights address a variety of specific problems such as guaranteeing fair trials, ending slavery, ensuring the availability of education, and preventing genocide. Some philosophers advocate very short lists of human rights but nevertheless accept plurality.

7. Human Rights are Universal

All living humans – or perhaps all living persons – have human rights. One does not have to be a particular kind of person or a member of some specific nation or religion to have human rights. Included in the idea of universality is some conception of independent existence. People have human rights independently of whether they are found in the practices, morality, or law of their country or culture. This idea of universality needs several qualifications, however. First, some rights, such as the right to vote, are held only by adult citizens or residents and apply only to voting in one's own country. Second, the human right to freedom of movement may be taken away temporarily from a person who is convicted of committing a serious crime. And third, some human rights treaties focus on the rights of vulnerable groups such as minorities, women, indigenous peoples, and children.

8. Human Rights have High-Priority

Human rights are matters of paramount importance and their violation a grave affront to justice. If human rights did not have high priority they would not have the ability to compete with other powerful considerations such as national stability and security, individual and national self-determination, and national and global prosperity. High priority does not mean, however, that human rights are absolute. As James Griffin says, human rights should be understood as "resistant to trade-offs, but not too resistant" (Griffin 2008). Further, there seems to be priority variation within human rights. For example, when the right to life conflicts with the right to privacy, the latter will generally be outweighed.

Let's now consider five other features or functions that might be added.

Should human rights be defined as inalienable?

Inalienability does not mean that rights are absolute or can never be overridden by other considerations. Rather it means that its holder cannot lose it temporarily or permanently by bad conduct or by voluntarily giving it up. It is doubtful that all human rights are inalienable in this sense. One who endorses both human rights and imprisonment as punishment for serious crimes must hold that people's rights to freedom of movement can be forfeited temporarily or permanently by just convictions of serious crimes. Perhaps it is sufficient to say that human rights are very hard to lose. (see Donnelly 2013: 10).

Should human rights be defined as minimal rights?

A number of philosophers have proposed the view that human rights are minimal in the sense of not being too numerous (a few dozen rights rather than hundreds or thousands), and not being too demanding. Their views suggest that human rights are—or should be—more concerned with avoiding the worst than with achieving the best. Henry Shue suggests that human rights concern the "lower limits on tolerable human conduct" rather than "great aspirations and exalted ideals" (Shue 1996). When human rights are modest standards they leave most legal and policy matters open to democratic decision-making at the national and local levels. This allows them to have high priority, to accommodate a great deal of cultural and institutional variation, and to leave open a large space for democratic decision-making at the national level. Still, there is no contradiction in the idea of an extremely expansive list of human rights and hence minimalism is not a defining feature of human rights. Minimalism is best seen as a normative prescription for what international human rights should be. Moderate forms of minimalism have considerable appeal, but not as part of the definition of human rights.

Should human rights be defined as always including moral rights?

Philosophers coming to human rights theory from ethics sometimes assume that human rights must be, at bottom, moral rather than legal rights. There is no contradiction, however, in people saying that they believe in human rights, but only when they are legal rights at the national or international levels. As Louis Henkin observed, "Political forces have mooted the principal philosophical objections, bridging the chasm between natural and positive law by converting natural human rights into positive legal rights" (Henkin 1978). Theorists who insist that the only human rights are legal rights may find, however, that the interpretations they can give of characteristics such as the universality of human rights and of their independent existence are fairly weak.

Should human rights be defined in terms of serving some sort of political function?

Instead of seeing human rights as grounded in some sort of independently existing moral reality, a theorist might see them as the norms of a highly useful political practice that humans have constructed or evolved. Such a view would see the idea of human rights as playing various political roles at the national and international levels and as serving thereby to protect urgent human or national interests. These political roles might include providing standards for international evaluations of how governments treat their people and as helping to specify when use of economic sanctions or military intervention is permissible. There are powerful advocates of this sort of view (e.g. Rawls 1999 and Beitz 2009). These theorists would add to the four defining elements above some set of political roles or functions. This view may be plausible for the very salient international human rights that have emerged in international law and politics in the last fifty years. But human rights can exist and function in contexts not involving international scrutiny and intervention such as a world with only one state. Imagine, for example, that an asteroid strike had killed everyone in all countries except New Zealand, leaving it the only state in existence. Surely the idea of human rights as well as many dimensions of human rights practice could continue in New Zealand, even though there would be no international relations, law, or politics. And if a few people were discovered to have survived in Iceland and were living without a government or state, New Zealanders would know that human rights governed how these people should be treated even though they were stateless. How deeply the idea of human rights must be rooted in international law and practice should not be settled by definitional fiat. We can allow, however, that the sorts of political functions that Rawls and Beitz describe are typically served by international human rights today.

THE EXISTENCE AND GROUNDS OF HUMAN RIGHTS

How Can Human Rights Exist?

The most obvious way in which human rights exist is as norms of national and international law created by enactment and judicial decisions. At the international level, human rights norms exist because of treaties that have turned them into international law. For example, the human right not to be held in slavery or servitude in Article 4 of the European Convention and in Article 8 of the International Covenant on Civil and Political Rights exists because these treaties establish it. At the national level, human rights norms exist because they have through legislative enactment, judicial decision, or custom become part of a country's law. For example, the right against slavery exists in the United States because the 13th Amendment to the U.S. Constitution prohibits slavery and servitude. When rights are embedded in international law we speak of them as human rights; but when they are enacted in national law we more frequently describe them as civil or constitutional rights.

Enactment in national and international law is one of the ways in which human rights exist. But many have suggested that this is not the only way. If human rights exist only because of enactment, their availability is contingent on domestic and international political developments. Many people have looked for a way to support the idea that human rights have roots that are deeper and less subject to human decisions than legal enactment. One version of this idea is that people are born with rights, that human rights are somehow innate or inherent in human beings. One way that a normative status could be inherent in humans is by being God-given. The U.S. Declaration of Independence (1776) claims that people are "endowed by their Creator" with natural rights to life, liberty, and the pursuit of happiness. On this view, God, the supreme lawmaker, enacted some basic human rights.

Rights plausibly attributed to divine decree must be very general and abstract (life, liberty, etc.) so that they can apply to thousands of years of human history, not just to recent centuries. But contemporary human rights are specific and many of them presuppose contemporary institutions (e.g., the right to a fair trial and the right to education). Even if people are born with God-given natural rights, we need to explain how to get from those general and abstract rights to the specific rights found in contemporary declarations and treaties.

Attributing human rights to God's commands may give them a secure status at the metaphysical level, but in a very diverse world it does not make them practically secure. Billions of people do not believe in the God of Christianity, Islam, and Judaism. If people do not believe in God, or in the sort of god that prescribes rights, then if you want to base human rights on theological beliefs you must persuade these people of a rights-supporting theological view. This is likely to be even harder than persuading them of human rights. Legal enactment at the national and international levels provides a far more secure status for practical purposes.

Human rights could also exist independently of legal enactment by being part of actual human moralities. All human groups seem to have moralities: imperative norms of behavior backed by reasons and values. These moralities contain specific norms (for example, a prohibition of the intentional murder of an innocent person) and specific values (for example, valuing human life). One way in which human rights could exist apart from divine or human enactment is as norms accepted in all or almost all actual human moralities. If almost all human groups have moralities containing norms prohibiting murder, these norms could constitute the human right to life. Human rights can be seen as basic moral norms shared by all or almost all accepted human moralities.

This view is attractive but has serious difficulties. Although worldwide acceptance of human rights has been increasing rapidly in recent decades, worldwide moral unanimity about human rights does not exist. Human rights declarations and treaties are intended to change existing norms, not just describe the existing moral consensus.

Yet another way of explaining the existence of human rights is to say that they exist most basically in true or justified ethical outlooks. On this account, to say that there is a human right against torture is mainly to assert that there are strong reasons for believing that it is always wrong to engage in torture and that protections should be provided against its practice. This approach would view the Universal Declaration as attempting to formulate a justified political morality. It was not merely trying to identify a pre-existing moral consensus; it was also trying to create a consensus that could be supported by very plausible moral and practical reasons. This approach requires commitment to the objectivity of such reasons. It holds that just as there are reliable ways of finding out how the physical world works, or what makes buildings sturdy and durable, there are ways of finding out what individuals may justifiably demand of each other and of governments. Even if unanimity about human rights is currently lacking, rational agreement is available to humans if they will commit themselves to open-minded and serious moral and political inquiry. If moral reasons exist independently of human construction, they can–when combined with premises about current institutions, problems, and resources–generate moral norms different from those currently accepted or enacted. The Universal Declaration seems to proceed on exactly this assumption. One problem with this view is that existence as good reasons seems a rather thin form of existence for human rights. But perhaps we can view this thinness as a practical rather than a theoretical problem, as something to be remedied by the formulation and enactment of legal norms. The best form of existence for human rights would combine robust legal existence with the sort of moral existence that comes from being supported by strong moral and practical reasons.

Human Agency as the Basis of Human Rights

A justification for human rights–whether teleological, consequentialist, deontological, or something else–should justify the main features of human rights including their mandatory character, their universality, and their high priority. This makes the construction of a good justification a daunting task.

Grounding human rights in human agency and autonomy has had strong advocates in recent decades. In *Human Rights: Essays on Justification and Application* (1982) Alan Gewirth offered an agency-based justification for human rights. He argued that denying the value of successful agency and action is not an option for a human being; having a life requires regarding the indispensable conditions of agency and action as necessary goods. Abstractly described, these conditions of successful agency are freedom and well-being. A prudent rational agent who must have freedom and well-being will assert a "prudential right claim" to them. Having demanded that others must respect her freedom and well-being, consistency requires her to recognize and respect the freedom and well-being of other persons. Since all other agents are in exactly the same position as she is of desperately needing freedom and well-being, consistency requires her to recognize and respect their freedom and well-being. She "logically must accept" that other people as agents have equal rights to freedom and well-being. These two abstract rights work alone and together to generate equal specific human rights of familiar sorts. Gewirth's aspiration was to provide an argument for human rights that applies to all human agents and that is inescapable. From a few hard-to-dispute facts and a principle of consistency he thinks we can derive two generic human rights – and from them, a list of more determinate rights.

A more recent attempt to base human rights on agency and autonomy is found in James Griffin's book, *On Human Rights* 2008. Griffin does not share Gewirth's goal of providing a logically inescapable argument for human rights, but his overall view shares key structural features with Gewirth's. These include starting the justification with the unique value of agency and autonomy, postulating some abstract rights, and making a place for a right to well-being within an agency-based approach.

In the current dispute between "moral" (or "orthodox") and "political" conceptions of human rights, Griffin strongly sides with those who see human rights as fundamentally moral rights. Their defining role, in Griffin's view, is protecting people's ability to form and pursue conceptions of a worthwhile life – a capacity that Griffin variously refers to as "autonomy," "normative agency," and "personhood." This ability to form, revise, and pursue conceptions of a worthwhile life is taken to be of paramount value, the exclusive source of human dignity, and thereby the basis of human rights. Griffin holds that people value this capacity "especially highly, often more highly than even our happiness".

"Practicalities" also shape human rights in Griffin's view. He describes practicalities as "a second ground" of human rights. They prescribe making the boundaries of rights clear by avoiding "too many complicated bends," enlarging rights a little to give them safety margins, and consulting facts about human nature and the nature of society. Accordingly, the justifying generic function that Griffin assigns to human rights is protecting normative agency while taking account of practicalities.

Griffin claims that human rights suffer even more than other normative concepts from an "indeterminacy of sense" that makes them vulnerable to proliferation (Griffin 2008: 14-15). He thinks that tying all human rights to the single value of normative agency while taking account of practicalities is the best way to remedy this malady. He criticizes the frequent invention of new human rights and the "ballooning of the content" of established rights. Still, Griffin is friendly towards most of the rights in the Universal Declaration of Human Rights. Beyond this, Griffin takes human right to include many rights in interpersonal morality. For example, Griffin thinks that a child's human right to education applies not just against governments but also against a child's parents.

Griffin's thesis that all human rights are grounded in normative agency is put forward not so much as a description but as a proposal, as the best way of giving human rights unity, coherence, and limits. Unfortunately, accepting and following this proposal is unlikely to yield effective barriers to proliferation or a sharp line between human rights and other moral norms. The main reason is one that Griffin himself recognizes: the "generative capacities" of normative agency are "quite great." Providing adequate protections of the three components of normative agency (autonomy, freedom, and minimal well-being) will encounter a lot of threats to these values and hence will require lots of rights. A better strategy here involves imposing demanding tests through the justificatory process—and particularly near its end when questions of burdensomeness and feasibility are being considered. Perhaps Griffin could build these tests into his notion of practicalities.

Griffin thinks that he can explain the universality of human rights by recognizing that normative agency is a threshold concept–once one is above the threshold one gets the same rights as everyone else. One's degree of normative agency does not matter. There are no "degrees of being a person" among competent adults. Treating normative agency in this way, however, is a normative policy, not just a fact about concepts. An alternative policy is possible, namely proportioning people's rights to their level of normative agency. This is what we do with children; their rights grow as they develop greater agency and responsibility. To exclude proportional rights, and to explain the egalitarian dimensions of human rights such as their universality and their character as *equal* rights to be enjoyed without discrimination, some additional ground pertaining to equality seems to be needed.

Political Conceptions of Human Rights

A political conception of human rights offers an account of what human rights are – or at least of what contemporary human rights are at the national and international levels. Advocates of political conceptions of human rights are often agnostic about universal *moral* rights while rejecting moral skepticism and thinking possible the provision of sound normative justifications for the content, normativity, and roles of human rights.

John Rawls introduced the idea of a political conception of human rights in his book, *The Law of Peoples* (Rawls 1999). The basic idea is that we can understand what human rights are and what their justification requires by identifying the main roles they play in some political sphere. In *The Law of Peoples* this sphere is international relations (and, secondarily, national politics). Rawls was attempting a normative reconstruction of international law and politics within today's international system, and this helps explain Rawls's focus on how human rights function within this system. Human rights within inter*personal* relations are not part of this sphere.

Rawls says that human rights are *a special class of urgent rights*. He seems to accept the definition of human rights given in Section 1 above. Besides saying that human rights are rights that are high priority or "urgent," Rawls also accepts that they are plural and universal. But Rawls was working on a narrower project than Gewirth and Griffin. The *international* human rights he was concerned with are also defined by their roles in helping define in various ways the normative structure of the global system. They provide content to other normative concepts such as legitimacy, sovereignty, permissible intervention, and membership in good standing in the international community.

The justificatory process for human rights and the other principles of the law of peoples is analogous to the one for principles of justice at the national level that Rawls described in *A Theory of Justice* (Rawls 1971). Instead of asking about the terms of cooperation that free and equal citizens would agree to under fair conditions, we ask about the terms of cooperation that free and equal *peoples* or countries would agree to under fair conditions. We imagine representatives of the world's countries meeting to choose the normative principles that constitute the basic international structure. These representatives are imagined to see the countries they represent as free (rightfully independent) and equal (equally worthy of respect and fair treatment). These representatives are also imagined to be choosing rationally in light of the fundamental interests of their country, to be reasonable in seeking to find and respect fair terms of cooperation, and impartial because they are behind a "veil of ignorance"– they lack information about the country they represent such as its size, wealth, and power. Rawls holds that under these conditions these representatives will unanimously choose principles for the global order that include some basic human rights.

Rawls advocated a modest list of human rights, one that leaves out many fundamental freedoms, rights of political participation, and equality rights. He did this for two reasons. One is that he wanted a list that is not parochial to the liberal democracies and that countries around the world would find attractive. The second reason is that he viewed serious violations of human rights as triggers of the permissibility of various kinds of intervention by other countries, and only the most important rights can play this role.

Leaving out any protection for equality and democracy is a high price to pay for assigning human rights the role of making international intervention permissible when they are seriously violated. We can accommodate Rawls's underlying idea without paying that price. To accept the idea that countries engaging in massive violations of the most important human rights are not to be tolerated we do not need to follow Rawls in equating international human rights with a heavily-pruned list. Instead we can work up a view–which is needed for other purposes anyway – of which human rights are the weightiest and then assign the intervention-permitting role to this subset.

Let's now turn to Charles Beitz's account of human rights in *The Idea of Human Rights* (Beitz 2009). His view shares many similarities with Rawls's but is more fully developed. Like Rawls, Beitz deals with human rights only as they have developed in contemporary international human rights practice. Beitz suggests that we can develop an understanding of human rights by attending to "the practical inferences that would be drawn by competent participants in the practice from what they regard as valid claims of human rights." Observations of what competent participants say and do inform the account of what human rights are. The focus is not on what human rights are at some deep philosophical level; it is rather on how they work by guiding actions within a recently emerged and still evolving discursive practice. The norms of the practice guide the interpretation and application of human rights, the appropriateness of criticism in terms of human rights, adjudication in human rights courts, and – perhaps most importantly – responding to serious violations of human rights. Beitz says that human rights are "matters of international concern" and that they are "potential triggers of transnational protective and remedial action."

Beitz does not agree with Rawls's view that these roles require an abbreviated list of human rights. He accepts that the requirements of human rights are weaker than the requirements of social justice at the national level, but denies that human rights are minimal or highly modest in other respects.

Beitz rightly suggests that a person can accept and use the idea of human rights without accepting any particular view about their foundations. It is less clear that he is right in suggesting that good justifications of human rights should avoid as far as possible controversial assumptions about religion, metaphysics, ideology, and intrinsic value (see the entry public reason). Beitz emphasizes the practical good that human rights do, not their reflection of some underlying moral reality. This makes human rights attractive to people from around the world with their diverse religious and philosophical traditions. The broad justification for human rights and their normativity that Beitz offers is that they protect "urgent individual interests against predictable dangers ("standard threats") to which they are vulnerable under typical circumstances of life in a modern world order composed of states."

WHICH RIGHTS ARE HUMAN RIGHTS?

Not every question of social justice or wise governance is a human rights issue. For example, a country could have too much income inequality or inadequate provision for higher education without violating any human rights. Deciding which norms should be counted as human rights is a matter of considerable difficulty. And there is continuing pressure to expand lists of human rights to include new areas. Many political movements would like to see their main concerns categorized as matters of human rights, since this would publicize, promote, and legitimize their concerns at the international level. A possible result of this is "human rights inflation," the devaluation of human rights caused by producing too much bad human rights currency.

One way to avoid rights inflation is to follow Cranston in insisting that human rights only deal with extremely important goods, protections, and freedoms. A supplementary approach is to impose several justificatory tests for specific human rights. For example, it could be required that a proposed human right not only deal with some very important good but also respond to a common and serious threat to that good, impose burdens on the addressees that are justifiable and no larger than necessary, and be feasible in most of the world's countries (see Nickel 2007). This approach restrains rights inflation with several tests, not just one master test.

Human rights are specific and problem-oriented. Historic bills of rights often begin with a list of complaints about the abuses of previous regimes or eras. Bills of rights may have preambles that speak grandly and abstractly of life, liberty, and the inherent dignity of persons, but their lists of rights contain specific norms addressed to familiar political, legal, or economic problems.

In deciding which specific rights are human rights it is possible to make either too little or too much of international documents such as the Universal Declaration and the European Convention. One makes too little of them by proceeding as if drawing up a list of important rights were a new question, never before addressed, and as if there were no practical wisdom to be found in the choices of rights that went into the historic documents. And one makes too much of them by presuming that those documents tell us everything we need to know about human rights. This approach involves a kind of fundamentalism: it holds that when a right is on the official lists of human rights that settles its status as a human right. But the process of identifying human rights in the United Nations and elsewhere was a political process with plenty of imperfections. There is little reason to take international diplomats as the most authoritative guides to which human rights there are. Further, even if a treaty could settle the issue of whether a certain right is a human right within international law, such a treaty cannot settle its weight. It may claim that the right is supported by weighty considerations, but it cannot make this so. If an international treaty enacted a right to visit national parks without charge as a human right, the ratification of that treaty would make free access to national parks a human right within international law. But it would not be able to make us believe that the right to visit national parks without charge was sufficiently important to be a real human right.

Civil and Political Rights

These rights are familiar from historic bills of rights such as the French Declaration of the Rights of Man and the Citizen (1789) and the U.S. Bill of Rights (1791). Contemporary sources include the first 21 Articles of the Universal Declaration, and such treaties as the European Convention, the International Covenant on Civil and Political Rights, the American Convention on Human Rights, and the African Charter on Human and People's Rights. Some representative formulations follow:

> Everyone has the right to freedom of thought and expression. This right includes freedom to seek, receive, and impart information and ideas of all kinds, regardless of frontiers, either orally, in writing, in print, in the form of art, or through any other medium of one's choice. (American Convention on Human Rights, Article 13.1)

Everyone has the right to freedom of peaceful assembly and to freedom of association with others, including the right to form and to join trade unions for the protection of his interests (European Convention, Article 11).

1. Every citizen shall have the right to participate freely in the government of his country, either directly or through freely chosen representatives in accordance with the provisions of the law. 2. Every citizen shall have the right of equal access to the public service of his country. 3. Every individual shall have the right of access to public property and services in strict equality of all persons before the law (African Charter, Article 13).

Most civil and political rights are not absolute—they can in some cases be overridden by other considerations. For example, the right to freedom of movement can be restricted by public and private property rights, by restraining orders related to domestic violence, and by legal punishments. Further, after a disaster such as a hurricane or earthquake free movement is often appropriately suspended to keep out the curious, to permit access of emergency vehicles and equipment, and to prevent looting. The International Covenant on Civil and Political Rights permits rights to be suspended during times "of public emergency which threatens the life of the nation" (Article 4). But it excludes some rights from suspension including the right to life, the prohibition of torture, the prohibition of slavery, the prohibition of ex post facto criminal laws, and freedom of thought and religion.

Rights of Women, Minorities and Groups

Equality of rights for historically disadvantaged or subordinated groups is a longstanding concern of the human rights movement. Human rights documents repeatedly emphasize that all people, including women and members of minority ethnic and religious groups, have equal human rights and should be able to enjoy them without discrimination. The right to freedom from discrimination figures prominently in the Universal Declaration and subsequent treaties. The Civil and Political Covenant, for example, commits participating states to respect and protect their people's rights "without distinction of any kind, such as race, color, sex, language, political or other opinion, national or social origin, property, birth, or social status".

A number of standard individual rights are especially important to ethnic and religious minorities, including rights to freedom of association, freedom of assembly, freedom of religion, and freedom from discrimination. Human rights documents also include rights that refer to minorities explicitly and give them special protections. For example, the Civil and Political Covenant in Article 27 says that persons belonging to ethnic, religious, or linguistic minorities "shall not be denied the right, in community with other members of their group, to enjoy their own culture, to profess and practice their own religion, or to use their own language."

Feminists have often protested that standard lists of human rights do not sufficiently take into account the different risks faced by women and men. For example, issues like domestic violence, reproductive choice, and trafficking of women and girls for sex work did not have a prominent place in early human rights documents and treaties. Lists of human rights have had to be expanded to include the degradation and violation of women. Violations of women's human rights often occur in the home at the hands of other family members, not in the street at the hands of the police. Most violence against women occurs in the "private" sphere. This has meant that governments cannot be seen as the only addressees of human rights and that the right to privacy of home and family needs qualifications to allow police to protect women within the home.

The issue of how formulations of human rights should respond to variations in the sorts of risks and dangers that different people face is difficult and arises not just in relation to gender but also in relation to age, profession, political affiliation, religion, and personal interests. Due process rights, for example, are much more useful to young people than they are to older people since the latter are far less likely to run afoul of the law.

Since 1964 the United Nations has mainly dealt with the rights of women and minorities through specialized treaties such as the International Convention on the Elimination of All Forms of Racial Discrimination(1965); the Convention on the Elimination of All Forms of Discrimination Against Women (1979); the Convention on the Rights of the Child (1989), the Convention on the Rights of Persons with Disabilities (2007) and also the Declaration on the Rights of Indigenous Peoples (2007). Specialized treaties allow international norms to address unique problems of particular groups such as assistance and care during pregnancy and childbearing in the case of women, custody issues in the case of children, and the loss of historic territories by indigenous peoples.

Minority groups are often targets of violence. Human rights norms call upon governments to refrain from such violence and to provide protections against it. This work is partly done by the right to life, which is a standard individual right. It is also done by the right against genocide which protects groups from attempts to destroy or decimate them. The Genocide Convention was one of the first human rights treaties after World War II. The right against genocide seems to be a group right. It is held by both individuals and groups and provides protection to groups as groups. It is largely negative in the sense that it requires governments and other agencies to refrain from destroying groups; but it also requires that legal and other protections against genocide be created at the national level.

Can a group right fit the general idea of human rights proposed earlier? Perhaps it can if we broaden the conception of who can hold human rights to include ethnic and religious groups. This can be made more palatable, perhaps, by recognizing that the beneficiaries of the right against genocide are individual humans who enjoy greater security against attempts to destroy the group to which they belong.

Environmental Rights

In spite of the danger of rights inflation, there are doubtless norms that should be counted as human rights but are not generally so treated. After all, there are lots of areas in which people's dignity and fundamental interests are threatened by governmental actions and omissions. Consider environmental rights, which are often defined as rights of animals or of nature itself. Conceived in this way they do not fit our general idea of human rights because the rightholders are not humans or human groups. But more modest formulations are possible; environmental rights can be understood as rights to an environment that is healthy and safe. Such a right is human-oriented: it does not directly address issues such as the claims of animals, biodiversity, or sustainable development.

A justification for this right must show that environmental problems pose serious threats to fundamental human interests, values, or norms; that governments may appropriately be burdened with the responsibility of protecting people against these threats; and that most governments actually have the ability to do this. This last requirement – feasibility – may be the most difficult. Environmental protection is expensive and difficult, and many governments will be unable to do very much of it while meeting other important responsibilities. The problem of feasibility in poorer countries might be addressed here in the same way that it was in the Social Covenant. That treaty commits governments not to the immediate realization of social rights for all, but rather to making the realization of such rights a high-priority goal and beginning to take steps towards its fulfillment.

Implementing a new right has opportunity costs. If no new resources are available, implementing a new right will mean that fewer resources are available for the implementation of existing rights. Rights are not magical sources of supply (Holmes and Sunstein 1999, Nickel 2007, ch. 5). This is not to deny, however, that successful implementation of a right can reduce threats in some areas and thereby reduce costs. For example, success in protecting the rights of minorities may reduce ethnic conflict and the threats to rights that it generates.

In 2012 the United Nations Human Rights Council appointed an Independent Expert on Human Rights and the Environment. The mandate for this position includes studying "human rights obligations relating to the enjoyment of a safe, clean, healthy and sustainable environment" and finding ways in which human rights can contribute to environmental protection.

Social Rights

The Universal Declaration included social or welfare rights that address matters such as education, food, and employment. Their inclusion has been the source of much controversy (see Beetham 1995). Social rights are often alleged to be statements of desirable goals but not really rights. The European Convention did not include them although it was later amended to include the right to education. Instead they were put into a separate treaty, the European Social Charter. When the United Nations began the process of putting the rights of the Universal Declaration into international law, it followed the model of the European system by treating economic and social standards in a treaty separate from the one dealing with civil and political rights. This treaty, the International Covenant on Economic, Social, and Cultural Rights (the "Social Covenant," 1966), treated these standards as rights – albeit rights to be progressively realized.

The Social Covenant's list of rights includes nondiscrimination and equality for women in economic and social life (Articles 2 and 3), freedom to work and opportunities to work (Article 4), fair pay and decent conditions of work (Article 7), the right to form trade unions and to strike (Article 8), social security (Article 9), special protections for mothers and children (Article 10), the right to adequate food, clothing, and housing (Article 11), the right to basic health services (Article 12), the right to education (Article 13), and the right to participate in cultural life and scientific progress (Article 15).

Article 2.1 of the Social Covenant sets out what each of the parties commits itself to do about this list, namely to "take steps, individually and through international assistance and co-operation…to the maximum of its available resources, with a view to achieving progressively the full realization of the rights recognized in the present Covenant." In contrast, the Civil and Political Covenant simply commits its signatories to "respect and to ensure to all individuals within its territory the rights recognized in the present Covenant" (Article 2.1). The contrast between these two levels of commitment has led some people to suspect that economic and social rights are really just valuable goals.

The system to monitor and promote compliance with the Social Covenant is modest since it mainly requires participating countries to make periodic reports on measures taken to comply with the treaty. Countries agree "to submit…reports on the measures which they have adopted and the progress made in achieving the observance of the rights recognized herein" (Article 16). A committee of experts, created by the Economic and Social Council in 1987, is given the job of looking at the progress reports from the participating countries. This body, the Committee on Economic, Social and Cultural Rights, studies the reports, discusses them with representatives of the governments reporting, and issues interpretive statements known as "General Comments" on the requirements of the treaty. A recent amendment to the treaty allows residents of countries that approve the amendment to submit complaints of violations to the Committee.

Why did the Social Covenant opt for progressive implementation and thereby treat its rights as being somewhat like goals? The main reason is that nearly half of the world's countries were in no position in terms of economic, institutional, and human resources to realize these standards fully or even largely. For many countries, noncompliance due to inability would have been certain if these standards had been treated as immediately binding. We will return to this topic below.

Opponents of social rights often deny them the status of human rights, restricting that standing to civil and political rights. Familiar objections to social rights include the following:

(1) they do not serve truly fundamental interests;

(2) they are too burdensome on governments and taxpayers; and

(3) they are not feasible in less-developed countries.

It is far from the case that most social rights pertain to superficial interests. Consider two examples: the right to an adequate standard of living and the right to free public education. These rights require governments to try to remedy widespread and serious evils such as hunger and ignorance. The importance of food and other basic material conditions of life is easy to show. These goods are essential to people's ability to live, function, and flourish. Without adequate access to these goods, interests in life, health, and liberty are endangered and serious illness and death are probable. Lack of access to educational opportunities typically limits (both absolutely and comparatively) people's abilities to participate fully and effectively in the political and economic life of their country. Lack of education increases the likelihood of unemployment and underemployment.

Another way to defend the importance of social rights is to show the highly useful support they provide to the full realization of civil and political rights. If a government succeeds in eliminating hunger and providing education to everyone this promotes people's abilities to know, use, and enjoy their liberties, due process rights, and rights of political participation. This is easiest to see in regard to education. Ignorance is a barrier to the realization of civil and political rights because uneducated people often do not know what rights they have and what they can do to use and defend them. It is also easy to see in the area of democratic participation. Education and a minimum income make it easier for people at the bottom economically to follow politics, participate in political campaigns, and to spend the time and money needed to go to the polls and vote.

The second objection is that social rights are too burdensome. It is very expensive to guarantee to everyone basic education and minimal material conditions of life. Perhaps social rights are too expensive or burdensome to be justified even in rich countries. Frequently the claim that social rights are too burdensome uses other, less controversial human rights as a standard of comparison, and suggests that social rights are substantially more burdensome or expensive than liberty rights. Suppose that we use as a basis of comparison liberty rights such as freedom of communication, association, and movement. These rights require both respect and protection from governments. And people cannot be adequately protected in their enjoyment of liberties such as these unless they also have security and due process rights. The costs of liberty, as it were, include the costs of law and criminal justice. Once we see this, liberty rights start to look a lot more costly. To provide effective liberties to communicate, associate, and move it is not enough for a society to make a prohibition of interference with these activities part of its law and accepted morality. An effective system of provision for these liberties will require a legal scheme that defines personal and property rights and protects these rights against invasions while ensuring due process to those accused of crimes. Providing such legal protection in the form of legislatures, police, courts, and prisons is extremely expensive.

Further, we should not think of social rights as simply giving everyone a free supply of the goods these rights protect. Guarantees of things like food and housing will be intolerably expensive and will undermine productivity if everyone simply receives a free supply. A viable system of social rights will require most people to provide these goods for themselves and their families through work as long as they are given the necessary opportunities, education, and infrastructure. Government-implemented social rights provide guarantees of availability, but governments should have to supply the requisite goods in only a small fraction of cases. Note that education is often an exception to this since many countries provide free public education irrespective of ability to pay.

Countries that do not accept and implement social rights still have to bear somehow the costs of providing for the needy since these countries—particularly if they recognize democratic rights of political participation—are unlikely to find it tolerable to allow sizeable parts of the population to starve and be homeless. If government does not supply food, clothing, and shelter to those unable to provide for themselves, then families, friends, and communities will have to shoulder this burden. It is only in the last century that government-sponsored social rights have taken over a substantial part of the burden of providing for the needy. The taxes associated with social rights are partial replacements for other burdensome duties, namely the duties of families and communities to provide adequate care for the unemployed, sick, disabled, and aged. Deciding whether to implement social rights is not a matter of deciding whether to bear such burdens, but rather of deciding whether to continue with total reliance on a system of informal provision that distributes assistance in a very spotty way and whose costs fall very unevenly on families, friends, and communities.

Once we recognize that liberty rights also carry high costs, that intelligent systems of provision for social rights supply the requisite goods to people in only a small minority of cases, and that these systems are substitutes for other, more local ways of providing for the needy, the difference in size between the costs of liberty rights and the costs of social rights ceases to seem so large.

Even if the burdens imposed by social rights are not excessive, it might still be wrong to impose them on individuals. Libertarians object to social rights as requiring impermissible taxation. Nozick, for example, says that "Taxation of earnings from labor is on a par with forced labor" (Nozick 1974: 169). This view is vulnerable to an attack asserting two things. First, taxation is permissible when it is used to support government-organized systems of humanitarian assistance that fulfill more effectively than charity duties of assistance that all individuals have. Second, property rights are not so strong that they can never be outweighed by the requirements of meeting other rights.

The third objection to social rights is that they are not feasible in many countries. It is very expensive to provide guarantees of subsistence, minimal public health measures, and basic education. The Social Covenant dealt with the issue of feasibility by calling for progressive implementation, that is, implementation as financial and other resources permit.

Standards that outrun the abilities of many of their addressees are good candidates for normative treatment as goals. Treating such standards as goals, which allows us to view them as largely aspirational rather than as imposing immediate duties, avoids massive problems of inability-based noncompliance. One may worry, however, that this is too much of a demotion. As norms, goals seem much weaker than rights. But goals can be formulated in ways that make them more like rights. Goals can be assigned addressees (the party who is to pursue the goal), beneficiaries, scopes that define the objective to be pursued, and a high level of priority. Strong reasons for the importance of these goals can be provided. And supervisory bodies can monitor levels of progress and pressure low-performing addressees to attend to and work on their goals.

Treating very demanding rights as goals has several advantages. One is that proposed goals that exceed one's abilities are not as farcical as proposed duties that exceed one's abilities. Creating grand lists of human rights that many countries cannot at present realize seems fraudulent to many people, and perhaps this fraudulence is reduced if we understand that these "rights" are really goals that countries should promote. Goals are inherently ability-calibrated. What you should do now about your goals depends on your abilities and other commitments. Goals coexist happily with low levels of ability to achieve them. Another advantage is that goals are flexible; addressees with different levels of ability can choose ways of pursuing the goals that suit their circumstances and means. Because of these attractions of goals, it will be worth exploring ways to transform very demanding human rights into goals. The transformation may be full or partial.

A right together with its supporting reasons might be divided into two parts. One part, call it the "demand side," sets out the rightholder's claim and the reasons why it is very valuable or important that this claim be fulfilled. In the right to a fair trial when one is arrested and accused of a crime` the demand side would set out the rightholder's claim to a fair trial and the reasons why that claim is very valuable or important. The other part, the "supply side," would set out the addressees' responsibilities in regard to the rightholder's claim. It would explain why this claim to a fair trial is a matter of duty, what the duties are, and why it is these particular addressees rather than other possible addressees that have the duty.

A goal that is similar to a right could also be divided into these two parts. The demand side would set out the beneficiary's claim or demand and the reasons why it is very desirable or important that this demand be fulfilled. For example, the demand side might set out the reasons why it is desirable for the beneficiary to have access to employment. And the supply side would set out the addressee's responsibility in regard to the beneficiary's demand. It would explain why promoting access to employment for the beneficiary should be a goal for the addressee. It does not impose duties on the addressee, but it shows that the addressee has good reasons for acting to satisfy the demand.

Since even a goal that is supported by good reasons imposes no duties—that is, fails to be mandatory in character—we may think that such goals are poor substitutes for rights and should not be called "rights." But it is possible to create right-goal mixtures that contain some mandatory elements and that therefore seem more like real rights. A minimal right-goal mixture would include a duty to try to realize the goal as quickly as possible. Here the demand side would set out the beneficiary's demand or claim and the reasons why it is very desirable or important that this demand be fulfilled. And the supply side would explain not only why the addressee has good reasons to pursue this goal, but also explain why the addressee has a duty to try to realize this goal with all deliberate speed. The economic and social rights in the Social Covenant seem to fit this model. The countries ratifying the Covenant agree to make it a matter of government duty to realize the list of rights as soon as possible. As we saw earlier, each of the Social Covenant's signatories has agreed to "take steps, individually and through international assistance and co-operation to the maximum of its available resources, with a view to achieving progressively the full realization of the rights recognized in the present Covenant." The signatories agree, on this interpretation, to make it a matter of duty to realize the listed rights as soon and as far as resources permit.

A problem with such a right-goal mixture is that it allows the addressee great discretion concerning *when* to do something about the right and *how much* to do. A panel supervising compliance with a human rights treaty may wish to remove some of this discretion by requiring that the addressees at least take some significant and good faith steps immediately and regularly and that these steps be documented. Duties to try are less vaporous if they are combined with duties that require immediate steps. Countries may be required to act in certain ways (e.g., make a good faith effort and be prepared to demonstrate that they have done so), set specific benchmarks and timetables, establish agencies to work on the goals, provide them with budgets, and use expert assistance from international agencies. To facilitate the monitoring of compliance the country may be required to collect data continuously concerning realization of the goals, make periodic reports, and allow its citizens to complain to the monitoring body about failures to pursue the goals energetically.

Insistence that human rights not be too demanding can be complemented by measures to enhance the ability of developing countries to realize human rights. Possible strategies for such a combined approach include using aid to increase the resources available for implementing rights, providing education to current and future officials, offering technical assistance concerning mechanisms of implementation, and battling corruption.

John Rawls proposed a duty of liberal democratic countries to aid poor or "burdened" countries. Rawls defines "burdened societies" as ones that "lack the political and cultural traditions, the human capital and know-how and, often, the material and technological resources needed to be well-ordered" (Rawls 1999). Rawls holds that well-off countries have a moral duty to assist burdened societies. Unfortunately Rawls does not provide much justification for this claim. In particular he does not use his idea of an international "original position" to work out how the justification for such a duty would go and what objections it would need to overcome.

A good defense of a duty of well-off countries to assist poor ones in realizing human rights would not automatically impose that duty on the citizens of the well-off countries (except, of course, through the taxes they pay). But perhaps citizens should share somehow in duties of international aid. One approach to explaining how and why citizens share in these duties involves viewing the citizens of a democratic country as having ultimate responsibility for the human rights duties of their government. If their government has a duty to respect or implement the right to a fair trial, or a duty to aid poor countries, its citizens share in that duty. They are required as voters, political agents, and taxpayers to try to promote and support their government's compliance with its human rights duties. This principle of shared duty is particularly attractive in democratic societies where the citizens are the ultimate source of political authority. This view makes individuals back-up addressees for the duties of their governments.

Thomas Pogge has taken a related but slightly different approach to generating individual duties from human rights that have governments as their primary addressees. Pogge emphasizes the Universal Declaration's Article 28 which says that "Everyone is entitled to a social and international order in which this the rights and freedoms set forth in this Declaration can be fully realized." Pogge sees in this Article a plausible norm, namely that both countries and individuals have negative duties not to be complicit in an international order that unfairly disadvantages poor countries and the people in them. A coercive political order, whether national or international, "must not avoidably restrict the freedom of some so as to render their access to basic necessities insecure –especially through official denial or deprivation. If it does, then all human agents have a negative duty, correlative to the postulated social and economic human rights, not to cooperate in upholding it unless they compensate for their cooperation by protecting its victims or by working for its reform. Those violating this duty share responsibility for the harms (insecure access to basic necessities) produced by the unjust institutional order in question" (Pogge 2002: 67).

WHAT MAKES A RIGHT FUNDAMENTAL?

Liberalism needs a theory of fundamental rights. Since rights belong to persons, a theory of rights should be linked to a conception of the person. The courts have never undertaken to develop such a conception. The implications of adopting competing positivist, deontological or empiricist conceptions of the person are explored. Because of the weaknesses of each, an eclectic politics of rights approach is advocated. On this approach, the validity of a claim of right is enhanced by its formal neutrality and congruity with legal precedent, but also depends on careful assessment of what recognition of the right would mean for actual persons in the concrete political situation.

Modern theories of the juridical function begin with the premise that ours is basically a democratic form of government, in which basic decisions are to be made by majority vote. Yet it is also a constitutional form of government, in which the powers of the majority are subject to definite limits. According to the doctrine adumbrated in the famous Carolene Products case (U.S. v. Carolene Products Co, 1938), those limits are breached when the majority seeks to violate fundamental rights, or to harm persons whom the political process cannot be relied upon to protect, or to impair the self-corrective processes designed into the political system. The Court did not then attempt to identify which rights are the most fundamental, beyond suggesting that the economic rights implicated in <169>ordinary commercial transactions are not among them. Within a few years, though, the Court had indicated that First Amendment rights were special, because of their central role in the self- corrective processes alluded to above: When we balance the Constitutional right of owners of property against those of the people to enjoy freedom of press and religion...we remain mindful of the fact that the latter occupy a preferred position...The First Amendment lies at the foundation of free government by free men (Marsh v. Alabama, 1946). It is worth noting that this can be interpreted as essentially a utilitarian argument for the primacy of First Amendment rights: their preservation is defended more as a long-term benefit for the society and the political system than as a need, desire or desert of the individual currently asserting the right. Thus Justice Frankfurter, citing Holmes, explained the rationale for the preferred position of free speech by arguing that the progress of civilization depends on maintaining the capacity for displacement of error (Kovacs v. Cooper, 1949). Yet, as he was keenly aware, the justice of an earlier generation had been equally convinced that the progress of civilization depends on free-market enterprise, largely immune to governmental regulation. It is not easy to show why the former belief is more scientific, less dogmatic than the latter. It is not only economic theories of progress that are subject to controversy and displacement.

Frankfurter's own response to this dilemma was to espouse judicial restraint in dealing with First Amendment claims as well as claims of economic rights. Courts, he held, were no more warranted in imposing their political than their economic predilections upon the elected agents of the people. Yet the denial that some rights are more fundamental than others has also appealed to certain judicial activists, who see the court's reluctance since 1937 to enforce property rights as an unprincipled surrender to political pressures, no longer warranted if it ever was. It is this perspective that seems to motivate such diverse pronouncements as Justice Stewart's insistence that property rights are personal rights (Lynch v. Household Finance Corp., 1972); Justice Stevens's attack on the multitiered approach to equal protection analysis (Craig v. Boren, 1976); and the Court's recent revival of ordinary scrutiny with teeth in striking down as irrational a statute that concededly did not impair a fundamental right or employ a suspect classification (Cleburne v. Cleburne Living Center, 1985). Apparently, the utilitarian or process-oriented approach to preferred freedoms has failed to commend itself to a stable, nonpartisan majority of the Supreme Court.

The Court has followed a similar path to fundamental rights in the context of the debate over incorporation of Bill of Rights guarantees pertaining to criminal procedures into the due process clause of the

Fourteenth Amendment. Here the prevailing approach has been to appeal to a concept of ordered liberty (Palko v. Connecticut, 1937), or the notions of justice of English-speaking peoples (Malinski v. New York, 1945) in order to identify those protections that are fundamental. Activist and restraint-oriented justice have often disagreed on results; but in methodological terms, all of them have looked unsystematically, and without rigorous empirical support, to historic pronouncements, ostensible current public opinion, and their own instincts in order to determine what shocks the conscience (Rochin v. California, 1952) or is repugnant to the traditions and conscience of our people (Snyder v. Massachusetts, 1934). Ultimately, one is apt to conclude that a right simply is fundamental when a majority of the Court says it is.

Conceptions of Persons and Rights

An alternative, and perhaps more promising, approach to the identification of fundamental rights would start from the axiomatic proposition that constitutional rights are personal rights (Regents of the University of California v. Bakke, 1978), and seek to derive a theory of rights from the relevant conception of a person. The first obstacle confronting such a project is that our jurisprudence, and especially our judiciary, has tended to shy away from exploring the concept of personhood. In fact, there is remarkably little material to work with, and that is mostly of little use to the present effort. The available literature suggests, however, that there are several ways of conceptualizing the relationship between personhood and rights, corresponding to several different ways of conceptualizing personhood itself.

One approach deserving mention is the legal-positivist. On this view, a person is simply what the law says it is including, in our society, ships and corporations, but not necessarily all members of our biological species (e.g., slaves or the unborn). Here, personhood is nothing more than a convenience, giving the entity access to the courts. It implies nothing of empirical or moral significance about the entity itself. Thus, it can tell us nothing about what specific rights the entity ought to have.

A related, but more substantive approach might be called the political-positivist. On this view, to be a person is to be recognized as a member of society. Whoever is so recognized is a person; whoever is not is not. Just as admission to citizenship in a specific political community is a matter of grace, not a matter of right, so too with membership in the broader human community. On this view, again, recognition will be a precondition for possessing rights, but the nature of the decision to recognize will not itself determine what rights it entails, because the decision is purely discretionary and need not depend on any particular facts about the applicant. Indeed, on the positivist approach the relationship may be just the opposite: the fact that all persons are accorded certain rights will determine the costs and benefits to society of admitting a given applicant, and personhood may be recognized or not for that reason alone.

Positivism of the legal and/or political stripe is reflected, though never expressly endorsed and argued for, in the record of Supreme Court decisions on slavery, corporate personhood, and abortion. In each case, the Court avoided any definition or principled analysis of personhood, simply appealing instead to the way it felt the law, the society, and/or the political branches of government had traditionally regarded the entity in question (Dred Scott v. Sanford, 1857; Santa Clara v. Southern Pacific Railroad Co., 1386; Roe v. Wade, 1973). In striking contrast, many of the same justice felt free to appeal to higher law or scientific principles when it came time to identify and construe the fundamental rights which attached to personhood, including, in particular, property rights.

Logically, a positivist approach to personhood suggests, if it does not absolutely require, a positivist approach to rights.On that approach, a person's rights are simply what the lawgiver says they are, and those rights are fundamental which the lawgiver has identified as such. Typically, as suggested above, the rationale for deeming a right fundamental, like the rationale for recognizing a person, would be a utilitarian one if indeed any rationale is provided or wanted in a positivist system.

A very different approach to personhood might be called the moral-philosophical. This view or family of views, sometimes seems to point to certain specific attributes of persons their self-consciousness, rationality, autonomy, and so forth as grounding their inclusion in the human community and their entitlement to certain rights. Philosophical approaches to personhood, or at least those of interest here, are typically linked to deontological theories of rights. Such theories identify a right as fundamental by linking it to what the person basically is. Insofar as they emphasize such attributes as moral agency and rationality as basic to personhood, they are focusing on (moral) desert rather than (biological) need or (psychological) desire as the wellspring of fundamental rights. Theories that ground a person's rights in the actions he or she has voluntarily performed, such as one's labor or one's contracts, are also desert-based.

A historical forebear of this approach was the theological one, defining the person as one possessing a soul. Ensoulment or rationality would seem to be a fact about the person that has important consequences for the theory of rights. Yet these factual concepts, in both their classical and modern forms, have proven conspicuously resistant to clear definition, let alone scientific measurement. More important, as Sandel (1982) points out in critique of Rawls, on close inspection it appears that these attributes of personhood are not strictly independent of and prior to the rights and responsibilities that are claimed to flow from personhood. Rather, typically the attributes are deliberately selected and defined so as to justify the particular normative consequences desired. Indeed, this strategy is openly embraced in Rawls's method of reflective equilibrium. Empirical attributes that get in the way are thus declared incidental, and not constitutive of the person. The facts that count are moral ones those that determine what we deserve. Typically, membership in the human species has implicitly been taken as a necessary and sufficient condition for personhood, with little attention paid to the issues posed by borderline cases such as immaturity or severe impairment.

The moral-philosophical approach has ancient roots, for example in Plato; in its modern form it is exemplified by Enlightenment thinkers like Kant and Hegel, and by contemporaries like Nozick, Rawls, Dworkin and Ackerman, whom Kant has influenced. Their central concern with the dignity and rights of persons is, not coincidentally, congruent with the logical structure and normative emphasis of liberal constitutionalism. Yet, as we have seen, the courts have avoided incorporating their approach into the law itself. Instead, they have tolerated the utilitarianism implicit in the positivist approach.

Another possible approach might be called the scientific-empirical. On this view, the question is not whether society has in fact accepted one as a member, but whether one actually possesses empirical characteristics that entitle one to be so recognized. Those characteristics might be biological, psychological, sociological, or what have you, so long as they are objectively demonstrable. Unlike the Kantian approach, the scientific approach allows that personhood could be a matter of degree. Unlike the positivist approach, the scientific approach to personhood entails a theory of human nature. The characteristics we identify as definitive of a person will have much to say about the basic needs and desires of persons. Thus, this approach should be far more fruitful than the positivist one for a theory of rights provided, of course, that the requisite facts can be established. Empirical approaches to personhood aspire to placing rights on a scientific basis, instead of an inherently controversial moral one. Thus, they appeal to generalizations about biological need and/or psychological desire, taking it as axiomatic that universal needs and desires are entitled to respect. In light of human diversity, though, science is unlikely to justify the equality of fundamental rights that has been a basic premise of Western moral philosophy.

The question of personhood has been approached in a scientific spirit by thinkers as diverse as Aristotle, Locke. Hume, and Marx. All sought to derive propositions about how we ought to live from propositions about how we naturally are, and to derive the latter from observations of the world of our senses. In recent years this approach has been discredited, partly by the severe difficulties experienced in establishing consensus about the scientific facts; partly by the argument that normative consequences would not flow from the facts, even if they could be established; and partly by revulsion against the kinds of inegalitarian policy inferences drawn by observers of human nature like Spencer, not to mention Nietzsche. Indeed, the argument that such theories as Spencer's have no place in our jurisprudence was a major element in the legal realists' assault, led by Holmes, on the view that property rights enjoy a preferred status in constitutional law (Lochner v. New York, 1905). Modern social science has so far failed to supply legal and philosophical thinkers with persuasive accounts either of what unites us or of what divides us. In the absence of such accounts, agnosticism and dogma have been the only available alternatives.

Philosophically, as Sandel (1982) points out, the difficulty is this. Liberalism needs a conception of the person that is sufficiently rich and realistic to have significant and constructive consequences one that respects the real differences between individuals and the hard choices that our specific form of life requires. At the same time, it needs a conception that is neutral as between different political factions and different private conceptions of the good one that upholds the equal dignity of all, and does not merely reflect or institutionalize some set of historically contingent and morally arbitrary biases. Almost regardless of the state of the evidence, these criteria will be difficult to meet simultaneously. Insofar as our conception of the person confines itself to what is demonstrably universal, it threatens to fall short of the first desideratum. Insofar as it incorporates the facts of human diversity and of our particular form of life, it threatens to fall short of the second. Thus, Rawls's persons in the original position are disembodied, declasses, and bereft of any particular values. Reason may well dictate that, ceteris paribus, they would rather have more income than have less, but, in the absence of more specific needs or desires, it turns out that their only rational option is to try to avoid a radically underspecified worst outcome. A real person who calculated in this way would strike us as more paranoid than rational. At the opposite extreme, Nozick's parties to the social contract have too much character: they seem possessed by a desire for unlimited acquisition of property. It is unclear why anyone not so possessed and surely many people are not would agree to a contract designed to further that goal above all others.

CONCEPTIONS OF NEUTRALITY

Modern liberal political and legal philosophers have in large part rejected the old search for an objective theory of the good, and have instead accepted the mandate of fairness or neutrality, recognizing that we will continue to differ in our visions of the good, and that a theory of rights cannot be expected to unify, stabilize or energize a society insofar as it gives exclusive or preferential recognition to the needs, desires, and contributions of some, while ignoring or downgrading the needs, desires, and contributions of others.

Several distinct approaches to realizing neutrality have surfaced in the recent literature. Nozick (1974) for instance, attains it by systematically blinding himself to the realities of groups and their power. All interactions in his world are between freely contracting individuals, essentially equal in power. More precisely, any inequality will be a manifestation of differences in talent or motivation that are not morally neutral, but deserve reward or punishment. The only restriction on the total freedom of individuals is that coercion is not permitted, but coercion is very narrowly defined, in terms of the use of force in the immediate situation. Otherwise, all are entitled to take what they desire and to keep what they have, even if others perish as a result. My desire is all, and your need is nothing; the right to life is explicitly subordinated to property rights. But, for Nozick, this choice is neutral because it leaves all survivors free to pursue their desires according to their talents.

Rawls (1971) shares Nozick's awareness of the difficulties that group power causes for a theory of individual rights, and he too responds by asking us to blind ourselves to group power. However, his approach is subtler and does not lead so quickly to ridiculous results. He allows us to remember that group power exists, and can threaten us, but he asks us to forget where we personally stand in the power structure. Thus our national calculations will consider not how to provide for our particular needs and desires, but rather how to design a framework within which we might best pursue those needs and desires, whoever we might be. This framework, unlike Nozick's will not blatantly legitimate pervasive inequalities; for Rawls does not attribute moral significance to accidents of nature that distribute talents unequally, or even to free choices that result in differential contributions to the aggregate social wealth. However, the framework does not convincingly guard against exploitation as effectively as it might. It is erected to solve an extremely vague array of hypothetical problems, instead of the specific ones that any real society must face in the light of its particular history and composition. The real work of applying general principles of fairness to those specific conditions remains to be done. That work will have to be done without the benefit of the veil of ignorance, and rules that seemed neutral out-of-context may seem less so when push comes to shove. Some of these latent questions come to the fore when we focus on the vagueness of Rawls's definition of the persons whose welfare must be considered in the original position. Some of his language in *A Theory of Justice* suggests that lineages and corporations might be represented; on the other hand, it is unclear how the theory precludes one from defending the enslavement of blacks by simply denying that they are persons. Thus, the structures of group power that are shut out at the front door may later gain access at the rear.

Dworkin (1981) agrees that the state must be neutral between competing notions of the good, but he holds, unlike Rawls, that equality is a principle prior to neutrality. Rawls (and Ackerman) seem to assume that these two criteria are equally fundamental and mutually consistent. Dworkin points out that this need not be the case, and he argues that of the two, equality is the more fundamental. The difficulty with this is that without a concept like neutrality, the meaning of equality is left radically unclear. Dworkin advocates sovereignty over a range of personal possessions essential to dignity as a fundamental right, thus translating the norm of equal concern for all persons to one of equal resources. The difficulty is that, like Nozick and Rawls. Dworkin seems to have discarded information without which rational decisions cannot be made. Treating persons as equals should not mean blinding ourselves to morally relevant differences between them, and it is the concept of neutrality that specifies which differences are morally relevant. By defining equality before we define neutrality, we risk interpreting equal resources to mean that all persons, regardless of age, size or health, must have equal food rations. At the same time, we also encounter serious difficulty in explaining why a democratic government should spend public funds on matters that are needed or desired only by a minority.

Ackerman's (1980) approach to neutrality is, like Rawls's, process-oriented. Ackerman does not ask us to forget what we know, but to disregard any claim that presupposes that one person or vision of the good has greater moral worth than another. For him, the central right is to a neutral justification for any exercise of power, public or private. Each individual is entitled to enter the marketplace of discourse and of action with a liberal education and a fair share of economic power to back him up. Within this basic structure of undominated equality, fair exchange of ideas and goods can occur. But, like Rawls and Dworkin, Ackerman has difficulty in spelling out the meaning of an equal start in life in a context of major differences in individual physical and mental endowments. He too simplifies his task by assuming such differences away. He too pursues his inquiry in a basically atomistic context, abstracted from the groups and institutions that are pervasive in our lives. Yet it is precisely these individual differences and groups relationships that give rise to the need for theories of fundamental rights in the first place. The questions remain: How can neutrality itself be defined in a politically neutral manner, without disregarding the morally significant differences among individuals? Indeed, is it valid to attribute morally significant qualities or even existence to persons, abstracted from and prior to their entry into specific social arrangements or political and legal institutions? Failure to deal satisfactorily with this issue is the core of the charge that liberalism, by its very axioms, is precluded from solving the problems it wishes to solve.

Much of the effort of the critical legal studies school has been devoted to showing that the formal categories of classical legal thought are inherently politically biased, self-contradictory, or both. Tushnet (1981) for example, has explored the dilemmas faced by antebellum Southern judges in dealing with rights and duties of slaves, whose status stood uneasily astride the person-property dichotomy. Horwitz (1979) has shown how an ostensibly neutral and well-settled law of property could be radically overhauled to accommodate the needs of emergent industrial capitalism. Even the very individualism of liberal thought has not escaped a radical criticism. Unger (1975) has shown, among other things, how an individualistic analysis of society tends to obscure both the phenomena of groups power and exploitation, and the extent to which human identity and self-realization are unthinkable outside the context of community life.

Granting the incisiveness of much of this criticism, the difficulty is in determining what it imports for a theory of fundamental rights. Efforts have been made to develop a new, more egalitarian theory of property rights. Not surprisingly, what seems more politically and morally neutral to critics of the status quo seems less so to its defenders. The new property, after some initial successes, has by now been pretty decisively rejected by the Supreme Court (Board of Regents v. Roth, 1972; San Antonio v. Rodriguez, 1973; Arnett v. Kennedy, 1974). If only neutral theories of rights are acceptable, and if there can be no such theory, what are we to put in its place? The critics sometimes seem to suggest that a passionate moral commitment is the answer. But the difficulty is that a neutral theory of fundamental rights was supposed to commend itself to support by general consensus indeed, on the social contract approach, by a unanimous agreement. This compact would ideally make the passionate individual pursuit of nonshared values possible and tolerable.

Now, partisan commitments are, by definition, incapable of doing the unifying and pacifying work that a liberal constitution is supposed to do, unless all parties but one are liquidated, whether by persuasion or armed struggle. Few it any of our law professors seem dedicated to armed struggle. At present, they must not only grant tolerance to those not yet persuaded, but require tolerance from a sometimes irate mainstream majority. In so doing, they seem to espouse the very liberal theories whose coherence and fairness they have denied. To defend this course on sheer pragmatic grounds is to acquiesce in the positivism of the status quo, and to leave those open to persuasion in doubt about the very thing they wish to know what would you do if in power?

THE POLITICS OF FUNDAMENTAL RIGHTS

From a liberal-constitutionalist point of view, the different criteria for establishing a right as fundamental reduce to two: procedural that the right has been recognized as such through a process accepted as valid; and substantive that the fundamental character of the right is supported by persuasive, principled arguments. Indeed, these criteria are not mutually independent. What makes the process valid is that it strives to hear and weigh impartially all relevant arguments. What makes arguments seem persuasive and principled is, in part, the impartial character of the forum and the expertise of the advocates who offer and the judges who accept the arguments. But the prestige of advocates and judges cannot be a sufficient condition for establishing rights. Otherwise, rights would be simply a reflection of power relationships, and recognition or nonrecognition of a right could be criticized only on the ground that actual power relations have been misperceived.

This positivist view fails to describe historical realities, because it misconceives the logic of rights as a language game in our society. There is indeed a politics of rights involved in establishing, securing, expanding or attacking a right. But this politics is distinguished from other kinds of politics by its particular logic, as well as by the specialized forums and personnel who dominate its activities. The norms of neutrality and universalism are especially important, for they must be seen to be honored in order for the system of rights to retain legitimacy. For all the logical weaknesses of these norms, they do serve to keep the process as open to all persons and all ideas as we presently know how to make it. The process is political in that claims cannot be recognized until they have been submitted through proper channels, which requires a modicum of resources and motivation. Moreover, the prospects for success may tend to improve as the political and economic resources of claimants increase. Nevertheless, the norms against overt status discrimination do constrain the form and content of acceptable claims. And if there is arguable bias in decision-making, we know how and where to pursue reform, even to the point of fundamental amendment of the system. The historical record reflects a secular trend toward greater openness and equality. Rights perhaps initially sought with very limited, selfish ends in view have come to be formulated, justified and applied in significantly broader terms. Thus the class of ultimate beneficiaries is broader than the original advocates of the right, including some who at first were not part of the system at all. Some of the initial victors may even wind up making significant sacrifices so that others can share in enjoyment of the newly established right.

In short, even if the original demand for and governmental recognition of a right were taken to reflect a calculus of power relations, the impact of its recognition would not be predictable from the same calculations. Even if the specific working out of the application of the ostensibly universal right over time were also conditioned by power relations, this conditioning would be governed by a different logic: the logic of legitimation and long-range hegemony, rather than the logic of short-run gains distributed according to the current balance of political forces. That is why positivism cannot provide a full account of why we have the rights we have today, nor is its dismissal of the question what rights we should have a plausible one. That is a question we have long been in the habit of asking; we go on asking it; and it is difficult to see what, if we ceased to ask it, we might do instead. As noted, the quest for answers has variously looked to philosophical conceptions of personhood, empirical generalizations about human needs and desires, and utilitarian arguments about the implications of social goals that enjoy consensual or majority community support. Arguments of the last sort are inconsistent with the axiom that rights belong to individuals. The other arguments tend to run afoul of charges of bias or of emptiness, depending on their degree of specificity.

Yet critics of liberalism attack a straw man in trying to show that the conceptual structure of liberal thought is marred by incoherence or contradictions and jumping thence to the conclusion that liberalism is not viable and should be abandoned in favor of another approach. What these critics overlook is the likelihood that similar havoc can be wrought with any conceptual system that undertakes to deal with fundamental, essentially contested moral, legal and political questions. But so what? When Goedel proved that Hilbert's project for the perfection of mathematics could not be realized, most mathematicians managed to carry on with their researches, and properly so. If we cannot have a system meeting certain criteria of logical perfection, still we can accomplish many other worthwhile things. If no argument is perfect, still some are better than others. A fairer test of liberal thought might look to the relative quality of political life in societies whereits concepts and procedures are used to shape and moderate conflict and to formulate collective goals, as compared to societies in which other sorts of language games are played. A political system is just insofar as it deals with the demands of all participants in ways that are generally accepted as legitimate provided, of course, that no one is wrongly excluded from participation, and that participant's acceptance is not invalidated by discernable coercion, manipulation, or the like. Granting that the definitions of these terms are highly contestable, we can and must attend closely to the nature of such contests and the fate of the contestants.

From this perspective, liberal constitutionalism possesses a viable system of fundamental rights insofar as it possesses workable, legitimate processes for asserting and deciding on claims that purport to trump other claims, even when the latter enjoy majority support and can plausibly be said to rest on recognized rights. The decisions in such cases must be supported by principled argument, and not merely by flat or appeal to expediency. Ultimately, however, the success of such arguments depends on empirical measures as well as conceptual analysis: directly or indirectly, we must consult the participants as to how well their needs, wants, and moral sentiments are being satisfied; and as to what would need to change in order to enhance their satisfaction. That the answers will be contingent on circumstances that changing situations may call for recognition of new fundamental rights, or redefinition of old ones is not inconsistent with the concept of rights, but flows directly from a correct understanding of what rights are about. Still, to speak of fundamental rights is to suggest that certain rights deserve to be, and normally will be, supported by the broadest and deepest consensus. Normally they will be the slowest to change, and in particular they will not be diminished or infringed without the most compelling justification which, by definition, could only be the recognition that some other right is even more fundamental. In more technical terms, of course, the Supreme Court has used the term fundamental to designate rights incorporated in the concept of due process, whose alleged infringement by national or state governments triggers a stricter than normal judicial scrutiny an easing of the normal presumption of constitutionality, and a shift of the burden of argument or of proof away from the citizen and onto the government.

Whether a given right is fundamental, or how fundamental it is, will depend on a weighing of one or more of these questions:

1. Is the right specifically identified as fundamental by a controlling text or authority, or logically entailed by a right so recognized?
2. Is the right empirically necessary to the realization of a recognized fundamental right?
3. Is possession of the right entailed by what it means to be a person, so that no person devoted to human dignity could reasonably prefer to live in a society in which the right was not recognized?

Typically, then, advocates of an unrecognized fundamental right will assert that in fact the right already exists, but that its scope and application have not yet been properly conceptualized, or that its logical significance within the whole system of rights has not yet been properly recognized; or they will assert that changed conditions or new empirical knowledge make out a case for recognizing a new right or upgrading an existing one, in order better to attain already established rights; or that current conceptions of human dignity require the recognition of a new right or upgrading of an existing one.

Arguments for downgrading a right would rest on similar grounds; but they should shoulder a far heavier burden of proof if we mean to take vested rights seriously.

Such arguments may be motivated by the short-run goals of a specific interest group, but, if so formulated, they could not be accepted as legitimate claims. Legitimacy demands an air of universality and timelessness, as well as a basis in current and widely appreciated fact. Even though a given right will not be of great value or urgent practical importance to all persons at all times, the argument that most any person might find it fundamentally important at some time is just the sort of argument that is needed.

2

Theory of Human Rights: Philosophy and Politics

Amartya Sen contends that a few concepts are as frequently invoked in contemporary political discussion as human rights. There is something deeply attractive in the idea that every person anywhere in the world, irrespective of citizenship or territorial legislation, has some basic rights, which others should respect. The moral appeal of human rights has been used for a variety of purposes, from resisting torture and arbitrary incarceration to demining the end of hunger and of medial neglect.

At the same time, the central idea of human rights as something that people have, and have even without any specific legislation, is seen by many as foundationally dubious and lacking in cogency. A recurrent question is, where do these rights come from? It is not usually disputed that the invoking of human rights can be politically powerful. Rather, the worries relate to what is taken to be the "softness" or mushiness of the conceptual grounding of human rights. Many philosophers and legal theorists see the rhetoric of human rights as just loose talk-perhaps kindly and well meaning forms of locution-but loose talk nevertheless.

Sen argues that the contrast between the widespread use of the idea of human rights and the intellectual skepticism about its conceptual soundness is not new. The U.S. Declaration of Independence, in 19776, took it to be "self-evident" that everyone is "endowed by their Creator with certain inalienable rights," and thirteen years later, the French declaration of" the rights of man asserted that 'men are born and remain free and equal in rights." But it did not take Jeremy Bentham long, in his *Anarchical Fallacies* written during 1791 and 1792 (aimed against the French "rights of man"), to purpose the total dismissal of all such claims. Bentham insisted that "natural rights is simple nonsense: natural and imprescriptibly rights, rhetorical nonsense, nonsense upon stilts," That suspicion remains every alive today, and despite persistent use of the idea of human rights in practical affairs, there are many who see the idea of human rights no more than "bawling upon paper," to use another of Bentham's barbed portrayals of natural right claims.

The dismissal of human rights is often comprehensive and is aimed against any belief in the existence of rights that people can have unconditionally, simple by virtue of their humanity (rather than having them contingently, on the basis of specific qualifications, such as citizenship rejection: they accept the general idea of human rights but exclude, from the acceptable list, specific classes of proposed rights, in particular the so-called economic and social rights, or welfare rights. These rights, which are sometimes referred to as second generation rights, such as a common entitlement to subsistence or to medical care, have mostly been added relatively recently to earlier enunciations of human rights, thereby vastly expanding the claimed domain of human rights. These additions have certainly taken the contemporary literature on human rights well beyond the eighteenth-century declaration that concentrated on a narrower class of "rights of man," including such demands as personal liberty and political freedom. These never inclusions have been subjected to more specialized skepticism, with the critics focusing on their feasibility problems and their dependence on specific social institution that may or may not exist.

Human Rights activists are often quite impatient with such critiques. The invoking of human rights tends to come mostly from those who are concerned with changing the world rather than interpreting it. It is not hard to understand their unwillingness to spend time trying to provide conceptual justification, given the great urgency to respond to terrible deprivations around the world. This proactive stance has had it practical rewards, since it has allowed immediate use of the colossal appeal of the idea of human rights to confront intense oppression or great misery, without having to wait for the theoretical air to clear. However, the conceptual doubts must also be satisfactorily addressed, if their idea of human rights is to command reasoned loyalty and to establish a secure intellectual standing. It is critically important to see the relationship between the force and appeal of human rights, on the one hand, and their reasoned justification and scrutinized use, on the other.

There is, thus, need for some theory and also for some defense of any proposed theory. The object of this article is to do just that, and to consider, in that context, the justification of the general idea of human fights and lo of the incurability of economic and social rights within the broad class of human rights. For such a theory to be viable it is necessary to clarify what kind of a claim is made by a declaration of human rights, and how such a claim can be defended, and furthermore how the diverse criticisms of the coherence, cogency and legitimacy of human rights (including economic and social rights) can be adequately addressed.

Indeed, a great many acts of legislation and legal conventions have been clearly inspired by a belief in some pre-existing rights of all human beings. This applies even to the adoption of the U.S. Constitution, including the Bill of Rights, linked to the normative vision of the U.S. Declaration of Independence (as was noted earlier). The difficult questions regarding the status and standing of human rights arise in the domain of ideas, before such legalization occurs. We also have to examine whether legislation is the pre-eminent, or even a necessary, route through which human rights can be pursued.

A theory of human rights must address the following questions in particular:

1. What kind of a statement does a declaration ethical of human rights make?
2. What makes human rights important freedom?
3. What duties and obligations to human rights reasons.
4. Through what forms of actions can human rights be promoted, and in particular whether legislation must be the principal, or even a necessary, means of implementation of human rights?
5. Can economic and social rights (the so-called second generation rights) be reasonably included among human rights?
6. Last but not least, how can proposals of human rights be defended or challenged, and how should their claim to a universal status be

assessed, especially in a world with much cultural variation and widely diverse practice?

(i) Human Rights can be seen as primarily ethical demands. They are not principally "legal," proto-legal" or 'ideal-legal" commands. Even though human rights can, and often do, inspire legislation, this is a further fact, rather than a constitutive characteristic of human rights.

(ii) The importance of human rights relates to the significance of the freedoms that form the subject matter of these rights. Both the opportunity aspect and the process aspect of freedoms can figure in human rights. To qualify as the basis of human rights, the freedoms to be defended or advanced must satisfy some "threshold conditions' of (i) special importance and (ii) social influence ability.

(iii) Human rights generate reasons for action for agents who are in a position to help in the promoting or safeguarding of the underlying freedoms. The included obligations primarily involve the duty to give reasonable consideration to the reasons for action and their practical implications, taking into account the relevant parameters of the individual case. The reasons for action can support both "perfect" obligations as well as "imperfect" ones, which are less precisely characterized. Even though they differ in content, imperfect obligations are correlative with human rights in much the same way as perfect obligations are. In particular, the acceptance of imperfect obligations goes beyond volunteered charity or elective virtues.

(iv) The implementation of human rights can go well beyond legislation, and a theory of human rights cannot be sensibly confined within the juridical model in which it is frequently incarcerated. For example, public recognition and agitation (including the monitoring of violations) can be part of the obligations-often imperfect-generated by the acknowledgment of human rights. Also, some recognized human rights are not ideally legislated, but are better promoted through other means, including public discussion, appraisal and advocacy.

(v) Human Rights can include significant and influenceable economic and social freedoms. If they cannot be realized because of inadequate institutionalization, then to work for institutional expansion or reform can be a part of the obligations generated by the recognition of these rights. The current can be promoted through institutional or political change does not, by itself, covert that claims into a non-right.

(vi) The universally of human rights relates to the idea of survivability in unobstructed discussion-open to participation by persons across national boundaries. Partisanship is avoided not so much by held by dominant voice in different societies across the world (including very repressive ones), but through an interactive process, in particular by examining what would survive in public discussion, given a reasonably free flow of information and uncurbed opportunity to discuss differing points of view. Adam Smith's insistence that ethical scrutiny requires examining moral beliefs from, inter alia, "a certain distance" has a direct bearing on the connection of human rights to global public reasoning.

HUMAN RIGHTS: ETHICS AND LAW

What kind an assertion does a declaration of human rights make? We would submit that proclamations of human rights are to be seen as articulations of ethical demands? They are, in this respect, comparable with pronouncements in utilitarian ethics, even though their respective substantive contents are, obviously, very different. Like other ethical claims that demand acceptance, there is an implicit presumption in making pronouncements on human rights that the underlying ethical claims will survive open and informed scrutiny. Indeed, the invoking of such an interactive process of critical scrutiny, open to information (including that about other societies) as well as to arguments coming from far as well as near, is a central feature of the theory of human rights proposed here. It differs both (i) from trying to justify the ethics of human rights in terms of shared- and already established-universal values (the uncomplicated "non partisan" view), and (ii) from abdicating any claim of adherence to universal values (and in this sense, eschewing any claim to being "non-partisan") in favour of a particular political conception that is suitable to the contemporary world.

These issues, which relate to the foundational discipline of ethical critique, will be examined later, in Section IX, in response to question (6). But the point to note for the moment, in answer to the first question, is that pronouncements of human rights are quintessentially ethical articulations, and they are not, in particular, putative legal claims, despite considerable confusion on this point, generated not least by Jeremy Bentham, the obsessive slayer of what he took to be legal pretensions. (We shall return later in this section to the nature of the misapprehension involved.)

A pronouncement of human rights includes an assertion of the importance of the corresponding freedoms- the freedoms that are identified and privileged in the formulation of the rights in question-and is indeed motivated by that importance. For example, the human right of not being tortured springs from the importance of freedom from torture for all. But it includes, furthermore, an affirmation of the need for others to consider what they can reasonably do to secure the freedom from torture for any person. For a would be torture, the demand is obviously quite straightforward, to wit, to refrain and desist. The demand takes the clear form of what Immanuel Kant called a perfect obligation. "However, for others too (that is, those other than they would be torturers) there are responsibilities, even though they are less specific and come in the general form of "imperfect obligations". The perfectly specified demand no to torture anyone is supplemented by the more general, and less exactly specified, requirement to consider the ways and means through which torture can be prevented and then to decide what one should, thus, reasonably do.

Even though recognitions of human rights (with their associated claims and obligation) are ethical affirmations, they need not, by themselves deliver a complete blueprint for evaluative assessment. An agreement on human rights does involve a firm commitment, to wit, to give reasonable consideration to the duties that follow from that ethical endorsement. But even with agreement on these affirmations, there can still be serious debates, particularly in the case of imperfect obligations, on –

(i) the ways in which the attention that is owed to human rights should be best paid ,

(ii) how the different types of human rights should be weighed against each other and their respective demands integrated together,

(iii) how the claims of human rights should be consolidated with other evaluative concerns that may also deserve ethical attention, and so on.

A theory of human rights can leave room for further discussions, disputations and arguments. The approach of open public reasoning, which is central to the understanding of human rights as proposed here, can definitively settle some disputes about coverage and content (including the identification of some clearly sustainable rights and others that would be hart to sustain), but may have to leave others, at least tentatively, unsettled. The admissibility of a domain of continued dispute is no embarrassment to a theory of human rights.

In practical applications of human rights, such debates are, such diabetes are, of course, quite common and entirely customary, particularly among human rights activists. What is being argued here is that the possibility of such debates-without losing the basic recognition of the importance of human rights-is not is just a feature of the general discipline of human rights including the underlying theory (rather than being an embarrassment to that discipline). An acknowledgment of the necessity to pay ethical attention to human rights, far from obliterating the need for such deliberation, actually invites it. A theory of human rights can, therefore, allow considerable internal variations, without losing the commonality of the agreed principle of attaching substantial importance to human rights (and to the corresponding freedoms and obligations) and of being committed to considering seriously how that importance should be appropriately reflected.

Variability of this kind is not only not an embarrassment; it tends to be standardly present in all general theories of substantive ethics. Indeed, a similar diversity can be found within utility-centered ethics, even though this feature of that large ethical discipline often receives little or no recognition. In the case of utility-based reasoning, variations can arise not only from the different ways in which utilities can be interpreted (as pleasures, fulfillment of desires, or realization of choices), nor only from the acknowledged heterogeneity of utilities themselves well recognized by both Aristotle and John Stuart Mill. They can also arise from the diversity of ways in which utilities can be used, whether by mere addition, or by multiplication, or through the addition of concave transformations of utility functions all of which have been proposed an pursued, within the discipline of utility-based evaluation. Further, the discipline of interpersonal comparison of utilities' may itself allow alternative procedures of quantification of utilities and go comfortably with accommodating permissible variations within specified classes of "partial comparability". The existence of different ways of making use of utility-based reasoning and alternative utilitarian procedures does not invalidate or even undermine the general approach of utility-centered ethics. And, similarly, the ethics of human rights is not nullified or thwarted by internal variations that it allows and incorporates.

Thus, the analogy between articulations of human rights and utilitarian declarations has considerable perspicacity, even though the great founder of modern utilitarianism, Jeremy Bentham, managed to miss that connection altogether in his classic work on natural rights in general and on the "rights of man" in particular. Bentham took the appropriate comparison to be that between the legal significance, respectively of:

(1) declarations of human rights, and

(2) actually legislated rights.

Not surprisingly, he found the former to be essentially lacking in legal status in the way the latter, obviously enough, would have. Bentham's dismissal of human rights came, thus, with amazingly swiftness.

It is easy to see that Bentham's rejection of the idea of natural "rights of man" depends substantially on the rhetoric of privileged use of the term of "rights," seeing it in its specifically legal interpretation. However, insofar as human rights are meant to be significant ethical claims, the pointer to the fact that they do not by themselves have legal or institutional force is obvious enough, but also quite irrelevant to the discipline of human rights. The appropriate comparison is, surely, between:

(1) a utility-based ethics (championed by Bentham himself), which sees intrinsic ethical importance in utilities but none in human rights or human freedoms,

(2) an ethics that makes room for the fundamental significance of human rights, linked with a diagnosis of the basic importance of human freedoms and the obligations generated by that diagnosis.

Just as utilitarian ethical reasoning takes the form of insisting that the utilities of the relevant persons must be taken into account in deciding on what should be done, the human rights approach demands that the acknowledged human rights must be given ethical recognition. The relevant comparison lies in this contrast, not in differentiating the legal force of legislated rights from the absence of any legal standing generated by an ethical recognition of rights (without any legislation or legal interpretation). Indeed, even as Bentham was busy in 1791 and 1792 writing down his dismissal of "rights of man", the reach and range of ethical interpretations of rights were being powerfully explored by Thomas Paine's *Rights of Man*, and by Mary Wollstonecraft's *A Vindication of the Rights of Woman*, both published during the period 1791 to 1792, though neither seemed to arouse Bentham's curiosity.

An ethical understanding of human rights goes not only against seeing them as legal demands, but also differs from a law-centered approach to human rights that sees them as if they are basically ground for law, almost "laws in waiting. "Ethical and legal rights do, of course, have motivational connections. In a rightly celebrated article "Are There any Natural Rights? Herbert Hart has argued that people speak of their moral rights mainly when advocating their incorporation in a legal systems. He added that the concept of a right "belongs to that branch of morality which is specifically concerned to determine when one person's freedom may be limited by another's and so to determine what actions may appropriately be made the subject of coercive legal rules" (1955`). Whereas Bentham saw rights as a "child of law," Hart's view takes the form, in effect, of seeing some natural rights as parents of law. They motivate and inspire specific legislations. Although Hart does not make any reference whatever to human rights in his article, the reasoning about the role of natural rights as inspiration for legislation can be seen to apply to the concept of human rights as well.

There can, in fact, the little doubt that the ideas of moral rights can serve, and has often served in practice, as the basis of new legislation. It has frequently been utilized in this was, and this is indeed an important use of human rights. That, for example, is precisely the way the diagnosis of inalienable rights was invoked in the U.S. Declaration of independence and reflected subsequently in the Bill of Rights, a route that has been well-trodden in the legislative history of many countries in the world. Providing inspiration for legislation in certainly one way in which the ethical force of human rights has been constructively deployed.

However, to acknowledge that such a connection exists is not the same as taking the relevance of human rights to lie exclusively in determining what should "appropriately be made the subject of coercive legal rules. 'it is important to see that the idea of human rights can be, and is, actually used in several other ways as well. Indeed, if human rights are seen as powerful moral claims, indeed as "moral rights") to use Hart's phrase, then surely we have reason for some catholicity in considering different venues for promoting these claims. The ways and means of advancing and implementing human rights need not, thus, be confined only to making new laws. For example, monitoring and other activist support, provided by such organizations as Human Rights Watch or Amnesty international or OXFAM or Medicines Sans Frontiers, can themselves help to advance the effective reach of acknowledged human rights.

Why are human rights important? Since declaration of human rights are ethical affirmations of the need to pay appropriate attention to the significance of freedoms incorporated in the formulation of human rights (as was discussed in the last section), an appropriate starting point must be the importance of freedoms of human beings to be so recognized. Note that while rights involve claims, freedoms, in contrast, are primarily descriptive characteristics of the conditions of persons.

By starting from the importance of freedoms as the appropriate human condition on which to concentrate, rather than on utilities, we get a motivating reason not only for celebrating our own rights and liberties, but also for out taking an interest in the significant freedoms of others, not just in their pleasures and desire-fulfillment. Bentham's insistence on choosing utility as the basis of ethical evaluation can be contrasted with the reasons for focusing instead are weighty and how the focus on freedoms can avoid some of the major pitfalls of concentrating only on utility in the form of pleasure or desire fulfillment. For example, the utilitarian calculus can suffer from valuation distortions resulting from the neglect of substantive deprivation of those who are chronically disadvantaged but who learn, by force of circumstances, to take pleasure in small mercies and get reconciled to cutting down their desire to "realistic proportions".

There have to be some "threshold conditions" of (i) importance and (ii) social influenceability for a freedom to figure within the interpersonal and interactive spectrum of human rights. Insofar as the idea of human rights demands public discussion and engagement, the agreement that would be sought is not only on whether some specific freedom of a particular person has any ethical importance whatsoever, but also whether its significance and its influenceability meet the threshold conditions for inclusion among the human rights on which the society should focus.

The threshold conditions may prevent, for a variety of reasons, particular freedoms from being an appropriate subject matter of human rights. To illustrate, it is not hard to argue that some importance should be attached to all four of the following freedoms:

(1) a person's freedom not to be assaulted;

(2) her freedom to receive medical care for a serious health problem;

(3) her freedom not to be called up regularly by her neighbors whom she detests;

(4) her freedom to achieve tranquility.

The presumed precision of legal rights is often contrasted with inescapable ambiguities in the ethical claims of human rights. This contrast, however, is not in itself a great embarrassment for ethical claims, including those of imperfect obligations, since a framework of normative reasoning can sensibly allow variations that cannot be sensibly accommodated in fully specified legal requirements. As Aristotle remarked in the *Nicomachean Ethics* (1893), we have "to look for precision in each class of things just so far as the nature of the subject admits."

In the laws of some countries, there is even a legal demand, which can hardly have extreme precision, for providing reasonable help to third parties. For example, in France there is provision for "criminal liability of omissions" in the failure to provide reasonable help to others suffering from particular types of transgressions. Not surprisingly, ambiguities in the application of such laws have proved to be quite large and have been the subject of considerable legal discussion in recent years. The ambiguity of duties of this type, whether in ethics or in law, would be difficult to escape if third party obligations of others in general are given some room, and this cannot be avoided for an adequate theory of human rights.

While the preceding analysis has been concerned with giving

reasonable consideration to actions in general that people can undertake in defending or advancing the human rights of others, it is the legislation of human rights, along with their institutionalization, that has tended to receive the lion's share of attention in the theoretical literature in this field. It is this legislative outlook that has also been firmly incorporated in much of the institutional understanding of human rights. However, while legislation is an important domain of public action, there are other ways and means which are also important and often effective in advancing the cause of recognized human rights.

First, under what can be called the 'recognition route" (to be distinguished from the "legalization of route"), there is acknowledgement but not necessarily and legalization or Institutional enforcement of a class of claims that are seen as fundamental human rights. The Universal Declaration of Human Rights, sponsored by the United Nations in 1948, which was perhaps the most important move that promoted global activities on human rights in the last century, falls solidly into this category. Subsequently, there has been a sequence of other international declarations, often through the United Nations, giving recognition, rather than a legal and coercive status, to various general demands, for example the "Declaration on the Rights to Development," signed in 1986. This approach is motivated by the idea that the ethical force of human rights is made more powerful in practice through giving it social recognition and an acknowledged status, even when no enforcement is instituted.

A second line of advance goes beyond recognition to active agitation. There can be organized advocacy urging compliance with certain basic claims of all human beings that are seen as human rights, and there can also be monitoring of violations of these rights and attempts to generate effective social pressure. The global NGOs have increasingly been involved in advancing human rights, through public discussion and support, on the one hand, and publicizing and criticizing violations, on the other. These efforts have come not only from dedicated human rights organizations, such as Human Rights Watch and Amnesty International, but also from broader organizations, such as OXFAM, Medicines Sans Frontiers, the Red Cross, Save the Children, and Action Aid. The rights involved in this "agitation route" may or may not have any legal starts in the country in question, but advocacy and support are not necessarily rendered useless by the absence of legal backing." Furthermore, even when some identified human rights have legal status, good enforcement of the relevant legislation may also call for public activism, which is to be distinguished from the process of legislation itself.

The third approach is, of course, that of "legislation. Even though the ethic of human rights must not be seen merely as "parents" of "human rights laws," it is certainly the case that many such legislations have been encouraged or inspired by considerations of human rights. Many actual laws have been enacted by individual states, or by associations of states, which gave legal force to certain rights seen as basic human rights. For example, the European Court of Human Rights, established in 1950 following the European Convention, can consider cases brought by individuals from the signatory states against violations of human rights. This has been supplemented by the Human Rights Act of 1998, aimed at incorporating the main provisions of the European Convention into domestic law, with an overseeing role of the European court to see "Just satisfaction" of the these provisions in domestic judgments. Many other examples can be given from different parts of the world. The 'legislative route" has had much active use.

There is an interesting question about the appropriate domain the legislative route. It would be a mistake to presume in general that if a human right is important, then it must be ideal to legislate it into a precisely specified legal right. For example, recognizing and defending a wife's moral rights to be consulted in family decisions, even in a traditionally sexist society, may well be extremely important, and can plausibly satisfy the threshold conditions needed to qualify as a human right. And yet the advocates of this human right, who emphasize, correctly, its far reaching ethical and political relevance, can quite possibly agree that it is not sensible to make this human into, in Herbert Hart's language, a "coercive legal rule". The necessary change would have to be brought about in other ways. Because of the importance of communication, advocacy, exposure and informed public discussion, human rights can have influence without necessarily depending on coercive legislation.

Similarly, the moral or political entitlement, which can easily be seen as a human right, of a somewhat slow speaker not to be snubbed in an open public meeting by a rudely articulate sprinter may well be important both for the self respect of the leisurely speaker and for public good, but it is not likely to be a good subject for punitive legislation. The protection of that human right would have to be sought elsewhere. The effectiveness of the human rights perspective does not rest on seeing them invariably as putative proposals for legislation.

ECONOMIC AND SOCIAL RIGHTS

Many critics are skeptical about extending the idea of human rights to include economic and social rights, such as the rights no to be hungry, or the right to basic education or to medical attention. Even though these rights did not figure in the classic presentations of rights human beings in, say, the U.S. Declaration of Independence, or French "rights of man," they are very much a part of the contemporary domain of what Cass Sunstein calls the "rights revolution." The legitimacy of including these claims within the general class of human rights has been challenged through two specific lines of reproach the institutionalization critique and the feasibility critique.

The institutionalization critique, which is aimed particularly at economic and social rights, relates to the general issue of the exact correspondence between authentic rights and precisely formulated correlate duties. Such a correspondence, it is argued, would exist only when a right is institutionalized.

Onora O' Neill has presented this line of criticism with force arguing that unfortunately much writing and rhetoric on rights heedlessly proclaim universal rights to goods and services, and in particular "welfare rights," as well as to other social, economic and cultural rights that are prominent in international Charters and Declarations, without showing what connects each presumed right-holder to some specific obligation-bearers, which leaves the content of these supposed rights wholly obscure. Some advocates of universal economic, social and cultural rights go no further than to emphasize that they can be institutionalized, which is true. But the point of difference is that they must be institutionalized: if they are not there is no right.

In responding to this significant criticism, we have to invoke the understanding, that obligations can be both perfect and imperfect. Even the classical "first generational" rights, like freedom from assault, can be seen as yielding imperfect obligations on others, as was illustrated with the example of the case of assault on Kitty Genovese in public view in New York. Depending on institutional possibilities, economic and social rights may similarly call for both perfect and imperfect obligations. There is a large area of fruitful public discussion and possibly effective pressure, concerning what the society and the state, even an impoverished one, can do to prevent violations of certain basic economic or social rights.

Indeed, the supportive activities of social organizations are often aimed precisely at institutional change, and these activities can be seen as part of imperfect obligations that individuals and groups have in a society where basic human rights are violated. Onora O'Neill is rights to emphasize the importance of institutions for the realizations of "welfare rights", but the ethical significance of these rights provide good grounds for seeking realization through institutional expansion and reform. This can be helped through a variety of approaches, including demanding and agitating for appropriate legislation, and the supplementation of legal demands by political recognition and social monitoring. To deny the ethical status of these claims would be to ignore the reasoning that motivates these constructive activities.

The feasibility critique proceeds from the argument that even with the best of efforts, it may not be feasible to arrange the realization of many of the alleged economic and social rights for all. This would have been only an empirical observation, but it is made into an allegedly powerful criticism of the acceptance of these claimed rights on the basis of the presumption, largely undefended, that recognized human rights must, of necessity, be wholly accomplishable. If this presumption were accepted that would have the effect of immediately putting many so-called economic and social rights outside the domain of possible human rights, especially in the poorer societies.

The traditional political and civil rights are not difficult to institute. For the most part, they required governments, and other people generally, to leave a man alone. The problems posed by claims to economic and social rights, however, are of another order altogether. How can governments of those parts of Asia, Africa, and South America where industrialization has hardly begun, be reasonably called upon to provided social security and holidays with pay for millions of people who inhabit those places and multiply so swiftly?

In assessing this line of rejection, we have to also why should complete feasibility be a condition of cogency of human rights when the objective is to work towards enhancing their actual realization. The understanding that some rights are not fully realized, and may not even be fully realizable under present circumstances, does not, in itself, entail anything like the conclusion that these are, therefore, not rights at all. Rather, the understanding suggests the need to work towards changing the prevailing circumstances to make the unrealized rights realizable, and ultimately, realized.

It is also worth noting in this context that the question of feasibility is not confined to economic and social rights only; it is a much more widespread problem. Even for liberties and autonomies, to guarantee that a person is "left alone", which Cranston seems to think is simple to guarantee, has never been particularly easy. If the current feasibility of guaranteeing complete and comprehensive fulfillment were made into a necessary condition for the cogency of every right, then not only economic and social rights, but also liberties, autonomies and even political rights may well fall far short of cogency.

How can we judge the acceptability of claims to human rights and assess the challenges they may face? How would such a disputation or a defense proceed? Like the assessment of other ethical claims, there must be some test of open and informed scrutiny and it is to such a scrutiny that we have to look in order to proceed to a disavowal or an affirmation. The status of these ethical claims must be dependent ultimately on their survivability in unobstructed secession. In this sense, the viability of human rights is linked with what John Rawls has called "public reasoning" and its role in "ethical objectivity.

Indeed, the connection between public reasoning and the formulation and use of human rights is extremely important to understand. Any general plausibility that these ethical claims, or their denials, have is dependent, on this theory, on their survival and flourishing when they encounter unobstructed secession and scrutiny, along with adequately wide informational availability. The force of a claim for a human right would be seriously undermined if it were possible to show that they are unlikely to survive open public scrutiny. But contrary to a commonly offered reason for skepticism and rejection, the case for human rights cannot be discarded simply by pointing to the fact that politically and socially repressive regimes do not seriously bother about human rights. Uncurbed critical scrutiny is essential for dismissal as well as for defense. Even as far as use to concerned, the fact that monitoring of violations of human rights and procedure of "naming and shaming" can be so effective is some indication of the reach of public reasoning when information becomes available and ethical arguments are allowed rather than suppressed.

However, it is important not to confine the domain of public reasoning to a given society only, especially in the case of human rights, in view of the inescapably non-parochial nature of these rights, which are meant to apply to all human being. This is in contrast with Rawls's inclination.

Particularly in his later works, to limit such public confrontation within the boundaries of each particular nation (or each "people," as Rawls calls this regional collectivity), for determining what would be just, at least in domestic affairs. We can demand, on the contrary, that the discussion include, even for domestic justice views also from "a certain distance", The necessity of this was powerfully identified by Adam Smith:

> We can never survey our own sentiments and motives, we can never from any judgment concerning them; unless we remove ourselves, as it were, from our own natural station , and endeavour to view them as at a certain distance from us. But we can do this in no other way than by endeavouring to view them with the eyes of other people, or as other people are likely to view them.

The universalist nature of Adam Smith's approach raises the question whether distant people can, in fact, provide useful scrutiny of local issues, given what are taken to be "uncrossable" barriers of culture. One of Edmund Burke's criticisms of the French declaration of the "right of man" and its universalist spirit was concerned with disputing the accept- ability of the notion in other cultures. Burke argued that "the liberties of infinite modifications, that cannot, or some similar, reason, the universality that underlies the notion of human rights is profoundly mistaken can be found in many other writing as well.

For example, Rosa Luxemburg a leading Marxist thinker and political leader in the early twentieth century, invoked a similar line of criticism of what she called the "metaphysical cliché of the type of 'rights of man' and 'rights of the citizen'." However, a scrutiny of Rosa Luxemburg's real concerns brings out the remarkable fact that she persistently invoked universalist principles herself, as is quite standard in the Marxist tradition (consider: "from each according to his ability, to each according to his needs"). Rather, Luxemburg was keen on emphasizing that the substantiation of these principles must depend on specific circumstances that obtain. Shorn of the rhetoric, there is, in fact, no particular difficulty in using basic universalist principles in general, while taking note of Luxemburg's pointer to the relevance of local circumstances and regional conditions in appropriately contingent, or parametric, specification of the exact demands of human rights.

However, a belief in uncrossable barriers between the values of different cultures has surfaced and resurfaced repeatedly over the centuries, and they are forcefully articulated today. The claim of magnificent uniqueness, and often of superiority, has sometimes come from critics of "Western values" varying from champions of regional ethics (well illustrated in the 1990s about the peerless excellence of "Asian values"), or religious or cultural separatists (with or without being accompanied by fundamentalism of one kind or another). Sometimes, however, the claim of uniqueness has come from Western particularists. A good example is Samuel Huntington's insistence that the "West was West long before it was modern" and his claim that "a sense of individualism and a tradition of individual rights and liberties" are "unique among civilized societies." Similarly, no less a historian of ideas than Gertrude Himmelfarb has argued that ideas of "justice", "right", "reason" and "love of humanity" are "predominantly, perhaps even uniquely, Western values."

Contrary to cultural stereotypes, the histories of different countries in the world have shown considerable variations over time as well as between different traditions within the same country. The championing of open public discussion, tolerating and encouraging different points of view, has a long history in many countries in the world. Indeed, some of the earliest open general meetings aimed specifically at settling disputes between different points of view took place in India in the so-called Buddhist councils, the first of which was held shortly after Gautama Buddha's death twenty-five hundred years ago. The grandest of these councils, the third, occurred under the patronage of Emperor Ashoka in the third century BC. Ashoka also tried to codify and propagate what must have been among the earliest formulations of rules for public discussion, a kind of ancient version of the nineteenth-century Robert's Rules of Order. He demanded, for example, "Restraint in regard to speech, so that there should be no extolment of one's own sect of disparagement of other sects on inappropriate occasions and it should be moderate even in appropriate occasions. Even when engaged in arguing, "other sects should be duly honoured in every way on all occasions."

To consider another historical example is early seventh-century Japan, the Buddhist Prince Shotoku, who was regent to his mother, Empress Suiko, produced the so-called constitution of seventeen articles, in 604 AD. The constitution insisted, much in the spirt of the Magna Carta to be signed six centuries later in 1215 AD: "Decisions on important matters should not be made by one person alone. They should be discussed with many."

When, in the twelfth century, he Jewish philosopher Maimonides had to flee an intolerant Europe to try to safeguard his human right to stick to his own religious beliefs and practice, he sought shelter in Emperor Saladin's Egypt (viz Fez and Palestine), and found an honored position in the court of this Muslim emperor. Several hundred years later, when, in Agra, the Moghul emperor of India, Akbar, was arguing and legislating, on the government's duty to uphold the right to religious freedom of all citizens, the European Inquisitions were still going on, and Giordano Bruno was burnt at the stake in Roma, in 1600.

In his autobiography, *Long Walk to Freedom*, Nelson Mandela describes how he learned about democracy and individual rights, as a young boy, by seeing the proceedings of the local meetings held in the regent's house in Mqhekezweni:

> Everyone who wanted to speak did so. It was democracy in its purest form. There may have been a hierarchy of importance among

> the speakers, but everyone was heard, chief and subject, warrior and medicine man, shopkeeper and farmer, landowner and laborer.

Not only are the differences on the subject of freedoms and rights that actually exist between societies often much exaggerated, but also there is, typically, little note taken of substantial variations within each local culture-over time and even at a point of time. What are taken to be "foreign" criticisms often correspond to internal criticisms from non-mainstream groups. If say, Iranian dissidents are imprisoned by an authoritarian regime precisely because of their heterodoxy, any suggestion that they should be seen as "ambassadors of Western values" rather than as "Iranian dissidents" would only add serious insult to manifest injury.

This issue is particularly important in determining what may be taken to be culturally "partisan" in a world of many cultural differences. Charles Beitz rejects, rightly, the plausibility of seeing the use of human rights, the plausibility of seeing the use of human rights as emanating from a "supposedly symmetrical relationship to the conception of political justice or legitimacy to be found in the world's cultures," and the goes on to seek their justification in terms of "the role they play in international relations." But how this "role" should be judged in terms of its acceptability, and in what sense should such an evaluation be culturally "partisan?" If the reasoning presented here is right, then we must distinguish between (1) the values that are dominantly favoured in a society, and (2) the values that could be expected to gain wider adherence and support when open discussion is allowed, when information about other societies becomes more freely available, and when disagreements with the established views can be expressed and defended without suppression and fear.

Being "non-partisan" requires respecting the participation of people from any corner of the earth, which is not the same thing as accepting the prevailing priorities in existing societies when information is extremely restricted and discussions and disagreements are not permitted. Widespread acceptability, which must be distinguished from pre-existing ubiquitous acceptance, is an important issue in any social evaluation, even in dealing with the role that human rights lay in international relations. There does, of course, exist considerable variation in the balance of manifest opinions and observed preconceptions in different countries and different societies?

These opinions and beliefs often reflect, as Adam Smith noted in a powerfully illuminating analysis, strong influence of existing practices in different parts of the world, along with a lack of broader intellectuals engagement. The need for open scrutiny, with unrestrained access to information is particularly great because of these connections. Which is precisely why Adam Smith's insistence on the necessity of viewing actions and practices from a "certain distance" is so important for substantive ethics in general and the understanding of human rights in particular.

In a chapter entitled "On the influence of Custom and Fashion upon the Sentiments of Moral Approbation and Disapprobation", Smith illustrated his contention:

> ... the murder of new-born infants was practice allowed of in almost all the states of Greece, even among the polite and civilized Athenians; and whenever the circumstances of the parent rendered it inconvenient to bring up the child, to abandon it to hunger, or to wild beasts, was regarded without blame or censure... uninterrupted custom had by this time to thoroughly authorized the practice, that not only the loose maxims of the world tolerated this barbarous prerogative, but even the doctrine of philosophers, which ought to have been more just and accurate, was led away by the established and upon this as upon many other occasions, instead of censuring, understand the abuse by farfetched consideration of public occasions to encourage. Plato is of the same opinion, and, with all that love of mankind which seems to animate all his writings, no where marks this practice with disapprobation..

What are taken to be perfectly "normal" and sensible" in an insulated society may not be able to survive a broad – based and less limited examination once thee parochial gut reactions are replaced by critical scrutiny, including an awareness of variations of practices and norms across the world.

Scrutiny from a distance may have something to offer in the assessment of practices as different from each other as the stoning of adulterous women in Taliban's Afghanistan and use of capital punishment in parts of the United States. This is the kind of issue that made Smith insist that "the eyes of the rest of mankind" must be invoked to understand whether a punishment appears equitable. Ultimately, the discipline of critical moral scrutiny requires, among other things, endeavouring to view (our sentiments and beliefs) with the eyes of other people, or as other people are likely to view them.

The need for interactions across the borders can be as important in rich societies as they are in poorer ones. The point to note here is not so much whether we are permitted to make cross-boundary scrutiny, but that the discipline of critical assessment of moral sentiments, no matter how locally established they are, demands that such scrutiny be undertaken.

The viability and universality of human rights are dependent on their ability to survive open critical scrutiny in public reasoning. The methodology of public scrutiny draws on Rawlsian understanding of "objectivity" in ethics, but the impartiality that is needed cannot be confined within the borders of a nation.

The fact that authoritarian orders are typically quite afraid of uncensored news media and of uncurbed public discussion, which make them resort often enough to suppression including censorship, intimidation, incarceration, and even execution provides some indirect evidence that the influence of public reasoning can indeed be quite large. That influence also lies behind the effectiveness of the interactive ways and means, including social recognition, informational monitoring and public agitation, which human rights activists tend to use. There is certainly a need for a fuller understanding of the associative nature of the acceptability of values, and this requires us to go well beyond lazy reliance on the given mores of the dominant social groups in the respective societies.

In conclusion, it can be said that despite their practical preoccupations, human rights activists have reason enough to pay attention to the skepticism that the idea of human rights generates among many legal and political theorists. These doubts have to be, and can be, addressed. But it is also important to note that the conceptual understanding of human rights, in turn, can benefit substantially from considering the reasoning that moves the activists and the range and effectiveness of practical actions they undertake, including recognition, monitoring and agitation, in addition to legislation. Not only is conceptual clarity important for practice, the richness of practice is also critically relevant for understanding the concept and reach of human rights. There is, we must conclude, no great deficit in the balance of trade between theory and practice.

PHILOSOPHY AND POLITICS OF HUMAN RIGHTS

In 1968, The United Nations celebrated the twentieth anniversary of the voting, by the United Nations General Assembly, of a universal declaration of the rights of man. The United Nations the organization that gathers together almost all of the states of the world (with the exception of China and various fragments of divided countries) but not humanity itself. The declaration, now twenty years old, was not accepted by member states as a basis for either legislation or juridical principles; it remains, today as it was yesterday, a simple, solemn and perhaps vain enumeration of the rights that states judge theoretically desirable to grant to individuals but that they shun considering as imperatives: intentions or objectives, perhaps: higher commands to a positive right, before which the leaders of state themselves must how, certainly not. No state, not even the United States, has given the rights of man, as proclaimed in 1948 by this assembly of states, a status equivalent to that of the amendments to the American Constitution on the basis of which the U.S. Supreme Court makes its decisions. This anniversary the year of the rights of man cannot fail to arouse mingled emotions in all of us. Is it an occasion for sadness or for joy? Remembrance of a lost hope or of a work in progress? Is the century of concentration camps, genocide, and the atomic bomb rendering the homage of vice to virtue when it evokes or invokes the rights of man? Or must we go still further: do the rights of man appertain to the philosophy of our time? In the eighteenth century, they were intrinsically linked to the rights of the citizen; personal and political rights were expressed in a liberal and universalist conception of the social order. In the twentieth century, they have been enlarged by economic and social rights. Does this represent a progression, in conformity with the logic of the philosophy of the Enlightenment? Or perhaps, on the pretext that carrying bourgeois statements to their completion by including in them the rights legitimacy claimed by socialists, have the drafters of the 1948 declaration confused incompatible ideas, brought together desirable objectives and categorical imperatives, without distinguishing between them, and, finally, emptied the concept of right of man of its content and significance by giving it an undefined extension?

We shall take as a point of departure a comparison between the first

French declaration of the rights of man (voted by the Constituent Assembly on August 23, 1789, accepted by King Louis XVI on October 3, and promulgated on November 3) and the universal declaration of the rights of man voted by the General Assembly of the United Nations in December 1948. In such a comparison, two propositions stand out very clearly: in essence, individual, political, and intellectual rights have not changed in the period from 1789 to 1948; jurists or statesmen continue to formulate them in the same terms. The 1948 declaration, however, devalues certain rights (such as property) that lie between political rights and economic rights, and it includes a section on social rights to which the members of the French Constituent Assembly gave no thought. We shall distinguish four categories of rights in this French declaration or perhaps it would be preferable to say four kinds of article.

1. The first category proclaims the egalitarian principle. Thus, in Article 1: Men are born and remain free and equal in rights. Social distinctions can be founded only on common utility. Or again, in article 6: The law must be the same for all, whether it protects or whether it punishes. All citizens, being equal in the eyes of the law, are equally admissible to all public dignities, places, and functions, in accordance with their capacity and without distinction other than that of their virtues and their talents. Pareto or an analytical philosopher would have no difficulty in demonstrating that common utility, for lack of a precise definition, does not make it possible to determine what social distinctions are justified. By the same token, there must be a standard of measurement for virtues and talents in order for society to reconcile equality and social distinction in accordance with justice.

The egalitarian principle finds an equally strong and more precise expression in the 1948 declaration: All human beings are born free and equal in dignity and rights. The term dignity belongs to the language of the twentieth century. It would be interesting to seek out its origin, the date on which it was incorporated into the classic terms (equality, liberty, and fraternity). Article 2 reinforces the egalitarian principle: Everyone is entitled to all the rights and freedoms set forth in this declaration, without distinction of any kind, such as race, color, sex, language, religion, political or other opinion, national or social origin, property, birth or other status. Article 7 goes on to affirm equality before the law and explicitly proscribes all discrimination; whereas Article 16 sets down the equality of man and woman in matters of marriage or divorce. And Article 23, in paragraph 2, offers the following rule: Everyone, without any discrimination, has the right to equal pay for equal work.

Obviously, formulas such as Men are born free and equal in rights cannot stand up under analysis (to be born free, in the proper sense of the term, signifies nothing), but they draw their inspiration from a philosophy we will follow Parsons in terming universalist. Equality before the law excludes privileged classes and inherited status even though it does not forbid the transmission of fortune or prestige from one generation to another. In 1789, of course, this egalitarian or universalist principle took on a revolutionary dimension against the estates of the Ancient Regime since it included the admissibility of all to all functions and called for reform of the tax structure, of which Article 13 (A common contribution is indispensable to the maintenance of public authority and the expenses of administration. It should be equally shared among all citizens, in proportion to their abilities) suggested changes that would bring about the liquidation of the fiscal privileges of the nobility and the clergy.

2. The articles that specify, in Gaetano Mosca's phrase, the democratic formula, belong to a second category. Representative of this, in the 1789 declaration, are Articles 3 (The source of all sovereignty resides essentially in the nation) and 6 (The law is the expression of the general will. All citizens have the right to contribute to its formation, personally or through their representatives). Article 21 of the 1948 declaration echoes this position: Everyone has the right to take part in the government of his country, directly or through freely chosen representatives. The will of the people shall be the basis of the authority of government; this will be expressed in periodic and genuine elections which shall be by universal and equal suffrage and shall be held by secret vote or by equivalent free voting procedures.

Even though both these declarations affirm the democratic idea, they differ in many respects. The 1789 declaration is manifestly directed toward limiting the action of the state (Article 5: The law has the right to prohibit only those actions prejudicial to society) and draws its inspiration from a philosophy enunciated both by Rousseau (The law is the expression of the general will) and by Montesquieu (article 16: No society in which the guarantee of rights is not assured nor the separation of powers determined can be said to have a constitution) The 1948 declaration seems more precise in its categorization of the democratic idea and in its reference to free elections. The latter represent another institutional translation of the democratic idea more democratic, from some points of view than separation of powers. But Article 12 of the 1948 declaration, which tends toward conservation of the rights to private life (no one shall be subjected to arbitrary interference with his privacy, family, home, or correspondence) does not suffice to conceal the gap between the nomocratic state envisaged by the members of the Constituent Assembly of 1789 and the modern state, in which achievement of social and economic rights is accorded a higher place than respect for individual rights.

3. Individual and intellectual liberties belong in a third category. They are summed up in articles 10 and 11 of the French declaration (No individual shall be molested because of his opinions, even religious opinions, provided that their manifestation does not disturb the public order established by law...Free communication of thoughts and opinions is one of the most precious rights of man; every citizen, therefore, may speak, write, and print freely, with the exception of being answerable for abuse of this liberty in cases determined by the law) Even the drafters of the 1789 declaration did not accept religious liberty without some difficulty and reticence (even religious opinions). By invoking disturbance of the public order brought on by a manifestation of opinion, the authorities of the time found a facile argument for limiting or prohibiting such manifestations. And in the same manner, the expression abuse of liberty authorizes all of the abuses of repression.

The 1948 declaration has a more liberal sound: freedom of thought, of conscience, and of religion (article 18); freedom of opinion and expression (article 19); freedom of peaceful assembly and association (article 20); and freedom of leave one's own country or to return to it, and freedom to find refuge from the persecution of a foreign state (article 14). The representatives of the communist nations were among those who signed this declaration: should this be considered a cause for rejoicing or indignation; should it be regarded as an expression of their ideal extending beyond the despotism of the present time or of their contempt for these bourgeois rituals?

4. Last, the administration of justice forms the subject of a fourth category of rights: article 7, 8, and 9 of the French declaration; articles 9, 10, and 11 of the universal declaration: No man may be accused, arrested, or detained except in cases determined by the law, and in accordance with forms prescribed by the law; nonretroactivity of laws (article 8 of 1789; article 11, paragraphs 2, of 1948); and presumption of innocence until a verdict of guilt (article 9 of the French declaration; article 11, paragraph 1, of the 1948 declaration). The universal declaration adds more of a supplementary formula than the element of a new idea: Fair and public hearing by an independent and impartial tribunal.

The historic, social, and political import of the French declaration was not lost on the most farsighted and most implacable of critics of the revolution, Edmund Burke. Analytically, the article stating that men are born free and equal in rights presents nothing of significance. Historically, it excludes hereditary distinctions of classes or estates. And, in the same way, other articles postulate the fact that functions prohibited to anyone by reasons of birth, fiscal exceptions inherited through tradition, and, in the final analysis, monarchy by divine right no longer exist. The author of Reflections on the French Revolution was therefore not mistaken when, in a certain sense, he encroached on the Marxist critique though on a basis of judgments of value in only a contrary sense and passionately denounced the revolutionary principles expressed in abstract language by the declaration of the rights of man. This declaration delivered the coup de grace to the hierarchic order of the Ancient Regime by stripping it of all legitimacy. The relative permanence of individual, political, and intellectual rights, between 1789 and 1948, can also be explained by its context of history. The Ancient Regime as Burke conceived it, with its reciprocal obligations, from above as well as Burke below, the rights and the duties defined by the place of each individual in the fabric of society, had been carried away with no hope of return by the revolutionary agony, though traces of it remained in Europe and in France throughout the nineteenth century and even during a part of the twentieth.

In terms of ideas as power, individual rights triumphed and destroyed institutions founded on contrary ideas. To what extent did they triumph in a positive sense, favoring or permitting the construction of a society in conformity with their demands or their logic? Marxists and democrats of liberal inspiration give contradictory answers to this question. They reached agreement, sincerely or hypoeritically, in drafting a declaration that adds economic and social rights to those four categories of rights we have mentioned above. But the democrat- liberals deny the fact that the democrat- socialists respect the individual rights of bourgeois tradition, and the democrat- socialists deny the idea that the society termed capitalist, whether bourgeois or liberal, achieves the economic and social rights.

Before attempting to interpret or comment on the dialogue between liberals and socialists relative to economic and social rights, we shall offer a few remarks on the changes that took place between 1789 and 1948 in the matter of the traditional rights whose four categories were previously summarized. The first such change concerns the right of property, and its significance must be readily apparent to any observer. In 1789, property formed a part of article 2, between liberty, on one side, and security and resistance to oppression, on the other. In 1948, it did not appear until article 17, following an article relative to the family and to marriage and preceding an article relative to freedom of thought, of conscience, and of religion. The right of property is expressed in ambiguous terms, acceptable both to the Marxists of the East and to the liberals of the West: Everyone has the right to own property alone as well as in association with others. No one shall be arbitrarily deprived of his property. Even in a socialist regime, certain goods may be the object of individual appropriation: the Soviet representatives were thus able to subscribe to such an article without violating their own principles. But in spite of everything, the moral devaluation of the right of property between 1789 and 1948 emerges clearly from the comparison of the two texts. Even a text drawn up exclusively by the Western powers and intended only for the use of the West would have marked more or less sharply a decline of the right of property in the hierarchy of values.

Even more than this devaluation of one right, a comparison between the two declarations makes clear the decline of all rights, of the very notion of the rights of man. The French declaration termed the right of property an inviolable and sacred right, which the drafters of the 1948 declaration would never have written. But neither would the latter have written that the aim of all political association is the conservation of the natural and unalienable rights of man. Such a formula in effect implies a philosophy of natural right. In other words, a philosophy by whose standards reason is called upon to determine the principles of the social order, valid everywhere and at all times; a philosophy that states, as its final goal for the collectivity, a guarantee of the rights of individuals, with the individual appearing as the sole reality of which a society is composed and, simultaneously, as the ultimate finality of the collective organization. This individualist philosophy of natural right survives here and there, but it no longer receives the assent of either legislators or influential thinkers, even in Europe or in liberal America. It is true that in the United States the amendments to the Constitution resembles a statement of the rights of man and give form to abstract principles in the light of which the Supreme Court decides the questions submitted to it. It seems, however, that even in the United States the amendments, like the rights of man, are considered as the supreme rules of a particular constitution and not as universal principles. Even the members of the American Congress would hesitate to take up again the French formula by which the goal of all political association is the conservation of the natural and unalienable rights of man. Moreover, if we suppose that they were to consider such an article, it would not have the meaning it assumed in the eyes of its authors at the end of the eighteenth century: those authors, in fact, did not entrust to the state the responsibility for promoting what we call today economic and social rights. They were far more concerned with limiting the established power, that of the monarch at first and that of the state in whatever form it might later take. The rights of man have not disappeared but they have changed in character: henceforth, they define or characterize the condition considered proper for all members of the collectivity, to be assured if necessary through the intervention of the state. Obviously, it is a logical step from traditional rights, restated from declaration to declaration, to the rights termed economic and social.

Before taking up the significance and status of these economic and social rights, we should like to pose a question that inevitably provokes contradictory replies. Were the socialists, by the representatives of regimes of the Soviet type, sincere in their agreement to traditional rights or were they not? When half the drafters of the 1948 declaration rendered only lip service to traditional rights and the other half was unresolved as to the meaning of the new rights, is there any cause for astonishment at the fact that it remains, twenty years later, what it was on the first day, a sort of appeal to the leaders of governments, an exhortation to conduct themselves in a decent manner?

Of the four categories of traditional rights that we have surveyed, the Soviet regimes accept the first that which translates into abstract language the idea of nondiscrimination and of equality before the law without reserve. Not that the Soviets do not sometimes violate the rules; but, then, Western nations do likewise. The claims of racial, ethnic, or religious minorities invoke violations, both overt and covert, of the universalism proclaimed as a maxim for any modern society.

The second category, that which translates the democratic formula, is not foreign to the authentic philosophy of the Soviet leaders and the peoples of Eastern Europe. The Marxist- Leninists claim to express and interpret the will of the masses. They organize ceremonies of acclamation and dub them elections, as if to symbolize their respect for a formula they do not apply but do not wish to repudiate and that they probably hope to apply some day, after having long held it in contempt. The Soviet leaders offer multiple justifications for the rule of the single party, sometimes as the vanguard of the proletariat, which is itself invested with a historic mission, and sometimes as the guide and representative of the entire people. Occasionally they put forth other arguments, such as the futility of elections in a country in which there no longer exists a class conflict or the greater importance of other forms of participation in the collective life, within the trade unions or the factories and farms. But no matter what the justification finally adopted may be, the spokesmen for the socialist regimes of tomorrow if not of today do not reject the democratic formula, the origin of sovereignty in the people.

The attitude of the Soviet regimes with regard to the rights of the third and fourth categories personal liberties and guarantees of impartial justice seems to me more ambiguous. At the present time, full and complete freedom of expression has not been granted to the citizens of any of the countries of Eastern Europe. At the very moment, the liberalization toward which the leaders of the Czechosloval government are striving is spreading terror in Warsaw and Moscow to such an extent that the men of the Kremlin are talking of a counterrevolutionary movement and of eventual action on the part of fraternal countries to reestablish or restore socialism. In the sense given to it by the Marxist-Leninists, socialism therefore seems to exclude liberty in the sense given to it by liberals of the entire world and even in the sense given to it by intellectuals and ordinary men formed under socialist regimes.

Marxist-Leninist socialism does not, however, reject freedom in the way fascism did. It does not deny personal and intellectual freedoms which the Stalin constitution of 1936 itself solemnly recognized and promised to all any more than it denies the sovereignty of the people, as amended by the guiding role of the Communist party. Ideologically, how is the reconciliation between principles and reality brought about? The arguments employed by the leaders of the regime oscillate between the old formula no freedom for the enemies of freedom and the pure and simple affirmation that the citizens of the Soviet Union effectively enjoy freedom of expression but have no desire to express anything that contradicts orthodox doctrine. To conclude on this point, let us say that the socialist regimes, which at first are ambitious to enrich formal freedoms by real freedom, have not, a half century after the October Revolution, succeeded in reestablishing the formal freedoms whose insufficiency Marx proclaimed but whose decay he would have indignantly denounced.

The same contradiction exists to an even greater degree with regard to the exercise of justice in the socialist regimes. Concentration camps, condemnation and execution of innocent people by the hundreds of thousands, confessions by individuals and groups accused of imaginary crimes: no regime before Stalin's had violated the rules of civilization relative to the administration of justice with so much brutality, so much cynicism, and such enormous, Kafkaesque lies. These violations of legality were attributed to the cult of personality an expression devoid of meaning except in the sense that it imputes to a single man the responsibility for all of these crimes. The fact remains and the evolution of the socialist regimes proves this every day that here again adherents of the Soviet system subscribe to the fourth category of the rights of man without hypocrisy and without illusion. Without hypocrisy, since they are not actually opposed in principle to an administration of justice in conformity with the ideal of the bourgeois West of the eighteenth century. Without illusion, since they are well aware of the enormous gap between the reality and the ideal. Despite all else socialist legality, which they invoke more and more frequently, differs in one essential point from liberal legality: the tribunals, even in theory, have no status of independence with relation to the state, which is itself in the service of the party. Insofar as minor offenses or common law crimes are concerned, socialist tribunals may come fairly close to tribunals of the liberal type; they are not, however, similar in matters of crimes against the state and this concept remains curiously elastic.

Such then, avoiding all polemics, the dialogue between a Marxist-Leninist and a liberal philosopher of the rights of man; rights that even if he does not apply them, the Marxist does not deny. The Marxist respects the principle of universalism, common to all modern societies; he admits the democratic formula while asking a translation for it other than that of free elections; he does not definitively exclude intellectual or personal freedoms although he refuses the benefit of them to the citizens of today; and he preaches socialist legality but shows no sign of resigning himself to the independence of tribunals.

Does the dialogue between a philosopher of the rights of man, as they have been formed by tradition, and a champion of economic and social rights, take on a character comparable to that of the preceding dialogue? The liberal does not reject the majority of economic and social rights, either in principle or in fact. The crux of the debate seems essentially theoretical.

Let us first recall the principle economic and social rights enumerated in the 1948 declaration: the right to marriage without any restriction due to race, nationality, or religion. The declaration evens adds to this the equality of rights of male and female with regard to marriage and divorce by requiring the free and full consent of the intending spouses. The declaration goes on to accord to each individual the right to social security (article 22), the right to work with the free choice of employment and an equal wage for equal work, the right to form a trade union or to belong to one, the right to repose and to leisure, the right to a standard of living adequate for the health and well-being of himself and of his family, and the right to an education (and even to an obligatory and free primary education). And finally, in article 28, the declaration includes the following formula: Everyone is entitled to a social and international order in which the rights and freedoms set forth in this declaration can be fully realized.

Does there exist a difference of nature or only one of degree between economic and social rights and the political and civil rights? In a little book entitled *Human Rights Today* (1962) the English writer Maurice Cranston devoted some pages to this problem and concluded there is a difference in nature. Economic and social rights, he wrote, constitute, so to speak, the lofty ideals of societies; they cannot be assimilated to categorical or unconditional rights. Two criteria permit and justify the distinction between rights and ideals: the criterion that Cranston terms practicability and that of paramount importance.

In order for one person to have a right, it is necessary that another have a duty that of respecting or of carrying out that right. Any state can normally assure the right to life, to freedom of expression, and to a trial of its citizens by a jury: however, the picture changes when it comes to the right to work, to social security, to paid vacations, to a decent standard of living, to obligatory and free primary education, and so on. The second criterion, which Cranston considers less decisive than the first, is easily applied to certain cases: Holidays with pay are excellent too; they contribute to the greatest happiness of the greatest number. But they are not a matter of paramount importance, like freedom of speech or equality before the law.

Does this second criterion have general significance? Is there a distinction of decisive importance in whether criminals are subject to the decision of a jury rather than to that of a professional judge? And if so, for whom? There are fewer criminals than workers. If importance is measured in terms of the number of individuals affected, the jury has less importance than holidays with pay. But is it not true that since anyone may be called before a tribunal, everyone is interested in the administration of justice? Remembering the situation of Russia under Stalin, let us admit this to be true. Yet even in this hypothesis, it is a matter less of a difference of nature than of degree unless we are to define importance in moral and not in material terms. The equitable administration of justice concerns us all because it calls into question values that are essential in our eyes. It is no longer a question of happiness but of morality. But in this hypothesis, the criterion supposes something that remains in question: the radical distinction between the universal rights of man and the objectives that a social order should set for itself.

The first criterion, that of practicability, of a duty correlative to rights, is also applicable at first estimate once a choice has been made of economic and social rights, expressed with excessive precision, and personal or intellectual rights, expressed in vague and abstract terms. The governments of the poorer nations do not have the material means to assure a decent standard of living to all or to guarantee a free and obligatory primary education to all children. How can we accord to all men a right to which there is no corresponding duty since no one can be held to the accomplishment of what he cannot accomplish?

The argument loses something of its force if economic and social rights are formulated in other, less precise, less restrictive terms. In order for the concept to seem less sharp, it would suffice to suppress rights such as those to paid vacations or to suppose that the right to work, to social security, or to a decent standard of living is understood with a reserve of common sense in terms of the resources available to the collectivity. Why should the state not have the same obligation to assure to all the standard of living compatible with the wealth (or the poverty) of the nation as to guarantee freedom of expression or equitable administration of justice? In what manner does the capacity or the power to accomplish these goals differ from one case to the other?

The question may be raised that the rulers of the state do not manipulate the distribution of incomes in accordance with their own will since such distribution is probably subject to a determinism that economists strive to understand and that the government leaders find difficult to control. The objection is just, but are the leaders of governments any more capable, at all times and everywhere, of achieving the rights of man relative to freedom of expression and to the democratic formula? As soon as one attempts to measure the real capacity of the effective leaders of the regime, or the multiple pressures to which they are subjected, there no longer exists any radical difference between the economic order and the political order: the leaders do not completely control either the one or the other.

According to Maurice Cranston, A human right by definition is a universal moral right, something which all men, everywhere, at all times, ought to have, something of which no one may be deprived without a grave affront of justice; something which is owing to every human being simply because he is human. In other words, Cranston is here taking up again, purely and simply, the philosophy of natural right, of the rights of man as men. It is in terms of this philosophy that he sets up a discrimination of principle between political and individual rights, on the one hand, and economic and social rights, on the other. The two criteria on which he supports his attempt to establish this discrimination are theoretically open to criticism. They are applicable to the simplest cases, to the most pronounced oppositions; they suppose essential discrimination but do not establish it.

The distinction between universal and categorical rights, on the one hand, and noble ideals, on the other, marks a return to the very philosophy whose particular character, in spite of its claim to universality, has been brought to light by all sociological thought and not simply by Marxism.

The French declaration of 1789 draws its significance less from its alleged universality than from the historic content that was both expressed and concealed in abstract formulas. Two centuries ago, the right to property was considered sacred; in our time, it has become relative, precarious, and revocable a universal right on the condition that it is expressed in terms that condemn neither Soviet nor Western practice. Each regime determines what may be the object of individual ownership. Generally speaking, one could state the dilemma in the following terms: either rights attain a certain sort of universality because, thanks to the vagueness of their conceptual structure, they allow of any institution whatever; or they retain some preciseness and lose their universality. The accused has the right to be judged according to fair procedures, but in every period and in every society the definition of fairness of procedures is subject to substantial variations. And in the same manner, participation in the government of the nation remains a universal right only on the condition that the institutions through whose intermediary such participation becomes effective are no longer specified.

The radical discrimination between universal rights and lofty ideals is vulnerable to the criticism that, from Nietzsche to Pareto, by way of Marx, brings to light the ruses of the will to power and of personal (or collective) interest. The Marxist seeks to unmask the predominant concern for personal freedoms, which are vital to some, in the refusal to place economic and social rights on the same level as the rights of liberal tradition. Do those rights decreed as universal and categorical and that act primarily to the profit of some present a greater importance than social security or the standard of living, which are profitable to all? Is not the inequality of the statutes attributed to these two kinds of rights the conscious or unconscious expression of a policy, legitimate but not evident as such? A liberal policy is not a universally valid philosophy.

Last, the radical distinction between categorical rights and lofty ideals is open to a final and more serious objection. Whether it is a matter of universal suffrage, freedom of expression, or guarantees of impartial justice, the rights of man demand an established order. They have not been gained without violence and they are not respected in a period of violence. Revolutionaries forget or scorn them and they cannot always do otherwise. In certain circumstances, the transformation of the social order with a view toward achievement of lofty ideals demands a resort to force. In such a case, the means judged necessary rightly or wrongly to attain the objectives fixed by economic and social rights exclude respect for personal or intellectual rights, for a period of uncertain duration. The rights of these two categories are not essentially incompatible, but they becomes so under specific conditions.

Obviously, the experience of the twentieth century has taught us the perils of sacrifice of traditional rights in the hope of realizing the lofty ideals of economic and social rights. Formal freedoms the right to the vote, personal freedoms do not suffice to guarantee a decent existence to all; they can expand only in a climate of real freedoms on condition of assuring security and a decent standard of living to the greatest number. The Marxists are right to remind us of this point. But there is available to us in this respect a pertinent reply: the suppression of traditional rights, though proclaimed at the beginning to be provisional, may remain in effect for a long time, and the producer does not always gain in real freedom what the citizen loses in formal freedom.

The aim of all political association is the preservation of the natural and unalienable rights of man. These rights are liberty, property, security, and resistance to oppression. If the men who govern, even in the West, were to seek to define the aim of all political association, what terms would they employ? Probably they would refer to equality (nondiscrimination), to economic security, and to the standard of living but certainly not to the preservation of the natural and unalienable rights of man. Thus, we return to the opposition already mentioned between a philosophy of rights, that tends to limit the power of the state, and a philosophy of rights confused with lofty ideals, which assigns to the state the crushing, perhaps unrealizable task of transforming the condition of man in society in compliance with certain requirements that were never manifested in the course of preceding centuries.

This ambitious, sociologically inspired philosophy prompts a refusal to hold strictly to the formal or the legal. Whether individuals are formally equal before the law signifies nothing so long as custom ignores this equality. In the United States, civil-rights legislation tends not only to compel the states or the schools to put into practice the equality that is an integral part of the American credo but also, on occasion, to curtail certain traditional rights that of the landowner, for example but prohibiting discriminatory practices. In this sense, legislation endeavors to alter custom.

Another example of this movement extending from the formal to the real can be found in the realm of education. The right to education signifies nothing if the family does not have the financial resources without which it would be unable to exercise this right. This necessarily has already resulted in free primary and even secondary education and in the multiplication of scholarships. But, in a later stage, we might question the advantages derived from their environment by the children of privileged families. Might it not be advisable to reestablish real equality by doing away, insofar as possible, with advantages that are reflected in a certain correlation between educational results and the social origin of students? Until the present time, it seems that no government anywhere has given supplementary points to candidates coming from the lower classes of society. But such a project has nonetheless been evoked. Carried to its logical end, it could imply, in a case in which the number of places available for higher education was limited, a numerous clauses for the children of the upper classes, in order to augment the degree of social mobility.

But let us set aside these projects, which are utopian at the present time, and which we have evoked here solely to shed light on the passage from the formal to the material. In poor societies, particularly in Africa, even a primary education for all is probably beyond the resources of the states. Thus, it will be the responsibility of these states to select those who are to receive a basic education. Of course, such a process of selection has also been at work in the past, but within and by society. Experience of the exclusion of the majority has not, in the common conscience, threatened the principle of the right of all to education. An unexercised right remains a right. Neither society nor the state was held responsible for furnishing to all the material means of exercising their rights. Sociological thought dispels this illusion of good conscience. And at the same time, it is concerned less with limiting the intervention of the state in order to protect the individual than with strengthening the public powers in order that they may permit every individual to exercise his rights.

In a certain sense, sociological thought has consecrated Nietzsche's, Marx's, or Pareto's criticism of eighteenth-century philosophy. It accepts historic relativism: every society organize itself in accordance with a certain system of standards or values, which are termed culture. So-called universal rights merit this description only on condition of being formulated in a language so vague that they lose all definite meaning. Of what significance is the right to property so long as the nature of the property open to individual ownership remains undetermined? Of what significance is political liberty so long as, from one period to another, there are constant changes in the institutional translation of participation of all in the government of the nation? This historic relativism now becomes an integral part of the common conscience and, profoundly marked by the sociological mode of thought, entails the technique of debunking, of bringing to light the interests or passions concealed behind these supposedly disinterested, passionless resolutions. But at the same time, the rights of man, stripped of their false universality, recover a historic significance, indeed a historic efficacy. The 1789 declaration cannot be separated either from the particular and nonuniversal philosophy that inspired it or from the bourgeois revolt against the Ancient Regime. Any declaration of rights appears finally as the idealized expression of the political or social order that a certain class or a certain civilization is attempting to realize. It at least permits condemnation of certain institutions (class distinctions) or affirmation of certain principles (non- discrimination), if not definition, on the basis of imperatives, of the precise composition of social organizations.

It is in this manner that the ambiguity of the universal declaration of rights of 1948 can be explained. That statement borrows from Western civilization the very practice of a declaration of rights: whereas other civilizations, though not ignorant of collective standards or of individual rights, are unaware of the theoretical and allegedly universal expression of such standards or rights. The Western origin of the declaration manifests itself, for example, in the articles relating to the family: nowhere is the free choice of a spouse or the equality of rights of male and female fully realized; in a strict sense, perhaps, Westerners play out for themselves the comedy of subscribing to such an ideal of the family. It is not the same thing for the men or women who belong to other cultures. Western philosophy granted lip service as an exemplary pattern. Another ambiguity of the 1948 declaration stems from the attempt at synthesis between a Marxist-Leninist conception and a liberal conception. The juxtaposition of traditional rights and economic and social rights was and remains acceptable both to the representatives of the Soviet Union and to those of the Western nations. Both camps in effect have set themselves the objective of accomplishing these two forms of rights. But this reconciliation leaves unanswered the real question, that of the relative importance of the two forms of rights.

Among the liberals, some, like Cranston, would reserve for the traditional rights a status different from that of economic and social rights. Others accept the theoretical equality of status but maintain the decisive importance of traditional rights on the level of political strategy.

Interpreted thus, the 1948 declaration, through its very ambiguity, fulfills the historic function of any such declaration: it criticizes modern society in the name of the ideals that this society has set for itself. According to sociological thought, all philosophy of natural right expresses and denies at the same time the society from which it emanates. It borrows its values and reproaches it for having betrayed them. The 1948 declaration, sometimes overly concrete, sometimes falsely universal, takes its place in the line of earlier declarations in spite of the defects natural to a collective work; it enjoins modern societies to maintain the traditional rights of individuals and to give to all the material means to make use of these rights. The drafts of the 1789 declaration wanted to limit the state in order to liberate the individual. The drafters of the 1948 declaration, without being fully aware of it, were prepared to give all powers to the state in order that it might guarantee security and a decent standard of living to all. The declaration of rights criticizes positive right in the name of the ideal to which the society subscribes. The 1948 declaration criticizes liberal society in the name of the socialist ideal and socialist society in the name of the liberal ideal.

3

Human Rights in Ancient Indian Tradition

The history of the philosophical discussion of human rights, of the dignity and brotherhood man, and of his common citizenship in the great society is long, it extends beyond the narrow limits of the Western tradition and its beginnings in the west as well as in the east coincide with the beginnings of philosophy.

The very right to live accrues to us only when we do the duty of citizenship of the world. From this one fundamental statement, perhaps it is easy enough to define the duties of Man and Woman and correlate every right to some corresponding duty to be first performed. Every other right can be shown to be usurpation hardly worth fighting for.

In the ongoing discourse on human rights search for a common basis for them in all traditions and cultures around the world has been one of the fundamental concerns. Absence of such basis has been obstruction the drawing of a universally agreeable list of these right and more than that the process of their interpretation and implementation. Of course the International Bill of Right and a few other UN Conventions seem to represent a consensus in this regard, not all countries have ratified them all. Some of those who have ratified have also expressed several reservations. Some other have also been expressing their difference of opinion collectively as, for example, some of the Asian countries did in the Bangkok Declaration before the Vienna World Conference on Human Rights in 1993. Although human rights have resolutely contested the claims made in the name of Asian values expressed in the Bangkok, Declaration, the controversies raised under the rubric of cultural diversities persist.

Serious doubts are expressed about the effectiveness of the international human rights instruments, which are alleged to be based on the historical experience of industrially advanced West not shared by the large section of the humanity inhabiting the rest of the world, particularly Asia and Africa. The concerns of this section of the world, it is argued, are different from the concerns of the West. Unless the concerns of this section of the world are given due in essence the Universal Declaration of Human Rights is a document whose underlying values are democratic and libertarian, based on the notion of atomized individuals possessed of certain inalienable rights in nature. These political values, as distinct from economic rights or communal rights, can be traced directly to the experience of France, England and the United States. The Declaration is predicated on the assumption that Western values are paramount and ought to extended to the non-Western world... Traditional cultures did not view the individual as autonomous and possessed of rights above and prior to society. Whatever the specific social relations, the individual was conceived of an integral part of a great whole, of a "group" within which one had a defined role and status.

The irrelevance of the Western conception of human rights founded on natural rights doctrines is not rooted solely in traditional cultural patterns, but is also a consequence of the articulated and modernized goals of Third World countries. The ideology of modernization and development that had attained universal status has come to be understood primarily in terms of economic development. The colonial experience of economic exploitation gave credence to the notion of human dignity as consisting of economic rights rather than civil or political rights. Freedom from starvation, the right for all to enjoy the material benefits of a developed economy, and freedom from exploitation by colonial powers became the articulated goals of many Third World countries. The strategies that evolved for the attainment of these goals incorporated an admixture of old concept and values frequently reinterpreted and redefined in light of contemporary realities and goals. Thus the state was to replace traditional group identities but the idea is an excuse for the promotion of a particular religious tradition and its promotion must therefore be opposed for that reason only, if no other.

The ides of human right, however, gains if it is related to different traditions. In the absence of such relationship it may be hard to push the idea in all the traditions. It becomes easily understandable and acceptable to the adherents of any tradition if it can be related to it. Such relationship invokes sympathy and help internalization of the idea while its absence leads to indifference and apathy or even revulsion. Like the historical experience mentioned above, close connection between the religious and cultural traditions is a well-recognized basis for the creation and realization of any national or international norms. Several studies on human right inclusive of India demonstrate the relevance of such connection. If any connection between the India traditions and the idea of human right can be found or established it helps in the realization of these rights. It is not that we must artificially create or incorporate connections which do not exist. But sincere effort is quintessential for the understanding of every tradition with the general assumption of some communion in the ultimate values and goals of life in all societies on earth. If we take that position and develop faith in the inherent goodness of every human being on earth in search of common happiness, the struggle for the realization of the human right will definitely succeed.

The enquiry also becomes relevant in view of the conflicting literature on human right in ancient Indian tradition. Such literature may be classified into three categories. Firstly, the one, which demonstrates deeper research and understanding of the India tradition as well as of the human rights, finds that the India tradition is not averse to the idea of human right but it does not contain the concept of human rights as known today emerging primarily from the West since the closing decade of the nineteenth century. Secondly, the one that argues that the tradition is fully in line with the modern concept of human right and supports it as much as Christianity or any other tradition does. Thirdly, the one that seems inspired by the emergence of consideration the human right movement may not succeed. In the interest of its success. it is pleased that the approach to human right must be reconsidered. Rethought and redrawn.

Some western enthusiasts also attribute the birth of the idea of human right to Christianity. Not only they attribute its birth to Christianity, they also argue that it is an attribute only of Christianity not found in other religious traditions. Such claims have led or lectured many scholars to idea in their respective religious tradition such as Judaism Islam,

Confucianism, Buddhism, and Hinduism. While search for the idea in different traditions should be helpful in its promotion, there are doubts whether the claim of its existence in one's own tradition to the exclusion of others helps it in any way. Such claim may rather lead the claimant lead the claimant to believe that only adherence or conversion to her and no other tradition can promote the idea and may therefore prompt the believers in that tradition to set on the task of propagating and establishing that tradition everywhere. If that is the likely consequence of the claim it will only harm the cause of human right by creating religious animosity and fundamentalism. It will naturally make the believers in others traditions conscious that was to retain the same supremacy as traditional groups. By the same token the state's responsibility is to free its people from colonial exploitation and to attain economic betterment. Essentially this is the conceptual framework that has structured the worldview of many Third World countries and within which human rights and human dignity are understood. Democratic government is perceived as an institutional frame work through which the goals of the state are to be achieved, an if it fails or becomes an impediment it can be dispensed with impunity.

In summary then it is evident that in most states in the world, human rights as defined by the West are rejected or, more accurately, are meaningless. Most states do not have a cultural heritage of individualism, and the doctrines of inalienable human rights have been neither disseminated nor assimilated... The cultural patterns, ideological underpinnings, and developmental goals of non-Western and socialist states are markedly at variance with the prescriptions of the Universal Declaration of Human Rights. Efforts to impose the Declaration as it currently stands not only reflect a moral chauvinism and ethnocentric but are also bound to fail.

The conceptualization of human rights is in need of rethinking. It should be recognized that the Western notion of human rights evolved historically, under a particular set of circumstances, in the most highly industrialized and developed areas of the world–areas that subsequently have dominated the rest of the world. Hence, rather than focusing on additional legal mechanisms for imposing the West's philosophic doctrines of the individual and inalienable human rights on the non-Western world, discussion of the issue of human rights should begin with the differing historical and contemporary circumstances of non-Western societies. Given differences in historical experience and contemporary conditions, what was a "natural" evolution in the West may not appear so "natural" in the Third World.

Hinduism in the recent years projects that the idea of human rights is opposed to the Indian tradition, which is based on the concept of duty and not rights. It is not that the last category of literature rejects the concerns behind the idea of human rights of achieving a just society. But it aims at creating a new approach for achieving the goals of human rights in the India society by seeking in its own religious and cultural traditions, which means the Hindu traditions. Some writings even by non-Hindu Western writers also seem supportive of such approach. Even if this last category of literature cannot be brushed aside as Hindu chauvinism, its tendency to monopolize the vast Indian tradition as Hindu is not free from difficulties in the present day India. Firstly, today Hindu means follower of a particular religion different from the followers of other religions. Secondly, India is not as theoretic state and should not therefore be indentified with any particular religion even if that religion is the most dominant one. Thirdly, as corollary to the foregoing, not only the religious overtones antagonize the followers of other religions but also convert an otherwise secular issue into a religious issue to be opposed and rejected by the followers of these other religions. That defeats the whole purpose of the exercise and the cause of human rights in its present or any proposed modified version. Such approach cannot and should not, therefore, be pursued.

The enquiry is confined to the India tradition. But is there anything like the Indian tradition and, if so, what is it? The answer to this question may be controversial. India is an ancient land with an ancient surviving civilization whose antiquity is not shared by any other existing civilization except the Chinese. In the course of its recorded history of over four thousand years India, apart from having its pre-Aryan inhabitants of different racial and ethnic origins commonly called the Dravidians, has attracted different people from around the world starting with the Aryans. The Aryans have been the earliest and the most dominant group to make India their home and to shape its identity. Others, who joined them later, include Iranians, Greeks, Parthians, Bactrians, Scythians, Huns, pre-Islamic Turks, early Christians, Jews and Zoroastrians. They entered either from the northwest by land or from the west by sea and became part of the rest of the population. The major influx of Muslims from the north started from tenth century onwards and ultimately established by Mogul Empire in the sixteenth century, which lasted until the middle of the nineteenth century when it was replaced by the British Empire. It is a matter of our living memory that under pressure from the people of India the British withdrew in 1947 dividing the land into India and Pakistan. The eastern part of the latter became Bangladesh in 1971. All the three countries share much of the traditions of the pre-partition India, but the present enquiry is confined to what is now India.

Despite or because of the mixing of so many racial, ethnic, religious and other identities, India was able to create and maintain an identity, which may safely be called the Indian identity and which the constitution as "the rich heritage of our composite culture". The early Aryans created the bases for this identity that stars taking shape in the four Vedas, whose antiquity is variously estimated between 6000 to 1000 BC. But it is generally agreed that they were all composed by 1000 BC. From then onwards a continual flow of rich literature from Brahmans. Upanishads, Smritis, Puranas, commentaries to digests preserved and strengthened that identity by weaving into it all the existing and acquired diversities of India. Perhaps no ancient civilization in the world has so much contemporary literature about it. More than five thousand authors had produced this literature before the British came to India in the eighteenth century. Just to have an idea of its enormity, Amartya Sen tells that only one of the epic, the Mahabharata authored by Vedavyasa is seventeen times the length of Iliad and Odyssey put together. The Mahabharata is only one of the several writing of Vedavyasa. This identity, as already noted, was continuously influenced by the entry of new people and developments in and outside India but was not destroyed or discontinued either by the Islamic or the British rule. At an early time in history the inhabitants of India came to be called as Hindus and their land as Hindustan by the foreigners. Thus initially and until after the arrival of Islam and other religions into country, the word Hindu denoted all inhabitants of a geographical area without any religious connotation. Hindu was synonym of Indian. It is the tradition of these people, which has created the Indian identity that continues to be the identity of India it is this identity, which I have named the Indian tradition in the present enquiry.

The enquiry may be alleged to be misleading, but it is not. It is not an enquiry into any religious tradition; it is an enquiry into the traditions of India vis-à-vis the modern conception of human rights. India has given birth to a tradition and culture, which is unique in many ways. One of its unique features is that is has never arrested or prevented the birth, growth or entry of new religions. It has given equal opportunity to all of them to grow, flourish and become e part of it. It has also not prevented people from having any or changing their religious beliefs and practices. It is not dogmatic, static or inflexible. It has given immense freedom to a person to believe, practice, preach and propagate whatever one considers appropriate for self and for others including the acceptance or non-acceptance of God. We are referring to that tradition to which Tagore and Iqbal have paid glowing tributes and of which Akbar the Great is as much part as Ashoka The Great.

The current ideas of human rights start from the French Declaration of Rights of Man and Citizen 1789 and the Bill of Rights in the Constitution of the United States in a specific historical and social context. If today those ideas are considered as talisman for the removal of human misery around the world they need to be related to all the people so as to make them universally understandable and acceptable. Unless that process is gone through mere declaration of human rights in the international and national documents will not be enough to achieve the stated goals. India's record in the participation and ratification of international declarations and their incorporation in its laws and the Constitution is appreciable. The Indian state has been making all possible efforts towards the realization of these rights at every level. But is has not yet been able to secure the desired results; the ground realities continue to be grim. This hiatus between theory and practice is often attributed to the age-old traditions of Indian people. The long held tradition of Karma and faith in God's justice leads the untouchable women to suffer violations of their rights notwithstanding the declaration and provision for enforcement of their rights in the Constitution and other laws. We intend to enquire whether such anti-human rights traditions are the only traditions of India or have they been merely manipulated for the advantage of a few to the disadvantage of many.

The enquiry also covers the claims of some Indian and a non-Indian scholars as well as public figures that India along with the rest of the Asian countries shares a traditions of human duties rather than of rights in which the focus in on the society and no one the individual and, therefore, it is not consistent with the current model of human rights that assigns central place to the individual.

RIGHTS IN INDIAN TRADITION

The antiquity, evolution and nature of the Indian tradition outlined above calls for a difficult, if not impossible, task to trace development of notion which are recent. Even if executed the task may not produce uniform and agreeable results because firstly, the tradition may be lacking the vocabulary or even ideas for matters that are comparatively modern and secondly, it may be uncertain and even contradictory in its contents and understanding. The current issue of human rights came into currency as late as the second quarter of the twentieth century, though it is traced back to some of the developments in the West in the last eighteenth century. But in line with the steps taken by the UNESCO in preparation for the UN Declaration of Human Rights, seeking opinion of thinkers around the world about their perception of human rights, as well as the intensive international drive for their recognition and application around the globe, many scholars and public figures are engaged in tracing their roots in different traditions, including the Indian to which we have referred to above.

Ancient as the Indian tradition is, no wonder if it did not have an expression in its classical language, i.e. the Sanskrit corresponding to "human rights" or ever "rights" as they are understood today. Perhaps no tradition including the most recent one will find exact corresponding egression in its traditional language carrying the same meaning as the expression "human rights" carries today. Even the languages in which this expression has evolved may have not assigned it the meaning that is assigned to it today. Search for an equivalent expression may lead us to nowhere. The traditional literature should, therefore, be examined by its intention and not literally and philologically. Let us look at the spirit of the human rights as we understand it and see whether that spirit is expressed somewhere in the corresponding traditional literature. Te spirit behind the expression human rights is the creation of a society in which each and every individual has the opportunity to realize one's best with equal freedom. The question is whether the Indian tradition recognized and supported the idea of such opportunity. If it did, it was supportive of human rights, otherwise not. As most of the ancient traditions are based on religion, tracing the antecedents of the human rights in these traditions, Paul Lauren generalizes: "Despite their vast differences, complex contradictions, internal paradoxes, cultural variations, and susceptibility to conflicting interpretation and fierce argumentation, all of great religious traditions share a universal interest in addressing the integrity, worth, and dignity of all persons and consequently, the duty toward other people who suffer without distinction". Starting with Hinduism, he states:

> In Hinduism, the world's oldest religion, for example, the ancient texts of the Vedas, Agamas, and Upanishads, among others partly written over three thousand years ago, continually stress that divine truth is universal and that religions belief must be a way of life. These scriptures address the existence of good and evil, wisdom, the necessity for moral behavior, and especially the importance of duty (dharma) and good conduct (sadachara) toward others suffering in need. They enjoin believers to fulfill faithfully their earthly responsibilities to all people beyond the self or family without distinction by practicing selfless concern for their pain, particularly charity and compassion for the hungry, the sick, the homeless, and the unfortunate, as discussed in the Manava Dharma Sutra (Treatise on Human Duties). All human life, despite the vast differences among individuals, is considered sacred, to be loved and respected without distinction as to family member or stranger, friend or enemy. For this reason, the foremost ethical principle of Hinduism – and one... that become so important to Mahatma Gandhi who in the twentieth century regarded himself as a deeply traditional and orthodox Hindu – is no injury to others. The edict stands directly and universally: "No injury (ahimsa) is not causing pain to any living being at any time through the actions of one's mind, speech, or body.

Buddhism, founded approximately 2,500 years ago in India by Siddhartha Gautama, also began by addressing the universal issues of human relationships, profound respect for the life of each person, and compassion in the face of pain suffered by fellow human beings. He explicitly attacked the rigid caste system of his day, democratically opening his order to all, stressing the worth of each individual regardless of their social or political position, and urging his followers to renounce differences 'of caste and rank and become the members of one and the same society' practicing universal brotherhood and equality. Scriptures like Triptika and Anguttara-Nikaya pay considerable attention to the enduring problem of human suffering (*dukha*), and stress that one's duty is to overcome selfish desires and private fulfillment by practicing charity and compassion (*karuna*) in the face of pain suffered by fellow human beings. Scriptures like Triptika and Anguttara-Nikaya pay considerable attention to the enduring problem of human suffering (*dukha*), and stress that one's duty is to overcome selfish and private fulfillment by significant contributions towards the evolution of international human rights. Firstly they established "values, normative standards, and ideals that proved to be enormously important sources of inspiration and strength for those who campaigned for human rights." Secondly, "by seeking to develop a moral imperative or universal sense of obligation toward humankind, these religious traditions helped establish an ingredient essential for any and all international human rights: a concept of responsibility to common humanity." And thirdly, "by developing concepts of duties." Quoting Gandhi that "The true source of rights is duty" he concludes that the "ideas about human duties led quite naturally to ideas about human rights."

Paul Lauren forcefully affirms that the seeds of human rights are found, as much in the ancient Indian tradition as in any other and that those seeds are not literally expressed in any tradition in the language in which they are expressed today. Secondly, it also demonstrates that there is nothing peculiar about the Indian tradition if it speaks of rights. In all traditions duties have led to rights. It is generally admitted that Sanskrit did not have an expression exactly corresponding to the English expression "right". In the current Hindu vocabulary, which is derived mainly from Sanskrit, the Sanskrit word "*adhikara*" is used for "right" and the word "*manavadhikar*" is used for "human rights" but the word "*adhikara*" did not always carry the sense of right in the early Sanskrit or even in early Hindi literature or usage. It had a positive connotation of right when it spoke of upper castes or classes while it had a negative connotation of liability when it spoke of the lower castes or classes including women. It was also used to denote power. Authority, competence or qualifications. Thus, though today the word "*adhikara*" is practicing charity and compassion (*karuna*) towards that in need, this ethic forms a part of Buddhism's Noble Eightfold Path that includes right thought, right speech, right action, and right effort toward "all beings." It also creates a religious tradition necessary to appreciate the Dalai Lama's more contemporary pronouncement that the world's problems will be solved only by showing kindness, love, and respect for all humanity as brothers and sisters and if we understand each other's fundamental humanity, respect each other's right, share each other's problems and sufferings.

Manu used the world '*Adhikara*' in the context of Brahmanas in a positive sense, but in the context of women in a negative way. Admitting that classic Sanskrit has no word corresponding to right and that the idea of 'just claim' is expressed by word "adhikar", Tulsidas says: "The word is hardly used in isolation but rather in the context either of the performance of some act or of an acquisition of some kind. Thus the word *adhikarin*, meaning a person having *adhikara*, almost always suggests that the person has either performed some dharma (prescribed duty) or has come to possess something, value of status".

Used for "right", it did not always convey that meaning in the ancient Sanskrit literature or even later religious books. Rather it supports inequality and discrimination among human being, which is contrary to the idea of "right" in the modern sense. Even in its positive sense "*adhikara*" carries the meaning of earning a right by one's action, Karma, and not possessing it as a natural attribute of being a human.

The ancient Sanskrit literature did not use the world "*adhikara*" frequently. As codes of conduct, Dharma Sutras emphasize more the duties of human than their rights; the word "*adhikara*" thus does not occur frequently. Like most other religions of the world, Hinduism emphasizes the duties of humans rather than their rights. Duties and rights being interrelated, it is possible to formulate ideas about rights from ideas about duties. Dharama Shastras use the term "dharma" more frequently than *adhikara*. Dharma implies justice and property as does the world "right" of the U.N. Declaration although the connotation of a "just claim" is not explicitly present. Yet, Dharma is the closest equivalent to "right". This connotation of *adhikara*, which is the nearest Indian equivalent to right, is based on two very interesting and philosophically significant interrelated ideas. To the Indian every right is acquired, i.e., it is not natural. Secondly the acquisition of any right is the result of one's action or one's status. Of these two basic ideas, the first may be called the idea of historicity and the second that of causality. Rights are earned and efforts made in acquiring them confer certain privileges upon persons who take the trouble to exert themselves. It is supported by karma philosophy "that a man gets what he works for". This is the moral basis for the rights.

The modern theory of rights that one has certain rights by virtue of being human is based on status and if that be so the animals must also have rights by being so. But animals don't have rights because they do not have volition. Thus comes the element of rationality in rights.

Dharma is perhaps the most fundamental word in the Indian tradition which could lead us to the discovery of a possible homeomorphic symbol corresponding to the Western notion of "Human Rights". Let us, therefore, turn to Dharma. Dharma is one of those Sanskrit words that defy all attempts at an exact rendering in English or any other tongue. After going through its use in different works on Dharmasastra at different stages of early Indian history, it is established how the world dharma passed through several transitions of meaning and how ultimately its most prominent significance came to be 'the privileges, duties and obligations of a man, his standard of conduct as a member of the Aryan community, as a member of one of the castes, as a person in a particular stage of life.

Derived from the Sanskrit root *dhr*, "sustain, support, uphold", *dharma* has a wide range of meaning: it is the essential foundation of something or of things in general, and thus signifies "truth", it is that which is established, customary, proper, and therefore means "traditional" or "ceremonial", it is one's duty, responsibility, imperative, and thereby "moral obligation", it is that which is right, virtuous, meritorious, and accordingly "ethical", and it is that which is required, precepted, or permitted through religious authority, and thus "legal."

The aggregate connotation here suggests that in South Asian cultures *dharma* represents "correctness," both in descriptive sense (the way things are) and in a prescriptive one (the way things should be), and reflects the inextricable connection in the religious thought of India between ontology, ritual ideology, social philosophy, ethics and canon law.

Dharma in the specific context of human right has finds the meaning of the word "multifocal": besides element, data, quality and origination, it means law, norm of conduct, character of things, right, truth, ritual, morality, justice, righteousness, religion, destiny, and many other things. Dharma as primordial is the order of the entire reality, that which keeps the world together. The individual's duty is to maintain his "right", it is to find one's place in relation to society, to the cosmos, and to the transcendental world. In order to have a just society, the modern West stresses notion of human rights. In order to have a dharma order, classical India stresses the notion of *swadharma*.

Dharma, as is apparent from its foregoing descriptions, contained elements of law, but it was much wider than positive law. It was not the creation of the king or the state; it was over and above them and king of the kings. It was based not on divine will but on reason and its sanction was derived not from any extrinsic or occidental agency, but from its internal logic that obedience to law will lead to welfare and it violation too misery. Perhaps for that reason conflicts between religion and the state were unknown in the ancient or even later Indian history. If ever a king deviated from his dharma he was compelled to abdicate.

The concept of Dharma, though central to Indian tradition, has not been static or dogmatic. It has evolved with the evolution of the society. From its early Vedic stage of determining the obligations of gods and cosmic order it moved to human beings creating *varna* and *ashrama* systems as early as the Brahmanas (c. 900-600 BC) classifying the society into four groups and the life of each individual into four stages. Along with that it incorporated the idea that every person who observed one's dharma not only helped the preservation of social order but also gained fame in this word and absolute happiness after death. From this sacerdotal and eschatological stance arises a normative dimension to dharma in which the term comes to mean the sum total of one's obligations by which one fits in with the natural and particularly the social world. Although these obligations are not univocal laid down at one place forever, the predominant of them are drawn from *Manavadharmasastra* or *Manusmriti* which determined them according to one's *varna* and *ashrama*. One's location in a particular *varna* depended upon his karma of this and past life. Therefore, one's obligation or dharma (*svadharma*) got merged into *varnashramadharma*, which depended upon one's birth – based on division of the four classes or *varnas*. *Varnashramadharma* was, however, not without exceptions. The *apaddharma* or obligations determined by emergency could supersede *varnasharmadharma*. The *varnashram* and apaddharma did not exhaust the entire dharma. Dharma also included sadharna (pertaining to everybody), samanya (common) or sanatana (eternal) dharma. According to this dharma all people, regardless of their varna and asharma, should observe some common obligations. Among others, the Arthasatra (c.300 BC) gives a representative list of such obligations, which includes refraining from injuring others (non-violence or Ahimsa), telling truth (satya), living purely, practicing goodwill, being forgiving, and exercise of patience at all times. While the Brahmanic tradition gave precedence to varnashramadharma over sadharandharma the Vedanta, Buddhism and Jainism taught that the demands of sadharandharma always overrule those of varnashramadharma. The Bhakti movement also added the dimension of submission of God for guidance in case of conflict between the varnasharama and sadharama dharma. In this connection it may also be noted that the sources of dharma also include sadachara and conscience, which respectively mean the actions of the honoured members of the society and the voice of one's conscience. Under this category dharma could be transformed to suit the changing conditions and advancement of the society.

Dharma in the Indian tradition is not laid down in any particular book of religion; it did not have an organization like church with monopoly to enunciate and enforce it, it does not have any fixed dogma or a set of dogmas and it has not only grown freely from within but has also borrowed liberally whatever was good and conducive for human well being in other traditions around the world in whose contact it came. Therefore, it promoted the creation of immense literature referred to above and let different religions and ideologies such as Jainism, Buddhism, Sikhism, Charvakas, and Lokayatas emerge, grow and survive. Its most important religious and philosophical wing – the Vedanta - , birth of Sikh religion, and interpretation of Indian tradition by great saints from Shankara, Ramanuja, Kabir, Raidas, Sufis, Ram Mohan Roy, Dayananda, Ramatirtha, Vivekananda to Arobindo Ghosh and others was influenced by the contacts with Christianity, Islam and other religious traditions. Interestingly, the ancient Indian tradition never claimed superiority over any other tradition, nor did it ever advocate its spread over other people and territories. It is unfortunate that its varnasharma aspect, which invoked universal logic, somehow degraded into the vagaries of birth-based discriminations and even the practice of untouchability. Unlike some other traditions, it did not go to the extent of excluding class or classes of people from the category of humans, but that is so consolation or justification for the unequal and ill treatment, which a large section of society met and continues meet in its name. The blame for such degradation and discrimination is attributed to the priestly or Brahmin class who did not rule the state but guided its rulers by the exposition of dharma. Although this kind of separation of powers between the ruler and enunciators of norms for ruling prevented the emergence of tyrants and totalitarian regimes and also the religious wars, witnessed in other traditions, it has left scandalous mark on the face of Indian tradition that cannot be justified under the conception of human rights in our time. Subject to this blot, the diverse and even opposite faiths, beliefs, ideologies, opinions and so on to grow and flourish is fully in line with the spirit of the human rights. For that reason when opportunity came to take independent decision in 1947, without much debate. India opted for a democratic republic and provided for a progressive bill of rights, including the affirmative rights, in its Constitution. In the international arena human rights has also always lent its positive support to them. In the words of Radhakrishnan:

> Tradition is something which is forever being worked out anew and recreated by the free activity of it followers. If a tradition does not grow, it only means that its followers have become spiritually dead. Throughout the history of Hinduism the leasers of thought and practice have been continually busy experimenting with new forms, developing new ideals to suit new conditions.

In view of such progressive and liberal nature of the Indian tradition, let us scrutinize it further in the context of our notion of human rights. If we pursue the difference between the varnasharama and sadharana dharma, it is eminently capable of subsuming the modern conception of human rights. Elaborating the two Kane concludes that all dharmasastra writers attached the highest importance to moral qualities (sadharana or samanya dharma) and enjoined them upon all with all the emphasis they could command; but as their main purpose was a practical one, viz, to guide people to rights acts in everyday life, they dealt more elaborately with the acts, rites and ceremonies that each person had to do with reference to his station in society. For that reason only and not for the reason that former was superior to the latter, the Dharmasastra writers are "found principally concerning themselves with varansrana dharma and not with sadharana dharma". Of course like any other aspect of dharma, saharana dharma was not laid down place forever, it is spread over the entire Dharamsastra literature. We have already noted it s description in the Arthasastra. We may also find it described variously in different writings on the Indian tradition, which may be availed of in the present context. For example, deriving the notion of law (dharma), Derrett says:

> The moral qualities of the nation, the ultimate virtues, must be subserved in any event. These were truth, abstention from injuring, freedom from anger, humanity, self-control, uprightness, abstention from theft, ritual purity, restraint of the appetites, generosity, compassion, nondiscrimination, forbearance, absence of envy, abstention from violence, patience, freedom from meanness, regard for the interest of others.

Puntambekar specifically uses them in connection with the preparation for the Universal Declaration of Human Rights. Naming them as ten freedoms drawn from Manu and Buddha says:

> They (Manu and Buddha) have propounded codes which were often essential human freedoms and controls or virtues necessary for a good life. They emphasis five freedoms or social assurances and five individual possessions or virtues.

The five social freedoms are:

(1) freedom from violence (Ahimsa),

(2) freedom from want (Asteya),

(3) freedom from exploitation (Aparigraha),

(4) freedom from violation or dishonor (Avyabichara), and

(5) freedom from early death and disease (Armitave and Aregya).

The five individual possessions or virtues are:

(1) absence of intolerance (Akrodha),

(2) Compassion or fellow feeling (Bhutadaya, Ahreha),

(3) Knowledge (Jnana, Vidya),

(4) freedom of thought and conscience (satya, sunrta), and

(5) freedom from fear (Abhaya).

Aware of the fact that they are not expressed in terms of freedoms in the ancient Indian tradition, he explains:

> Human freedoms require as counterparts human virtues or controls. To think in terms of freedoms without corresponding virtues lead to a lopsided view of life and stagnation or even a deterioration of personality, and also to chaos and conflict society.

As at the time of his writing India was under foreign rule, he also pleaded for freedom from foreign rule because such "rule is a damnable thing." For Gandhi and other Hindu reformers, both priests and rulers have duties to all that can be the basis of universal rights, and all people have, in addition to their particular occupational duties, a common dharma of fundamental duties, of which the most important are truth telling (satya) and not harming living beings (ahimsa). ... Most educated modern Hindus would agree theoretically with the emphasis to the common dharma, not only of Hindus but of all human beings. Hindu culture increasingly emphasizes one's 'common dharma' (sadharana dharma) over the 'specialized dharma' (visesa dharma) of caste rules, rituals and duties. The first promotes activities for public self are and attracts progressive reformers: Human rights advocates might locate here a convergent indigenous Indian impulse. Despite its rather anemic social history, 'common dharma 'still provides the strongest ideological plank from within the tradition to all those marginal, weak, exploited, and protesting. Many major reformers (from Buddha and Kabir to Raidas) made this dharma their moral terra firma for attaching the birth-based jati or caste dharma and its inequities, while modern reformers like Ambedkar and Gandhi tried to render common dharma the soil for sowing the seeds of modern India's tolerant and civic public culture.

There is support for the human rights even in the difference between the varnashramadharma and svadharma, which even Manu recognized. The idea of svadharma, if not understood as rigid code of law, can be a contribution in the field of human rights in its suggestion that differences be taken seriously" and that different people may have different rights and duties, each human being deserves and should have equal consideration and equal concern. Such interpretation of equality is the universal norm, which can be used even for the humanization of varnashramadharma.

Rights and Duties

Critics as well as the defenders of the Hindu tradition often rely on the absence of reference to rights and meticulous details of duties of persons in it to deny the existence of human rights in it. This is not a unique feature of the Indian tradition. All ancient traditions speak of duties and hardly of any rights. The Indian tradition may, appear to be especially prominent in this regard because of its meticulous enunciation of varnasrama dharma. Otherwise it shares that tradition with others.

Historically until long after the French and US declarations of rights, not all Western thinkers had supported the idea of rights. The idea that the rights of man could be a starting point for political morality was regarded by Jeremy Bentham and other utilitarian's as wild and pernicious nonsense. Expectedly, Karl Marx said, "none of the so called rights of man goes beyond egoistic man,... an individual withdrawn behind his private interests and whims and separated from the community. Even until today intense discussions continue on the justification of rights-based world. In order to bring precision in the rights-based argument and theories only as late as in 1919 Hohfeld drew a chart of jural relations distinguishing rights from privileges, powers and immunities. It is in that relationship that a right in strict sense in one person imposes duty on another against whom he has the right. But in other situations duties are not imposed though absence of right, disability and liability may arise. In this strict sense freedom is not right and, therefore, subjects no one to duty, through it creates absence of duty in the subject of freedom. If a right so defined always creates a corresponding duty, could it not be argued that existence of duty in one person towards another is as good as the creation of right in the later. The main objection to such argument is that what happens if the person on whom duty is imposed does not perform it. The answer is that in either case it is a breach of law, which could be corrected by legal action. Just as legal action could be instituted for the enforcement of rights, it could also be instituted for the enforcement of duties. But because in the West the concept of human rights developed against the state, perhaps theoretically and strategically state could not be subjected to duties unless the existence of rights was recognized in the individual preceding the creation of the state. Therefore, the rights theory developed the way it has done. It is now being pursued in spite of several difficulties being faced in its operation in respect of human rights of individuals inter se such as of children against parents or of spouses between them or of old parents against their earning and able children. In such situations rights model does not work well, rather it transfers realization of rights to the state, unless the people are also taught to perform their duties. As the Indian tradition dealt with such situations only and did not face the problem with the state, it taught people to perform their duty well according to their station in society and stage in life. Perhaps it could be one of the reasons that Gandhi saw the primacy of duties over the rights. In Indian conditions where people are neither aware nor capable of enforcing their rights, imposition of legally enforceable duties could protect the rights better than merely the declaration of rights. It could also help in humanizing the public authorities towards respecting the civil and political as well as social and economic rights.

Gandhi had another reason too. At the time of writing his letter, India was still under British rule. Gandhi had no doubt that no country or people had the right to rule others. So long as a person is under the rule of another or lacks Swaraj (self rule), he is incapable of enjoying any rights to be claimed-duty of the outside ruler to withdraw it rule. If both side thus performed their duties, the rights of the ruled get realized automatically. In the absence of performance of that duty, no rights could be expected. In his statement perhaps Gandhi was also reminding the future rulers of independent India that in order to justify their rule they had to perform their duties, as it was every ruler's dharma.

Scholars also give an additional explanation for the absence of rights and presence of duties in the Indian tradition. They say that the Western declarations of rights such as of the United States or France are manifestos of liberation, an insistence that rights previously denied now be recognized, they imply reclamation of the lost ground. In India "there is also the accumulated tradition of the language of the British courts, in which thousands and thousands of litigants sought preservation or restoration of inherited rights and privileges, not least the symbolic honors supposedly awarded, not by the British, but by the Sovereign of the Universe enshrined in the temple." As there were no Indian counterparts of Hennery VIII or of any other absolute ruler and dharma was king over kings, which imposed on them the duty to uphold dharma by imposing the prescribed penalties on this violators, the occasion to make a demand for rights never arose. Such occasion was created for the first time by the British rule against which the people of India began to make the demand of rights towards the end of the nineteenth century.

The assertion of 'rights' in its last analysis would mean some act that would not be in accordance with the interest of some other. 'I have the right to do this or that' is an assertion which becomes necessary only when in going to realize my desire with reference to them I come in conflict with the interest of some other. Such an assertion would scarcely be necessary in a society where everyone will do only that which at the same time inures to the benefit of all else.

The Indian tradition required the individuals to refrain from doing evil and intruding upon the will of others and to rise above the ego. One can say that such denial or effacement of self by the individual is not consistent with the culture of rights. We must, however, not ignore that the concept of rights is not an expression of individual ego but of common good to humanity.

Perhaps it is to remind the individual of this common good that now the West also is reflecting on the relevance of duties. It is now demanding a universal declaration of duties too on the lines of the Declaration of Human Rights. The Inter Action Council consisting of 25 former heads of state and government has already prepared a draft of Universal Declaration of Human Responsibilities for adoption by the United Nations. Many are critical of the Indian Constitution insofar as it provided only for the rights on the Western style without providing for the duties of the individual. They are not satisfied even with the directive principles of state policy imposing certain duties on the state. The Constitution was amended in 1976 introducing a few duties of the individual. It is unclear whether the amendment was encouraged by the Indian tradition or the socialist model of the West. In view of the fact that the socialist model is now gone and the

West is also discussing a universal declaration of duties, the duties model of Indian tradition may required further enunciation and exploration.

We need not enter into the niceties of the difference between the individual and the person to explain the argument of uniqueness of human rights in the West because of the position of the individual in the Judeo-Christian heritage. The primordially controlling religious concept for the Jewish understanding of human being is its creation in the image of God. By virtue of reflecting the divine image, absolute worth is accorded to human being. From this Jewish heritage, Western rights acquired their absolute character as attendant to the human being of every individual.

Within its Christian heritage, however, divine regard for human being was perfected by the Son of God in the person of Jesus Christ. Through Christ, humanity is freed from sin, redeemed before God, and exists in a state of grace.

The Christian understanding of human rights is entirely a function of the extraordinary value divinely granted to human being through the person of Jesus Christ. This value is not only absolute; it is fait accompli. Human rights language within the Christian religious tradition addresses itself to this divine regard, and is accordingly dictated by the Word of God revealed through Jesus Christ.

One may ask that if it were so why did it not occur to the Jewish and Christian world until the end of nineteenth century and why even after its occurrence human rights continued and continue to be violated in many ways in that part of the world? Ignoring, however, the facts and concentrating on the principles, so far as this argument goes to support the idea of human rights in Jewish or Christian tradition or in both. But it is used to deny the idea of human rights in other traditions, as many to deny it in the Hindu tradition. It is true that the ancient Indian tradition does not speak of original sin and subsequent redemption or of divine law and "words of God" uttered at the initiation of the creation. Even if some works incorporating such tradition are said to be uttered by the prophets or incarnation and not to anyone beyond. But describing the origins of universe the Manavadharmasastra says that dividing his own body, the Lord became half male and half female; with that (female) he produced association with the first. Spirituality, not materialism, became its ideal. Therefore, in spite of Bhagavadgita's strong message to fight for one's rights the dominant goal of such fight turns into moksha rather than material gains. To be indifferent to this worldly and to be concerned about the otherworldly gains became an ideal for the individual. Perhaps, for that reason, he cared more for the freedom to make speculations about the other world and another life rather than the recognition of his material interests in this life. To a considerable extent, it is true, these traditions still guide the life of an average Indian in matters of claims of his rights.

But besides this otherworldly and spiritual aspects of the Indian tradition, its other aspects such as those expressed in sadharama dharma, living in harmony with nature and other beings, not being guided all the time by self-interest but also caring for the interest of others, keeping one's need and desires within limits as Gandhi did in our own times, performance of one's obligations religiously instead of putting forward, one's real and imaginary claims perpetually, are some of the fundamental issues for the understanding and application of the human rights. They raise the foundational question about the model of human rights. Should that model lead to further conflicts and clashes or should it lead to peace and harmony? There are cultures and traditions that promote conflicts and clashes and others that promote peace and harmony. The Indians tradition falls in the latter category.

For assigning special place to human rights in Christianity we can quote two commandments for the Bible. "You shall love the Lord your God with all your heart, and with all your soul, and with all your mind" and "You shall love your neighbor as yourself". In the Indian tradition volumes of literature on Bhakti staring from the Pauranas and including the Bhagvadgita and subsequent epical works of Chaitanya, Surdas, Tulsi, Mira, Nanak, Kabir and so many others are full of the first commandment and more. And equally the second commandment is expressed at more than one place such as "Do not do to others what you do not like to be done to yourself". Perhaps it sounds as if I am speaking for a particular religion. We would have never done so but for dispelling some of the notions people carry about traditions other their own which in no way serve the cause of human rights.

To deny the conception of individual autonomy in the Indian traditional reliance is also placed on the often-quoted verse from the sastric literature, which says: "for the family sacrifice the individual: for the community the family; for the country the community; and for the soul the whole". The verse expresses the supremacy of the self over everything else. Nothing can and must come in the way of realization of one's self. The core of the verse does not contradict the rest of the Indian tradition, nor does it promote ego or self-interest. It simply amplifies the importance of the self of every human being, which every other human being must respect everyman for the simple fact that his manhood is capable of reaching perfection.

Reliance on any religion to found the current idea of human rights is not necessary. To claim that a particular religion alone and no other in the world provides such foundation is dangerous. In no way it serves the cause of human rights. In the evolution of the idea of human rights every religion has something to contribute. As religion plays a significant role in the lives of the people, relating the idea of human rights to their religion helps them in its understanding and application. Beyond that the idea must be founded on rationality as most other ideas in the modern world are founded. If India's record of human rights is dismal the foregoing discussion must help in understanding that it is not entirely due to its religious traditions. Religious tradition have of course been manipulated to introduce birth based discriminations and practice of untouchability, but they were only serious aberrations by their beneficiaries which need to be clarified and removed. The study of tradition must help in explaining and removing those aberrations.

In view of our shared belief that a universal regime of human rights will lead to the creation of an ideal society in which each one of us will have equal opportunity of realizing one's best, any and every step towards the realization of that goal is worth making. In India the state, innumerable NGOs, groups and individuals are seriously engaged in the task of realizing the goal. The goal, however, is not yet in sight. Why it is so? Are we not serious enough in our task or are we making mistakes in its performance? Two types of answers seem to be coming. Firstly, the Western model of human rights is not suitable for India. The two answers are interconnected. It is like hen and egg story. Unless we have an agreed model of human rights we cannot we examine its base in our tradition. Therefore, we must first have a model before we examine its foundations in our tradition. But we cannot have a model founded on our traditions without knowing the traditions. The task is therefore problematic.

Without entering into the more difficult question of developing a model, let us examine the Indian tradition in the light of the current model reflected in the International Bill of Rights. The Indian tradition is, however, so complex that any description of it will invite controversies. To minimize the controversy we have rather confined to the ancient tradition as gathered primarily from the Dharmasastra literature. That literature is not one book or set of books but rather innumerable books written in a long course of time of about four thousand years in different parts of the country from north to south and east to west. It is formidable task to bring it within a uniform tradition. The only unifying force is the authority of the Vedas which this literature does not challenger. This acceptance of the Vedas as the ultimate authority doing with various other factors may be called as one unifying factor of that tradition which gives it an identity. That identity came to be called at some point of time in India's history as Hindu, even though initially and for long time the word Hindu continued to cover all people in a geographical area. It started acquiring a religious connotation as a distinguishing mark between the followers of Islam and the rest. That distinction was sanctified in law during the British rule from the end of eighteenth century onwards, which divided the natives into Hindus and Muslims and the rest as British or Europeans. As the gap between the Hindus and Muslims was further widened during the British rule from the beginning of the twentieth century, which ultimately resulted in the division of the country, the use of the word now generates communal links. Therefore, even though it is mentioned twice at one place in the Constitution, the current tradition of India also recognizes and must recognize, as it has done in the past, the existence of other sub-traditions including Islamic and Christian.

The pre-Islamic and pre-Christian tradition which has given India a unique place among the major traditions of the world may have many characteristics. Its most striking characteristic is its freedom from any dogma; freedom to every individual to decide what one considers best for oneself; freedom to say whatever one considers good for the rest of the society and even the freedom to recognize or deny the existence of God or any supernatural power. Even in its belief in God it "believes in the evolution of our knowledge of God." It does not distinguish ideas of God as true and false, adopting one particular idea as the standard for the whole human race. It is an evolutionary tradition building itself constantly all the time. Believing in such liberalism and evolution of the Indian tradition, it should not out rightly reject an idea of human rights simply for the reason that it comes from the West. Its ideal has always been composite and plural. The deeper insight into the institutions of the different countries discloses that it is the same universal reason which permeates the universe, and its touch makes the whole world kin. Therefore, so long as the present conception of human rights can reason out its vision of a better society, Indian tradition does not and shall not come in its way. It is adequately evident from the importation of that conception in the Constitution of India and the endorsement of the International Bill of Rights and other human rights conventions by India.

The fact, however, is that such incorporation endorsement of the human rights idea has not yet produced the desired results. It is not that the human rights record has not improved from what it was in the pre-independence days, but it has not been able to create that hope and determination for pursuing it with which the idea was launched. Therefore, questions arise whether the idea of human rights in its present from suits the Indian tradition or does it need modification or replacement in the light of our tradition and experience rarely anyone holds the view that the idea must be totally replaced. But from the very beginning in line with Gandhi people have been exploring with the idea of emphasizing on duties besides or instead of the rights. The idea is not so bizarre or against the current idea of human rights if understood in the spirit in which it was expressed in the ancient Indian tradition. It imposed heavier duties and responsibilities on the rulers and privileged classes of the society than on the others. "The higher the man, the fewer are his rights and the more numerous his duties. As once the great human rights advocate, Palkhivala, argued before the Supreme Court, in India the common man needed the fundamental rights more than the rich and powerful. The rich and powerful could take care of their rights from their own resources, while the common man could not. And here lies the difference in the perception of the human rights in the Indian mind, which did not perceive and experienced so much danger from the state, except during the British rule, as from the privileged sections in the society. It is that privileged class of the society whether within or outside the state that continues to disregard the human rights of the masses. This class is also exploiting the current human rights model to the advantage without regard to or against the human rights of masses. Therefore, the skepticisms on the current model are not baseless. Could we conceive of a model for India, which instead of or in addition to individual rights imposes legally enforceable duties on the state and other bodies acting under the colour of state? The question requires urgent attention in the light of privatization and globalization creating imminent chances for the exploitation of the weak by the strong. The answer to this question does not lie merely in the campaign for the awareness of the existing rights of the individual.

The Indian tradition needs to be studied carefully and thoroughly from the point of view of human rights. Such study is more relevant now than ever before because of the false notions being held and spreads about it out of its ignorance. A careful study may not support the birth-based discrimination and the practice of untouchability as they came to be. Much of what is propagated in the name of Indian tradition may be found baseless and much of it could be explained in the context of social, historical and political changes. Dharmasastra expressly tells "one should not observe but give up what was once Dharma, if it has come to be hatful to the people and if it would end in unhappiness." Today the Indian tradition does not need to guard itself in isolation against the foreign rulers; it has its own rule, swaraj, Varna system was a classification of functions not opposed to equality. "One becomes a Brahmin by his deeds not by his family or birth, even a Chandala is a Brahmin if he is of pure character", says Manu. "Conduct counts and not birth." The Mahabharata elaborates "that man is known as brahmana in whom are seen truthfulness, generosity, absence of hate, absence of wickedness, restraint for avoiding wrong-doing, compassion and a life of austerity; if these signs are observed in a sudra and are not found in a brahmana, then the sudra is not a sudra and the Brahmana is not a Brahmana." Similarly untouchability was initially connected with the impurity of acts and not with birth. The openness of the tradition to rationality must be highlighted and utilized to remove anything that is irrational.

Seen in that perspective the Indian tradition is not only receptive to any notion of human rights, but if can also enrich that notion. Cautioning against the universalizing of the Western notion of human rights, we can move on towards a new vision; of human rights based in the Indian tradition. Human rights are not human only. They concern equally the entire cosmic display of the universe, from which even the Gods are not absent. The animals, all the sentient beings and the supposedly inanimate creatures, and also involved in the interaction concerning human rights. Many traditional cultures are centered on God, and some other cultures basically cosmocentric. The culture which has come up with the notice of human rights is decisively anthropocentric. Perhaps we may now be prepared for a cosmotheandric vision of reality in which the Divine, the Human and the Cosmic are integrated into a whole, more or less, according to the performance of our truly human rights.

The Indian tradition does not claim superiority over any other tradition. Nor does it lay down universal standards for other traditions. It is so not because of its poverty or weakness but because of its eternal spirit of liberty that it is never too sure to be right. Any tradition that lacks that spirit cannot form sound basis of universal human rights. The endeavour to universalize the human rights must, therefore, be based on worldview that takes into account all traditions and demands of the world. Similarly all world traditions without uprooting their cultures and giving up possible solutions to their human rights problems within them must be open to be part of the worldview. Instead of being scared of one another they must get inspired by the spirit of togetherness in the common cause of humanity. Rabindranath Tagore, the late poet laureate, inspires "when I can acknowledge the poets and artists of other countries as my own, let me feel with unalloyed gladness that all the great glories of man are mine".

4

Human Rights in the Western Tradition

The purpose of this chapter is to contribute to the ongoing debate on human rights, by exploring to what extent they are Western, and what might be done to make them more universal. Whatever is Western, from Christianity via some of the colonial languages and Western science and technology to Western history and development models in general, tends to be conceived of as universal. The West is so powerful that such ideas as Western history = universal history and Western culture = universal culture are found not only among Westerners. The high level of acceptance of Western development models (called modernization) implies an acceptance of the model character of both Western history and Western culture. Formulated in more Hegelian terms, "there has been and still is an underlying assumption that humanity has had a crystallization point for early self-realization in the West". By implication, Western human rights = universal human rights has gained almost automatic acceptance.

But regardless of the strength of this tradition, pretending that something is universal does not make it universal in any operational or meaningful sense. Humanity is badly served if all shoe factories turn out shoes of size 40 and car factories cars for right-hand drive only. Simplifying to universal = West + non-West, there are actually three problems here, not only that of imposing West on non-West when it does not fit, and not having non-West benefit from its own human rights tradition. There is also the problem of the West not benefiting from the non-Western tradition. Loser, the whole world.

The reaction or over-reaction to the present asymmetry could easily lead to an asymmetry with the three corresponding problems: imposing non-West on the West; not having the West benefit from its own tradition; and not having the non-West benefit from the (liberal) Western tradition. The last is often used as an argument not only against any change but against even looking into the problem. Those who argue that the human rights tradition is Western are seen as arguing against the human rights tradition in general; deliberately or not supporting repressive regimes in particular. The position taken here, however, is openness to all six problems. But given the Western background for the human rights tradition the task right now is to analyze that tradition and then bring in the non-West tradition.

The key entry points for discussing this problem are time in the sense of history as basic, i.e. structural, change, and space in the sense of culture. How did human rights originate historically and grow structurally, and what kind of cultural imprint does the human rights tradition carry? But first some conceptualization of human rights is indispensable. A human right will be conceived of here as a norm, concerning, indeed protecting, the rock bottom of human existence. There is a link to basic human needs which potentially would make human rights applicable to human beings everywhere. As for any norms, there are norm-senders who lay down the borderline between the prescribed, the indifferent, and the proscribed. There are norm-receivers whose acceptance of the norm (meaning that the norm has been received, not only registered) implies inclusion of the prescribed and exclusion of the proscribed from their action repertories. And there are norm-objects in principle the centerpiece of the construction-for whom a human right implies a claim on the norm-receivers if they omit the prescribed acts and/or commit the proscribed acts.

Human rights can be seen as parts of a contract or covenant between the state and the human beings/citizens. For international human rights a three-tier world context with three constructs is needed: individuals, states, and communities/organizations of states. This particular social construction came slowly into being after the decline of the Middle Ages. The Westphalia system of 1648 and the Concert of Europe of 1815; the emergence of international governmental and people's organizations and of international law (the Hague system) in the nineteenth century building a community of states; and the organizations of the League of Nations (1919) and the United

Nations (1945) serve as important stepping stones and convenient anchoring points for process analysis. If history is the record of social change and social change is interpreted as structural change, then there is not only a story but a history to be told here, and it has been told many times.

Reciprocal systems of rights and duties must be as old as human beings themselves. The concrete normative content varies, with *lex talionis*, in positive or negative formulations or both, often used as a meta- norm. In *lex talionis*, self-reference is the anchoring point for behaviour towards other. The bottom line of the ethical budget is what will ultimately benefit myself, in other words, the meta-norm is ego-centered: Do unto others what you want others to do to you.

But there is also a god-centered reference, probably equally universal. The question is what kind of god, what kind of theology as opposed to the anthropology underlying lex talionis. The distinction is between an immanent god inside us, making humans (in Buddhism all sentient beings) imbued with that substance sacred; and a transcendental god outside, even outside Planet Earth (Thou who art in Heaven). In the immanent case the rights of Other and the duties of Self would be anchored in the unity of humans in addition to the sacredness of Other, and lex talionis comes in the back door through the assumption that hurting Other is also hurting Self. In the transcendental case the rights of Other and the duties of Self derive from the duties to a transcendental god as formulated in the Judeo-Christian Ten Commandments. There is still horizontal reciprocity, but not as a useful, well-tested traffic rule for human behavior or because unity of life implies symbiosis. The commandments are our duty to God as a vertical, transcendental ethics as opposed to horizontal, immanent ethics.

This logic is expressed with apodictic clarity in Matthew 25: 40 (positive version) and Matthew 25: 45 (negative version): When you did it to those my brothers you were doing it to me. When you refused to help the least of these my brothers, you were refusing help to me. This horizontal behavior is vertically anchored ethically.

But who is to judge? Ultimately Thou who art in heaven. But before that ultimate judgement his representatives, the clerical hierarchy. Being closest to a transcendental god they also came up on top of the social hierarchy when feudalism was crystallized during the Middle Ages. The abstract duty to the Father in Heaven was mirrored in the more concrete duty to the father in church.

The rest of the story can now be told quickly, using the principle of structural inertia or isomorphism through time. Two logically related processes took place: aristocracy replaced clergy on top of the social hierarchy and the top aristocrat, the king/emperor, took on god-like characteristics, being increasingly omnipresent, omniscient, and omnipotent. This does not mean that clergy and god came second in the temporal order constituted by aristocracy and king, but that they constituted a spiritual order on a side-track, no longer in the center of society. The relative significance of the two orders then becomes the focus of politics, the trend being secularization, implying increasing marginalization both of clergy and god, even to the point of the latter being declared dead or at least dying. Conceivably this is what happened in the Soviet Union under perestroika, with the second, ideological order, the Party, being marginalized and even history, the homologue of god, receding into the background and the old god coming up again.

Transition formulas were found and are still used. The king became rex gratia dei, and theology (Luther) produced the teaching of the two orders, essentially reproducing the clever biblical distinction between what is of Caesar and what is of God, with the admonition to give unto each his due. Gradually the king and aristocracy were then replaced by cabinet and bureaucracy, meaning the state; with the old order, the ancient regime, marginalized if they were not executed. What remained was and is the essence, the structural relation between state and citizen being patterned on the relation between state and citizen being patterned on the relation between God and Christian. That these two transformations replacing entrenched powers were not easy is borne out clearly by the drama of European history. They would have been considerably more problematic had isomorohism not been preserved. The actors change, but the structure remains the same. The essence of a crime such as murder is no longer against God but against the state; the victim comes second. The state is not merely a third party but is directly offended, and like God entirely justified in administering punishment; doing it to me.

The king being only a local primus inter pares and the state being one among several, however, neither king nor state could be more than local gods, however omnipresent, omniscient, and omnipotent. The search for a single and universal super-king and/or super-state still continues. Napoleon, refusing to be crowned by the pope, placing the crown on himself, tried to cast himself in the first role. The United Nations has been cast in the second. US resistance to the UN might be understood not only as power struggle in the temporal order between US and UN, but also as a US refusal to let the UN play god-like roles, thereby replacing the spiritual order. But with the UN system both norm-sender and norm- receivers were in place, US misgiving notwithstanding.

We still have to account for the third construct, the individuals, in whom the rights are vested, as norm-objects. Imagine a hunter-gatherer, or pastoral nomadic community with people woven together in structures that take the shape of nets of rights and duties. The interaction net is made in such a way that everybody is relatively well protected. Human beings are of course physical/biologically recognizable in this network. And the more densely the net is spun, the more difficult or meaningless will it be to detach the individual from the network.

Individualizing Judaism/Christianity/Islam with a transcendental god emphasizes the knots, and union-orientated Hinduism/Buddhism with a more immanent god-concept the nets. Transcendental religions endow human beings with individual souls as that which can attain union with god. Immanent religions depend less on that concept, which is rejected out of hand in radical Buddhism. But occidental religions also have immanent, net-orientated, collectivist aspects. There was also legitimation from below in the voice of the people, with *vox populi, vox dei* as the obvious transition formula, meaning that God also speaks through the people. And the whole tradition of democracy took shape and is still taking shape.

The relations between individuals within a state were increasingly regulated by national (or municipal laws, and between states increasingly through international law. It is in this context that human rights should be seen as an imaginative complex construct combining elements of national and international law. Human rights are based on both of them and contribute to both of them. The human rights are implemented as concrete actions engaged in by the state. They are of two kinds, the negative human rights focusing on the proscribed acts the state should abstain from, i.e. on domesticating, restraining the state, making the state obey due process of law in principle created and upheld by the state. And then there is the second kind, the prescribed acts of commission the state should engage in. The negative human rights limit state power, the positive human rights define the state as a provider, with the individuals having claims on the state, not only against the state as for the negative rights.

The civil and political rights are often seen as being more of the first kind, and the economic, social and cultural rights as more of the second. The original French Declaration of 1789, and the Universal Declaration of Human Rights of 10 December 1948, can be seen as combining the two elements, and that also applies to the two Covenants of 16 December 1966. But the balance between focus on acts of omission and acts of commission moved in the direction of the latter, supported by the idea of an increasingly interventionist state. The latter extends the contractual power of the state as provider, one reason why one of these Covenants is not yet ratified by the US, and one reason why this trend may now be reversed.

However, this distinction is less important and also mainly semantic, like the distinction between freedom from and freedom to much depending on what kind of words are used and whether or not negative particles are made use of. More important is the social structure of a human right.

The very term human rights focuses our attention on human individuals and on something called rights. The right is then conceived of as wrested from or conceded by the state, whether it is called inherent and inalienable or not. However, any social system analysis between actors organized in two or three tiers would cry eloquently for some image of reciprocity. If the state gives or concedes rights to individuals, what must the individuals give back to the state in return? And whatever it is, could this not possibly be called (human) duties.

We shall call them human duties, indicating that the very phrase human rights is actually a misnomer for the more complete, but awkward, human rights/duties. Human rights may even be seen as a propaganda formulation, relatively similar (and not by chance) to the phrasing used in economic theory when economists talk about goods and services and never about bads and disservices. State and capital may both prefer to be represented by mystifying euphemisms. And the fundamental thesis of this section is that any single-minded focus on human rights, and not on duties, is like reading one side of an insurance contract, overlooking the small print on the reverse.

Correspondingly, the state is embedded in a state system, which may or may not give rise to a community or even an organization of states. The state organization is only a norm-sender if the state, at least to some extent, makes itself accountable to the state organization, which implies readiness to be evaluated by the norms it has agreed to receive, the human rights norms. The question is what the state receives in return for making itself accountable. The answer suggested is legitimacy bestowed upon the state by the state community. Here we could imagine a process. The state community accepts a new state and confers on it the status as a bonafide member of the state system. The new member will immediately be exposed to the human rights norms, and since these are institutionalized norms, no matter how weak, an element of accountability is established. With increasing accountability/fulfillment there will be increasing legitimacy. Of the two, accountability and fulfillment, the former is probably more important than the latter. A state may have a high level of fulfillment but it makes itself impenetrable to outside scrutiny. On the other hand, states may also make themselves fully accountable, exposing all their failures and shortcomings. The latter is probably more a member of the system than the former, subjecting itself to review. In accountability there is a heavy element of submissiveness dear to the norm-sender/ law-giver. Fulfillment without accountability smacks of arrogance; of being accountable only to oneself. Even more arrogant would be accountability while at the same time refusing to receive the norms from the organization of states and receiving them from elsewhere, including being one's own norm-sender.

Thus, there is a complicated balance at work here. Human rights should not be identified with an individual right merely because the norm-object is an individual. Located in the interface between international and national law, in a sense as customary parts of both of them, the human rights serve an important integrative function in the total world normative system by tying the three tiers together.

We cannot go further in the exploration of this phenomenon without looking at the duties. Between the emerging state and the emerging individuals a new contract social was forged. We have seen nothing like the end of that process yet. But one key to the phenomenon is found precisely in the title of the original French document, referring not only to the rights of man but also to the rights of citizen. A man stands for a person in a more absolute, perhaps even universal sense, whatever that might mean. But he or she is a citizen only relative to his or her own state, and more particularly to the state of which he or she is a citizen. The duties that immediately come to one's mind would be the duty (particularly of men) to produce and (particularly of women) to reproduce; in other words, to make the state rich in terms of non-human and human capital. Then there is the economic duty to pay taxes and the political duty to be law-obedient, or at least not to work against the political machinery. And finally there is the military duty (particularly for men) to sacrifice one's own life, for the cause defined by the state in the interstate system.

These are heavy duties; the last to lay down one's own life even extreme. It is important to see the rise of obligatory war service, from pertaining only to a caste of warriors to affecting all able-bodied men and women, and ultimately involving everybody as non-protesting victims in increasingly totalizing wars, in the light of increasing scope for human rights. Total rights in principle entitle the state to demand total duties in return. The total provider is entitled to total commitment. The state finally gives emancipation to women, but the state takes it back as military service. The state gives, the state takes, the name of the state be praised, for this is where the god like substance has been transferred. Basic question: is this a good deal?

In this process the state has a very rational argument: if the state has to provide for all items in these international checking lists of rights, then the state simply need more resources. For this to happen the citizens have to work hard, producing a surplus, directly and indirectly, that can be used to provide for what not only the citizens but the whole world system demands of the state. The citizen would have the duty to provide the state with the means with which the state can provide for the citizen and fulfill its obligation to the state system; and the duty to make use of his or her rights, to claim but not to over-claim, thereby legitimizing further the calls to duty from the state. He or she will not be able to extricate himself/herself from the duties by not claiming the rights. Refusal to go to school cannot be exchanged for refusal to do military service. A right implies the duty to claim that right. Not to claim the right destroys the construction of the right as natural, inborn, inalienable.

This is important because it also serves to illustrate why there is no contradiction between a state being high in fulfillment of human rights for the citizens and at the same time highly aggressive in the interstate system, with a high level of ability to mobilize the citizens for that type of aggression. Both of the United States (relatively high on civil/political rights) and the former Soviet Union (relatively high on social/economic rights) in this connection may be cited. They both worked out contracts with their citizens. And they both succeeded, to some extent, in making the citizens pay less attention to the neglected human rights (high level of unemployment in the United States, and misery; high level of political repression in the Soviet Union) because so much else was relatively well provided for. There may be other states in the world system with a very low level of provision for any kind of right, and consequently also unable to mobilize their population unless they have other sources to draw upon, such as normative power in the shape of intact religious myths and beliefs, and visions of missionary rights and duties. With the human rights a contractual rather than a normative basis for mobilizing the population was/is institutionalized as a very powerful way of exchanging rights for duties. The individual has a claim on the state, and so has the state on the individual.

However that may be, there can be no doubt that human rights as an institution are linked to a particular historical phase in the evolution in the West of the modern state system. More particularly, they are linked to a strong and central state with considerable resources at its disposal, otherwise many of the rights the implementation of which could be quite costly simply become vacuous. What emerges is a powerful provider in our midst, some kind of latter-day god, not only omnipresent, omniscient and omnipotent, but also benevolent, as a welfare state, l'etat providence (as opposed to l'etat gendarme) should be. Human rights balance omniscience and omnipotence with benevolence, of the negative and positive kinds mentioned. But as the construction has emerged, state omniscience and omnipotence come as parts of the bargain. With obedient citizens dutifully claiming their rights and exercising their duties they can become quite formidable in their consequence. Till we make up one day, realizing that total freedoms, in the shape of rights, have made us totally unfree, trapped by duties. And not only in bondage to the state, but also to an organization of states that bestows legitimacy on a state that bestows rights on its citizens in return for accountability and duties. Weber's iron cage? Giddens's surveillance society? The question remains: Is this a good deal?

What is Western about this construction generated by Western history is not the content of the norms, but the construction itself:

1. The norm-triad gradient expresses the vertical slope of an ethics of rights and duties from above rather than human compassion;
2. The construction gives the universal and regional organizations of states increasing legitimacy, leading to a more centralized world society;
3. The construction gives the state increasing legitimacy, leading to a more centralized national society;
4. The construction detaches the individual knot even more from nets of reciprocity and solidarity, leading to more alienation.

HUMAN RIGHTS: A CIVILIZATIONAL-CULTURAL PERSPECTIVE

The approach taken will be less historical, more synchronous, seeing Western civilization as one major macro-culture, among others. The question to be answered is to what extent, and precisely how, the content of the human rights as we know them in their totality serves as a carrier of western civilization as opposed to other civilizations, with a relatively clearly expressed and consistent Western bias. The question to be asked is not whether this is good or bad; only whether it is the case.

For the exploration of this problem a vision of Western civilization is needed. The present vision is based on cosmology analysis. Civilizations are then explored along seven dimensions for their assumptions about space, time, knowledge, nature, persons, societies, and the transpersonal, the last in the West meaning God. The particular stand taken by Western civilization along these seven dimensions is indicated as hypotheses, and what then follows is an exploration of the extent to which human rights can be seen as an exemplification of that particular civilizational position.

Space: The Western assumption is that the world can be divided into three parts: a center, which is in the West; a periphery waiting to receive whatever comes from the West; and a recalcitrant evil refusing to receive the word, and the goods and services that follow, and to be incorporated as second-class West. In this image of the spatial arrangement of the world there are actually three ideas: centralism, with the West as the causal center of the world; universalism, with the idea that what is good for the West is good for the world; and a good/evil dichotomy marginalizing evil, trying to beat evil with crusades or deter it with atom bombs.

The human rights tradition can be seen in this light. Not only did it originate historically in the West and has been propagated from the West, the tradition could only have originated in the West. The Universal Declaration of Human Rights was accepted by a predominantly Western United Nations and might have faced many more problems in Vienna in 1993. In the first years it was disseminated and propagated, and still is, from the West towards the rest of the world. In the Cold War, dominating East-West relations during almost the entire period since the 1948 Universal Declaration, the civil and political human rights on which the West sees itself as being particularly strong have been emphasized more than the social and economic rights where the socialist countries tended to see themselves as stronger. And most Western countries rank above most Third World countries on both kinds of human rights.

Whatever the reason may be, one more dimension has been institutionalized whereby the center can remain the center and the periphery the periphery. This enables countries in the West to appoint themselves judges over the rest of the world, distributing certificates of high and low levels of fulfillment. The objection to this argument would be that the West simply is, as also evidenced by the fact that there are more people wanting to migrate into the West than into other parts of the world. And the counter-objection is that this is so because the West has the power to define what is best. The obvious hypothesis is that a norm (such as right to care for the aged within the family itself, as opposed to old-age homes) more adhered to in the non-West than in the West would have a hard time being accepted as a human right as long as the West has the power to prevent it. The Third World might rank higher, and the West does not appreciate that. Moreover, wealth is always attractive.

Time: The Western time perspective combines progress with asymptotic convergence to an ideal, possibly with a crisis before that state of affairs is attained. The human rights conceptualization is to a large extent of that kind. There seem to be two processes at work. On the one hand, there is a given set of human rights and the painstaking, sometimes quick, sometimes slow, process of states fulfilling the norms, hopefully converging asymptotically to that ideal world. But there is also the second process of expanding the set of norms, identifying new human rights, institutionalizing them, thereby modeling Utopian society through a process of norm expansion. Combined, these two processes will always cement the leadership of the leaders, by definition already fairly high on implementing norms. But seeing others catching up they can still retain leadership of and distance from other countries by adding new rules to the game. At the end of the process is Utopia with all rights fulfilled all over. The process gives to the center the right to define what Utopia looks like. And the Western center will tend to define it in such a way that they themselves are given permanent residency, or at least the first position on the waiting line.

Knowledge: The Western knowledge structure is atomistic and deductive, as opposed to the holistic/dialectic combination that can be found in many other cultures. The fragmentary, atomistic aspect is reflected in two ways: the individual as the unit of norm fulfillment, as opposed to the group, and the single human rights norm as the unit of account. Instead of holistic judgements of whole countries as Christian or civilized comes the atomistic and empirical mapping of human rights fulfillment for m individuals on n variables of human rights. The matrix is formidable, like an enormous chessboard where red lights indicate deficiencies to be eliminated through adequate norm enforcement. Again this is not a question of good or bad, only of noting an unmistakably Western epistemology at work with the great attention given to the social atom, the individual; and to the conceptual atom, the specific HR variable. At the world level the atom is the country, not the system.

Nature: The Western perspective is that of domination over nature, meaning that humans have the right to manipulate nature more or less as they want. One particular aspect of this is the unlimited right to kill animals for human consumption, even to expose them to highly painful experiments, presumably for human betterment through insight gained in matters relating to health and disease. Humans are the end; nature is means. Animals and plants do not have legal standing, hence no rights.

This anthropocentric perspective is fully reflected in the human rights tradition, even in the very name, human rights. Animal rights are now (jokingly) being considered. Nature's rights might be around the corner, but they are late in coming, possibly too late to save important species. Moreover, who will be the norm-senders when the directly concerned parties animals and plants are not articulating in a manner understandable to the norm-receivers, the states? Articulation has to be mediated through human beings, such as animal and nature lovers, and their articulation may be far from reliable. Leaving that point aside, it is clear that in the lack of consideration for non-human nature a position has been taken, and that position is in agreement with Western civilization in general. The human rights as they emerged remain anthropocentric.

Persons: The Western position, in Freudian terms is based on strong egos (individualism); sometimes using (moral) superegos to control the id, their bodies, sometimes the other way round. The common element is the sense of ownership of the body, and an individual relation to the superego, privatizing both the body and the superego. From this follow two important aspects of the Western approach, the sacredness of the individual body, and spirit of the individual.

Societies: The Western position combines verticality and post-medieval individualism in a strongly competitive system defining winners and losers. The model sketched above of the human rights concept reinforces that structure. There is the primacy of the national and international levels over the local level. Individuals are subjected to the state as citizens (subjects), even if entitled to human rights in return. However, with perhaps as much as 90 per cent of the global economic assets centrally controlled inside states, and most of the remaining decision-making at the international level, almost nothing is left to the local level because local assets are small and ultimately tied up with central decisions. With this pattern repeated is administrative and political decisions vertically certainly has some backing in reality. A focus on the word right alone makes it not look like that; coupled with the word duty it becomes more clear.

But this vertically is found in most social constructions. What makes for Westernness is the way it is coupled to individualism in strongly competitive relations. Human rights become individual rights to the extent that individuals are the norm-objects, the units to which the norms are related and in which they are ultimately fulfilled. This excludes collective rights such as peoples' rights and other group rights. Women, age groups, indigenous groups, ancient peoples, non-Western cultures pocketed inside Western societies are such groups, at the bottom of society often engaged in efforts to imitate the states subjugating them. More than most, they are in need of human rights protection to preserve and enhance their group characteristics, not only as individuals inside a given social structure. Denial of such collective rights is verticality at work. The individualizing prospect of human rights deprives these underprivileged groups as such of their major political asset: mobilization and organized struggle as a group. In some cases their grievances may be adequately redressed by extending individual rights. Group rights become a matter of urgency the moment the group as a whole wants something different from what can be granted to the sum of individuals, such as national sovereignty under the doctrine of national self-determination, the only collective right that seems to be solidly enshrined. All these struggles have been and are uphill.

This has an important consequence. The individualizing condition for benefiting from the rights is not only that people reciprocate with duties, but also that they accept the rights as individuals, not as groups. The right to education means each individual's right to have access to the public schools as defined by and organized by the state, and as run by the dominant group. It does not necessarily mean the right of a group of individuals with some shared (ascribed or achieved) characteristics to institutionalize their own type of education. The only exception would be in connection with religion and language, for a very simple reason: they are the raw material out of which most nation states are wrought, which is the reason urgent group claims have to be met at some point. Failure to implement these rights easily leads to an explosive situation. But teaching the vernacular is still not the same as teaching in the vernacular, and this is where the state often draws the line.

As rights are also coupled with such duties as taxation and conscription to enable the state to do what the state deems necessary in order to secure the rights, the question of reciprocity arises. Thus, if money is needed for the welfare state then the state might believe in hydro-electric plants in order to provide energy cheaply in a marketable form, and to make a profit on the sale of that energy. In doing so the state might act against the interests of such groups as native populations or nature lovers. But as there are (almost) no group rights, only individual rights, for humans in general and for categories, there is at present no way in which this would be rejected as counteracting human rights. Individual members of a native group more deprived than the average may secure legal redress on the basis of human rights. Not the group as an organization; mainly the category of individuals. The state would tend not to like group rights standing in the way of the nation-building enterprise, preferring direct lines of command to the social atoms, the individuals.

The transpersonal: The Western perspective also presupposes an overriding, transcendental principle. It was god in the old days; one or more of the successors to god nowadays. These successors, were the king, the state, the people, and the state organization (the League of Nations, the United Nations, etc.). The state is then constructed in the image of a benevolent, omnipresent, omniscient and omnipotent king, possibly receiving legitimacy both from the state community and from the people. The human rights tradition contributes to this construction as the enlightened state receives an increasing number of norms, implements them in the form of human rights, and is even able to extract such duties from the citizenry as being compliant hostages to nuclear deterrence, meaning potential collective extermination. The new social contract looks like the old one with allegiance to the authority, in return for protection and assistance. The state elevates itself through an act of levitation to the transcendental levels of even deciding over omnicide, through weapons of mass destruction, while standing on top of a growing human rights mountain.

It is not where the human rights are located on any single one of these seven dimensions that counts. It is the whole package that is unmistakably Western. Propagation of human rights, consequently, is also propagation of Western civilization, and partly intended as such. This in itself does not make the Western human rights tradition wrong. But it certainly leads to two important questions. What, if anything, is so specifically Western that it should not form part of a universal declaration? And what could other civilizations, major or minor by today's thinking, contribute to a universal declaration? The questions are not new. But the failure to address them effectively is problematic.

The Problems: Ten Pointers to the Future

Let us first ask the question: what are the concrete consequences of this massive Western structural/cultural export in terms of contradictions that have shown up, and may sooner or later show up more clearly, both within and between states, and ultimately for individuals? The answer has to be ambivalent:

1. A system for increasing protection and provision for increasing numbers of individuals on an increasing number of HR dimensions;
2. The reinforcement of centralizing tendencies both in world, regional and national societies, based on a vertical reciprocity imposing accountability on states and duties on the citizens within an increasingly homogenizing world culture; and
3. The destruction of alternative structures and cultures; as a consequence of the four structural problems and the seven cultural export problems.

Accepting the first consequence but not the other two, the problem is how to address them without losing what has been gained. This may look formidable the way it has been formulated, but actually directs our attention, in a relatively systematic manner, to concrete problems for which solutions may exist if not today then tomorrow. Some of them are already being contemplated.

The problem of the steep norm-triad gradient the solution does not lie in the abolition of the UNGA state-individual triad, but in surrounding it with other triads. Limiting ourselves to mundane, not transcendental, actors we could divide norm-senders and norm-receivers into universal, regional, national, sub-national (group), and individual. If we assume that the norm-object remains the individual, and that the purpose of the whole construction is to safeguard basic human needs.

Obviously, universal as sender has already been interpreted to mean UN organizations other than the UNGA, such as UNESCO, WHO, FAO, ILO, and UNICEF to take some examples relating directly to more specific human needs. And regional as sender has been interpreted to mean Europe, Africa, and the Pacific. These interpretations could also apply to the receiver side, with the UNGA in fact saying that in addition to the states, Specialized Agencies and the regions should also be responsible for the enactment of human rights. Moreover, these two approaches could increasingly be combined. They are both minor variations within the present human rights discourse and structure and should not encounter resistance for reasons of structure, only when new content is introduced. According to the general theory, such changes would give more authority to other parts of the UN and to regions, thereby decentralizing along functional and geographical lines, not concentrating the ultimate, universal normative emission in one sender (UNGA), and the delicate balance between enacting rights and cashing in on duties in one receiver only (the state).

However, more interesting innovative combinations could be explored. In line with a tendency found many places in the world towards devolution within the state, how about leaving the task of enacting some rights to the local level, provinces, or even to municipalities? This would be in line with the philosophy underlying federalism, and again in line with strong political traditions. There is also the possibility of being more flexible, leaving to the local population to decide who should be the norm-receiver. If the choice is in favor of a subnational unit then that unit would have a direct link to the norm-sender, bypassing the nation state, a formula that would loosen world society, making it more similar to national societies with multiple channels of command and communication.

The problems appear the moment we consider senders and receivers that are non-territorial, nonstake, like International Peoples' Organizations (IPOs) and Transnational Corporations (TNCs), and senders that are interest groups, national or inter/transnational, such as occupational groups (trade unions), age and gender groups, racial and ethnic groups. And yet, why could not TNCs be given the task of implementing some basic human needs in addition to, or instead of, some of the things they are doing? If successful they would benefit even if they have to pay the price of making themselves more accountable. In line with the general arguments the point is not to let the state off the hook of accountability, but to extend accountability to other world actors. The point is not that the UNGA should cease norm-production, but that several major organizations could send universal (not only regional) norms with human rights status when, for instance, the Catholic Church is doing so. ILO is a good, positive example.

Would this not add up to too many norms from too many sources? People raised in monotheistic cultures with one spiritual authority would be predisposed to agree; others might have more training in moral diversity. The argument would be that it is in our interest to spin a dense normative web of norms by and large pointing in the same basic human needs direction, dispersing both authority and credit. Above all this is an argument in favor of taking civil society seriously, not only the three-tier state construction based on the state system.

The Problem of World Power Concentration

The problem is not a world central authority able to disburse goods and services, but a world government with heavy machinery for coercive enforcement and a singular, universalistic world culture. Projecting from nation states, some conclude that this would be the solution, not contemplating the amount of coercive machinery needed to extract compliance from recalcitrant states, or whether punishment as a means of securing general and individual prevention of crimes will work any better at the international than the national levels. Multiplying senders and receivers is probably the best antidote to over-centralization. And the notion of universal human rights essentially drawn from only one civilization with one sender only, UNGA, with a Security Council (Western dominated) equipped to enforce compliance, is a recipe for regional and national revolts. The similarity with the Christian Crusades (1095-1291) is only too obvious.

The Problem of National Power Concentration

Here some fairly concrete suggestions can be made. If the problem is that rights too easily translate into implicit duties, then the solution is to make those duties explicit and challenge them! Two such duties are taxation and conscription; the former challenged by the right, the latter by the left. We could easily imagine two new human rights here: the right of the individual to refuse military service, and the right of the individual to strike a bargain with the state, unpackaging the state package of services, accepting (and paying) for some, rejecting (and not paying) for others (like insurance policies). A deconstruction not only of the state discourse but of the state itself, in other words.

The Problem of Individual Alienation

Again, no simple institutional solution is around the corner. What we are looking for is the dense cocoon of a net of reciprocal rights and duties, from individuals, to individuals, and about individuals. Neither, rights only nor duties only will do. The general word is compassion, within a unity-of-being ethos, a relatively clear normative content in some fields, and ethical intuition in the rest. In short, a richer ethical culture than we have in many places of the world today where waning faith in God as the ultimate norm-sender has coincided with waxing alienation not only from the human Other, but also from Self.

The Problem of Balanced Normative Input

The Judeo-Christian normative culture is richly represented in the HR tradition. Three contributions stand out: the sacredness of the individual human body (against torture, for instance), the sacredness of the individual human spirit (against repression of expression and impression, for instance) and equal treatment, regardless of gender, race, class, nation. These are major inputs to a universal normative culture. Moreover, they can also be used against toxic pollution (industry) to the body, and spiritual pollution (mass media) to the spirit.

But how about Islam? How could an institution like the *Zakat*, making individual almsgiving for the satisfaction of the basic needs of others an obligation, be fitted into the scheme? In that case the norm-receiver would be the individual, as would also the norm-object. The norm-sender for the Muslim is Allah. But why not let the UN reproduce an Islamic norm for the benefit of non-Muslims?

In a similar vein, a very important normative culture could be lifted from Hinduism-Jainism-Buddhism: ahimsa, non-violence. Why should not states and others, as norm-receivers, be given the task of working systematically for the reduction of violence of all kinds when they are given the task of working systematically for the reduction of violence of all kinds when they are given the task of working systematically for the reduction of disease of all kinds? Particularly as violence is becoming a major cause of death. Because the state wants to retain its monopoly on physical violence in its power repertory for internal or external use, but not disease.

Correspondingly, from the Chinese tradition could come a respect for the family as a unit, partly by having the family as a norm- receiver for basic needs provision, partly by having the family as a norm-object to be protected by the state. And from the Japanese tradition could come a point that might sound like a joke but is not: the right not to have vacation. In a more serious vein: how could the famous article 9 of the Japanese Constitution (the Japanese people forever renounce war as a sovereign right of its nation and the threat or use of force as means of settling international disputes) become a part of world culture? Japan wants to be equal, but why not try to raise others to the Japanese constitutional level rather than lower Japan to their level by circumventing article 9? Even if article 9 was forced upon them by the victor rather than emerging out of the Japanese tradition? The answer is not found in the UN Charter with its two-tier normative structure; the sender being the San Francisco Conference (26 June 1945) and the receivers, the member states. The interesting construction would be to introduce the UNGA as norm-sender for article 9, with a blank instead of the word Japanese and then use the citizens of any country as norm-receivers controlling the war-renunciation that is in fact realized by the state, which then becomes the norm-object.

And then there are the countless minor cultures; indigenous, native. We are still rich. But we are undermining that richness by reducing the cultural and structural diversity in the world just as we are reducing the bio-diversity needed for ecological balance. The meta-norm would be to preserve and increase cultural and structural diversity so that an ever richer human rights tradition could be created.

The Problem of the Final State

The final state, assumes our ability today to have an image of the end of the process. If there is one thing we can learn from history, a good example would be that this ability is limited, or zero. Like any process the HR process is filled with contradictions, and we ourselves are parts of that contradiction. At the roots of positivism as epistemology lies the idea that the future is built into the present; at the roots of dialectics the notion of reality as self-transcending into new phases/stages that are not only unknown but also unknowable (if we knew them we would already be halfway there). Hard positivism, in the sense just defined, would have to be rejected. A softer positivism, however, assuming that we have to work from where we are and that the near future is relatively knowable on that basis, becomes more acceptable.

The Problem of Atomism/Deductivism

This is less of a problem. The issue can be formulated very simply: do we or do we not know what we are doing when we are propagating human rights? What is the essence of the human rights exercise? The flat operational answer, The International Bill of Human Rights defines the exercise in extension but not in intention. The essence as seen by the present author lies in the relation to basic human needs. The beautifully structured text by McDougal, Lasswell, and Chen defines eight areas respect, power, enlightenment, well-being, wealth, skill, affection, and rectitude (sometimes adding security which could be fitted into basic needs categories. What matters is not the number, or the term, but the willingness to develop a discourse both at the atomistic (the single norms) and the holistic (packages of norms) levels. Both will always have to be revised, but then we at least know what we are trying to revise.

The Problem of Anthropocentrism

There are two very different ways of approaching the problem of animal and plant rights: extension of compassion to all sentiment beings, i.e. the unity-of-life principle, regarding them as sacred because they possess life; and an indirect lex talionis, do (don't do) unto animals/plants so that they can (cannot) continue serving you. The perspectives can be referred to as biocentric and homocentric respectively, and it is not obvious that they exclude each other. Immanent Buddhism would tend to favor the former, the occidental transcendental religions the latter, since they are homocentric. In either case non-human forms of life would be included as norm-objects; in other words, a major change of the norm-triad. We are probably not ready for it yet, but we might see the homocentric perspective as a start, keeping biocentric rooting for later.

The Problem of the Strong Egos

This is seen as the source of valuable Western contributions to a world dialogue, with give-and-take aiming at truly universal human rights (so far we have heard only from the West). But precisely these strong Western egos may be insensitive to the softer voices from the subjugated discourses of the weaker egos.

The Problem of Social Individualism

This is the problem of group rights, with groups as norm-objects, ultimately also as norm-receivers. The problem is whether the group rights differ from the aggregate or sum of individual rights. If they do not differ no problem arises; individualism prevails. If they differ, the group running the state will prefer the aggregate of individual rights in order to assimilate the group into the dominant (majority or not) structure and culture. If the subjugated group still insists on group rights, then the actio popularis is at least potentially available and may last forever. Finally, if there are no individual rights counterparts the group right may sail through easily. The classical example is national self- determination, with no individual counterpart. And as to the opposite case (no group rights counterpart), most civil and political rights may serve as an example. The freedom of expression, for instance, is clearly the aggregate of individual freedoms as only individuals express themselves.

But this does not work for many of the social, economic and cultural rights. Access to the schools run by the dominant group is not the same as running schools oneself, perhaps not as deep as the difference between some other group's religious service and one's own, but in that general direction. There is a difference between access to the dominant system of health care and running one's own health-care system; all of this because the faith in a universally valid curriculum and a universally valid health care is challenged, like the faith in a universally valid religion.

And, possibly the most important one: the difference between group property and the aggregate of individual property; the latter is the famous right to have private property, the former is collectivism, common property, *res communis*. In all probability this is the most sticky issue, the script underlying them all, informing people whether they should oppose or endorse group rights. Recognition of groups other than nations (with the right to own states) might lead to group property defying a basic expression of individualism.

Correspondingly, social development, as part of the right to development, is not the same as aggregate human development: just as peace as the right of a nation in the world is not the same as peace as the sum of rights of citizens in the society. In these two examples of collective rights the problem may be that of finding individual-level equivalents rather than group-level equivalents of individual rights. However, regardless of how problematic this correspondence may be the fact is that the human condition has not only an individual but also a group mode, both surrounded by strong feelings. Consequently, group rights will always be on the agenda: not only those that have no individual right homologue, but also others, whenever it makes a difference. It usually does.

The Problem of Transcendentalism

The Western formula has been to have a strong god/strong king/strong state, and compensate by strengthening the individual. Other societies, such as many tribal orders, have had neither one nor the other. Then there are the despotic orders based on strong states and weak individuals. And, of course, the fourth possibility, strong individuals inside weak states, bringing to mind such remarkable constructions as Iceland and the Faroe islands.

Many aspects of the Western formula will probably remain for a long time. But the formula can be diluted with norm-senders and norm-receivers other than states; and with norm-receivers and norm-objects other than individuals. Indeed, if we play on the full richness of civil society there is enough work to do, deepening and broadening the human rights tradition for generations to come.

5

Human Rights Movement in Contemporary India

The relationship between individual and the state determines the frameworks of human rights. This framework is an unprecedented challenge today. After tracing the evolution of the civil rights movement in India in the age of colonialism and its trajectory towards maturity in the post-Independence period, many scholars emphasise the need to focus particularly on economic, social and cultural rights in a third world context such as India's, and more so in the present age of globalisation, arguing that this will in turn pave the way for the achievement of civil and political rights.

In this age of globalisation, the very framework of society is undergoing great transformation. While the nation-state remains the fundamental constituent element of the international community, its role is changing in the face of the expansion of the global market. The global market, clearly dominated and controlled by the imperialists, is assuming an aggressive control over more and more -aspects of our lives. Frameworks of human rights – cast largely in terms of the individual's relationship with the state are facing an unprecedented challenge. According to the direct or indirect proponents of globalisation, economic development – in other words, the spread and deepening of the market – should precede over everything else. But what is this economic development? Whose development? Whose economy? Does it ensure people's basic welfare and rights? The grim reality is that the global economy is not at present working in favour of the poor countries or of the poor; rather the rich countries and the rich are becoming richer and the poor poorer. There is a lot of debate about the extent to which economic growth leads to the realisation of economic rights.

In this context, it should be emphasised that quality and security of life cannot be measured solely in terms of the market or economic development, economic growth or per capita income. Genuine sustainable development is a more-holistic process, embracing the place of individuals- in civil society, their personal security and their capacity to determine and realise their potential. As the United Nations Development Programme states;

> The concept of human development is much broader than the conventional theories of economic development. It analyses all issues in society – whether economic growth, trade, employment, political freedom or cultural values – from the perspective of the people. It thus focuses on enlarging human choices.

In this way, the process of development brings together the full range of human rights – civil, cultural, economic, political and social – into one indivisible and interdependent whole. Freedom from fear and extrication from want are the two sides of the same coin. That is why, in the Preamble to the International Covenant of Economic, Social and Cultural Rights, one of the cornerstones of international human rights law, it has been clearly and unambiguously accepted that "the ideal of free human beings enjoying freedom from fear and want can only be achieved if conditions are created whereby everyone may enjoy his economic, social and cultural rights, as well as his civil and political rights". In 1993, the world conference of the governments of the different countries on human rights in Vienna clearly declared that "All human rights are universal and indivisible, interdependent and interrelated. The international community must treat human rights globally in a fair and equal manner, on the same footing and with the same emphasis."

It must be emphasised that the concept of human rights is not an abstract idea, independent of class division, but is basically dependant on the specific stage of the social development of any country. There cannot be any unchangeable, pure and abstract concept of human rights, independent of a specific society, universally applicable to all countries across time. The experience of the development of human society has shown that the social and economic progress achieved through the continuous development of the productive forces helps to develop the concept of human rights. A primary consciousness regarding human rights can be traced even to the early stages of human society, but in the absence of an appropriate social base, it could not develop, not to speak of its realisation. The unprecedented development of the social productive forces in Europe under capitalism through the industrial revolution created that social base by challenging the old feudal, monarchical and religious authority, and gradually thereby shaped the concept that "human beings are born free and equal in dignity and rights". And, in this context it must be emphasised that though the aspiration for equality and dignity of all human beings, reflecting the essence of human rights, was inherent in the culture and civilisation of the different stages of human society.

The historical trajectory of democratic transformation of European autocracies has hinged upon the successful assertion of three important components of human freedom:

(i) freedom of expression;

(ii) freedom from arbitrary imprisonment;

(iii) freedom from custodial violence.

The legitimisation of these freedoms as the inalienable civil and political rights of all citizens against the state constitutes a historical landmark in the evolution of liberal democracies, initially in Europe, and subsequently in other parts of the advanced countries.

Civil Rights Movement in India

In India, the civil rights movement began during the colonial period in close association with the national liberation movement. Though the movement did not acquire any organisational form before 1936, its genesis can be traced from the early 19th century, when the embryo of the civil libertarian consciousness was manifested through the demand for the freedom of expression and also for the freedom of the press, equality before the law, protection against racial discrimination, etc. And the ground for an organised effort to develop the civil liberties movement was gradually being prepared by different significant events like the adoption of the Declaration of Rights in a special session of the Congress (1918), the spontaneous agitation against the Rowlatt Act (1919), the historic meeting at Calcutta addressed by Rabindranath Tagore amongst others to protest against police firing in Hijli Jail on the political prisoners (1931), leading to efforts to form a Citizens' Committee for championing the cause of the release of political prisoners and safe-guarding individual freedom, etc. The 1920s and 1930s was a significant period in the history of India's freedom movement. Mass movements against colonial rule were gradually spreading and assuming an organised form. The All India Trade Union Congress, the All India Students' Federation, the All India Kisan Sabha, the Progressive Writers' Association, etc, were founded. The All India Trade Union Congress was gathering strength on the basis of the much cherished unity of different factions leading the working class. All these movements actually set the foundation and the background for an organisation to launch the civil rights movement.

Ultimately, on 24 August 1936, the All India Civil Liberties Union (ICLU) was founded in Bombay with Jawaharlal Nehru as the main initiator. Rabindranath Tagore was elected as the president, - Sarojini Naidu as the working president, and - K B Menon as the general secretary and a 21-member executive committee which included Jawaharlal Nehru, Abul Kalam Azad, Sarat Chandra Bose, Rajendra Prasad, Vallabhbhai Patel, Jayaprakash Narayan, etc. The inherent spirit of the ICLU was precisely reflected in the closing sentence of Nehru's address at the inaugural session: "The idea of civil liberty is to have the right to oppose the government".

We must keep in mind there must be some basic distinction in the civil rights movement in any country between its colonial and postcolonial phases. But at the very outset it must not be forgotten that in spite of a post-second world war revolutionary upsurge all over India against imperialist domination, India's freedom was achieved basically through a compromise with the imperialists, thereby handing over power to the bourgeoisie, dependant on the imperialists in alliance with the feudal elements. As a consequence, human rights of the common labouring people were not at all guaranteed, nor were such rights expected to be ensured. The Constitution of India, framed after the adoption of the UDHR, of which India was a signatory, no doubt, has ensured the inclusion of some fundamental rights like right to life, expression, press, association, mobility, etc. But even in this "rights-giving" constitution, provisions have been included to take away all the fundamental rights on one or other excuses.

And again, rights to work and shelter have not been included in the Constitution in spite of the demand repeatedly raised by the people as well as by civil rights organisations. Consequently, the unbridled persecution as well as exploitation of the common labouring people continues. Naturally the people fought and have been fighting during the whole of the post-independence period for service and other means of livelihood, land for cultivation and housing, for better wages and living conditions, exercising their constitutional democratic rights to fight for these demands. But the State takes recourse to persecution and torture, imprisonment and police brutalities, like lathi charge and firing, unashamedly suppressing all basic democratic and legal norms and grossly violating all the fundamental rights enshrined in the Constitution.

The civil and democratic rights movements began to develop in postcolonial India just side by side with the process of transfer of political power from the British imperialists to the Indian ruling classes. The first organisation that came up was in 1947, the Madras Civil Liberties Union (MCLU). In the meantime a Bombay Civil Liberties Conference was held on 1-2 January 1949. The same year, MCLU organised an All India Civil Liberties Conference in Madras on 16-17 July. Significantly, even then, just after India's independence, apprehensions were expressed in the conference that the limited civil liberties- enjoyed under the British rule would be "the first casualty" in independent India. In 1948, the Communist Party of India (CPI) was banned and an all-out severe repression on its members and sympathisers unfolded. A civil liberties committee was formed in West Bengal in the same year. Eminent scientists, lawyers and academic intellectuals like Meghnad Saha, Sarat Chandra Bose, N C Chatterjee, Khitish Chattopadhyay, etc joined this movement against the government's onslaught on civil and democratic rights, particularly of political workers.

In the post-independence period the members and the supporters of the undivided CPI mainly organised and took the lead in the civil rights movement at different junctures of time. This created a couple of problems. First, the movement used to become active only when the communists were under state repression and persecution. But when state repression against the communists receded, the movement practically evaporated. This lack of continuity was, no doubt, detrimental to the building up of a strong and organised movement. Second, and most importantly, since the communists' main commitment and devotion were to their party programmes, it was virtually impossible to frame policies and develop and organise the civil liberties movement independently on a broader basis beyond the boundary set forth by the party, so that the interests of the broad section of the masses in general be served.

A resurgence of the civil liberties movement began only in the 1970s of the last century on a new and more or less independent plane. With the formation of the Association for the Protection of Democratic Rights (APDR) in West Bengal in 1972, there began the present and undoubtedly new and higher phase of the movement. Thus a new chapter in the process of evolution and development of the human rights movement in India was inaugurated. The movement acquired, an independent theoretical and organisational foundation leading to a continuous existence and a set of ongoing activities. In Andhra too, Andhra Pradesh Civil Liberties Committee (APCLC) was formed in 1974. Gradually this movement, no doubt, became a permanent feature of Indian society, spreading to Delhi, Maharashtra, Assam, Punjab, Kashmir, Chhattisgarh, Tamil Nadu, etc. APDR was formed in West Bengal at a time of the most heinous attack on democratic rights, when state terrorism appeared in its most barbarous form through mass killings, murder in police and judicial custody, fake encounters and atrocious and continuous attacks on mass movements of labouring people. Naturally the main demands at that time centred on putting an end to all those inhuman, illegal and undemocratic acts of the state, release of all political prisoners and the repeal of the black acts like MISA. International support came from the international civil rights organisations like Amnesty International. The movement got tremendous support from the people. But in June 1975 the most draconian internal Emergency was imposed in India, taking away by a stroke of the pen, all the basic civil rights of a citizen -enshrined in the Constitution of India.

Emergency and its Aftermath

Taking advantage of this, the Government of West Bengal banned APDR and arrested some leading activists most of whom had to languish in jail without any meaningful trial for the whole Emergency period, i.e., about 21 months. During this infamous Emergency period, an all India civil rights organisation, the People's Union for Civil Liberties and

Democratic Rights (PUCLDR) gradually took shape in 1976, with Jayaprakash Narayan as its moral spirit. In the 1977 parliamentary elections, the repressive government was defeated, and PUCLDR played a significant role in mobilising the people against the ruling clique. After the withdrawal of the Emergency, there developed a high tide of mass movement demanding the release of all political prisoners, which had to be included in the election manifesto of the Left Front (LF) in West Bengal. Consequently, the newly elected LF government had to release all political prisoners, and the ban order on APDR had to be withdrawn. Subsequently, a number of civil rights organisations have been formed, regionally or on a national basis in almost all the states.

Though a democratic atmosphere prevailed after the withdrawal of the Emergency and the installation of a new government in New Delhi, it was apprehended by the civil rights workers that state terrorism, police atrocities as well as attacks on mass movements and human rights would continue in some form or the other. The experience of the next four decades confirmed these apprehensions. All the anti-people acts of the State continued, although on a smaller scale. And APDR played its role as before. But it was felt at the same time that public opinion as well as movements, as far as possible, should be built not only for safeguarding political and civil rights, but also for the general economic and social rights of the people. With this contention, the basic aims and objectives of APDR were aligned with the UDHR. Consequently, protection of the -human and civil rights of even non-political people came under the purview of APDR. At present APDR has been fighting not only against state terrorism, violation of political and human rights and police atrocities, but also against indiscriminate non-state terrorism, and in favour of the people's right for livelihood, education, medical facilities, and against globalisation, environmental pollution, communalism, fundamentalism, etc.

On this specific issue of what should be the viewpoint of the civil rights organisations to any government or political party, a clear difference of opinion emerged. When the Janata Party came to power after the fall of the Congress government at the centre in 1977, the national leaders of the PUCLDR refused to criticise or condemn the government even after the killing of workers in Kanpur and mine workers in Dalli Rajhara.

Consequently, the Delhi unit came out of the organisation and built a separate one, the People's Union for Democratic Rights (PUDR). In fact, in the context of increasing criminalisation and corruption of the political parties and brutalisation of state terror, even assaults on democratic rights activists, the civil liberties organisations like APDR, PUDR, etc, have emerged as significant social forces in many states, which both the central and state governments have to reckon with. That no doubt signals the maturity of the civil rights movement.

The Age of Globalisation and Human Rights

In conventional analysis, liberal western theorists equate human rights, in a general sense, only with the civil and political rights, thereby basically almost negating the economic, social and cultural rights of the people of the third world, and also the latter's right to develop independently and without any interference by the imperialist nations. This will naturally be conducive to the maintenance of the economic domination of the imperialists on the third world. The UDHR of 1948 itself shows overwhelming concern for political and civil rights and gives meager attention to economic, social and cultural rights. Though the International Covenant on Economic, Social and Cultural Rights adopted by the United Nations in 1966 – largely through the insistence of the third world countries seeks to rectify the imbalance, human rights continue to be equated with only political and civil rights. On the other hand, liberal western theorists want to interpret human rights only in an individualistic sense, showing no concern for the sense of the collective, or of the collective interests of the people, or the country itself. Their aim is to impose their own reality-induced mentality on the people of the third world who face a completely different reality and background. The aspiration for the freedom and development of the individual self of the post-renaissance advanced capitalist countries, basically liberated from the domination of feudalism and the church of the middle ages, has almost no similarity with the fundamental aspiration of the people of the third world, still gasping under the bondage of imperialism (direct or indirect), feudalism and religious fundamentalism. The spirit of the international covenants of 1966 and the declaration of development of third world countries of 1986, adopted by the United Nations in spite of the stiff resistance by the advanced countries, has rightly led to the Tehran declaration of 1986: "The Civil and Political Rights cannot be fully realised without fully realising the economic, social and cultural rights".

In order to secure the most basic of all human rights – the right to life, along with the fulfilment of the ideal enshrined in the Preamble to the UDHR (of "enjoying freedom from fear and want"), conditions must be created to achieve and secure human- rights to food, to clothing, to shelter, to education, to health, to employment, etc, which are fundamental to the very survival of the vast majority of the human race in Asia, Africa and Latin America. Life and liberty, food and freedom, must go hand in hand if we want to develop an integrated and real vision of human rights for these people, one which does not revolve around the individual, but is centred on a notion of the rights of the collective, the community, the nation. It is obvious that this vision is simply contrary, almost inimical, to the goal of achieving mainly the civil and political rights of individuals, following the dictate of liberal western champions of human rights. This follows from the colonial experience of the third world countries. Subjected to alien and exploitative colonial domination for centuries, fighting for freedom came to mean fighting for the freedom of not merely the individual, but for the people as a whole. This explains why freedom as well as the basic economic, social and cultural rights to these people becomes a composite collective ideal, intertwined with the quest of whole communities for human dignity and social justice, "free of hunger and want". And this should be the primary understanding for redefining and developing a basic concept of human rights relevant to the people of the third world, far away from the concept as understood and propagated so long by the liberal western theorists of human rights, and almost imitated by us, the human rights activists of countries like India, shamelessly, though perhaps unconsciously.

Once we accept that for the people of the third world, the right to live is the most important and decisive human right to realise and secure, it also becomes evident that even in the 21st century, the most scandalous obstacle to the realisation of that right is colonialism or domination of imperialists in different avatars, and their aggression and exploitation, control and domination over the third world. This again basically encourages and perpetuates racial discrimination, fundamentalism and communalism as well as almost all the backward norms and practices of precapitalist society, whichever become helpful to the continuation of that domination. Imperialism arrogantly tramples upon the national independence and sovereignty of the third world countries, controls and captures their natural resources and wealth, raw materials and produced goods, thereby depriving them of their legitimate incomes. During the post-second world war period, most of the 150 major localised wars took place in the third world, with the direct or indirect backing of imperialist countries, and obviously the people of these countries became the cannon fodder of those wars. In the last 100 years, at least six million people have been killed by imperialists, directly or indirectly.

Economically too, due to the exploitation and manipulation of imperialism and their stooges, the living conditions in these countries for most of the people are becoming more and more precarious. This process has actually been evident for the last few centuries with the emergence of capitalism, and especially its highest phase, imperialism. It has been tremendously accentuated in the last few decades with the emergence of the economics of globalisation, based on neo-liberal economic doctrine. Perhaps it would be better to take the help of Lewis Carroll's famous allegory *Through the Looking Glass* to under-stand the phenomenon of globalisation.

In Lewis Carroll's allegory, Alice and the Queen were running hand in hand in the Red Queen's garden, and the Queen was running so fast that it was very difficult for Alice to keep pace with her. But still the Queen kept crying "Faster! Faster!" The most curious part of the thing to Alice was that the trees and the other things round them never changed their places at all; however fast they went, they never seemed to pass anything. An astonished Alice exclaimed: "Well, in our country, you'd generally get to somewhere else – if you ran for a long time as we've been doing"-. But the Queen retorted: "A slow sort of country! Now, here, you see, it takes all the running you can do, to keep in the same place. If you want to get somewhere else, you must run at least twice as fast as that"!

Think of the Red Queen's garden as capitalism. The relentless search for markets and profits brings about rapid changes in production and space, industry and commerce, occupation and locale, with profound effects on the organisation of classes and states. It is through this ferocious process of extension and change that capitalism preserves itself, remains capitalistic, and perpetuates basically the same system. This paradox, or rather this dialectic, can only properly be grasped if we understand that the "bourgeoisie can not exist without constantly revolutionising the instruments of production, and thereby relations of production, and with them the whole relations of society" (Karl Marx). This was not an understanding merely appropriate to what happened to the world in the first half of the 19th century: it is no less appropriate to under-standing what has happened over the second half of the 20th century and also in the first decade of the present century, and to what is taking place in the world today in the context of globalisation. Now think of Alice, frantically running along-side the Red Queen, as the representative of the third world. You will begin to grasp the real significance of globalisation to them. They must keep on running in order to keep pace in the face of deprivation and poverty, brought about by the fierce plunder of the imperialists for more and more profit, but still basically unable to satisfy their basic needs of life – for food and shelter, for health and education and culture.

And from the point of view of imperialism, historically speaking, its most severe crisis burst out towards the end of the 1920s, ultimately resulting in the Second World War. The ferocity of this continuous period of crises forced the imperialists to give greater attention to plundering the third world's natural resources – land, minerals, water, and even air. The process of globalisation is nothing but the programmatic manifestation of this more acute phase of imperialist plunder based on the hydra-headed doctrine of neoliberalism. The Indian ruling classes began to traverse this path of globalisation since 1991.

The gurus and disciples of globalisation described it as the panacea for all economic woes and ills; they claimed that the only path to prosperity is to adhere to free-market principles. The nations of the third world, in particular, are being urged to deregulate and open up their economies to free trade and foreign investment, to ensure their speedy transition to the status of developed economies. But it has already been proved that globalisation has brought, in its wake, great inequities, mass impoverishment and despair; that it has fractured society more acutely along the existing fault lines of class, colour, gender and community, while almost irreversibly widening the gap between the rich and the poor, both in terms of individuals and nations; that it has caused the flow of capital across international borders, which has been responsible for financial and economic crises in many countries and regions; that it has enriched a small minority of persons and corporations within nations and within the international system, marginalising and violating the basic human rights of millions of workers, peasants and farmers and indigenous communities.

Though globalisation has been portrayed as turning the whole world into one global village, leading to unprecedented enjoyment of human rights for everyone together with the spread of the highly cherished values of democracy, freedom and justice, in reality, it has turned the world into a global market for goods and services, dominated and steered by the powerful, gigantic transnational corporations and governed by the rule of profit, thereby trampling upon the basic human rights of the people in the world, particularly in the third world countries. The governments of these third world countries are abiding by the multilateral agreements that are deepening the process of globalisation, thereby violating the basic human rights of the people. These agreements and policies have had adverse effects on the right to work, the right to food, the right to health, the right to education, and the right to development. In their drive for profits, companies, in particular, the TNCs, have been restructuring their operations on a global scale. The result has been massive- unemployment. In 1995, the International Labour Organisation announced that one-third of the world's workforce.

In India, only 8 per cent of the labour force is in the formal economy while 92 per cent work in the informal economy with no legal protection or security, and are subject to ruthless exploitation. Workers in developing countries have been forced into a race to the bottom, and the bottom means slave like conditions. Consequently, the calorie intake of the poor has declined. The Trade Related Aspects of Intellectual Property Rights Agreement of the World Trade Organisation prevents countries from producing low cost generic drugs, robbing poor patients of their rights to health. Policies promoting globalisation by introducing the market mechanism into the provision of healthcare obviously make such services less available to the poor. The privatisation of health and hospital services also makes the poor suffer as services become more oriented towards those who can pay. The lives of at least one to two million children on average are lost every year. The right to education has also been adversely affected by privatisation policies and the turning of education into a profit generating enterprise in developing countries.

The consequences of violations of human rights are revealed by the widening gap between the rich and the poor, both at the global and the local levels, as reflected in international statistics:

(1) Half the world – nearly three billion people – live on less than two dollars a day.

(2) The wealthiest nation on earth has the widest gap between rich and poor of any industrialised nation.

(3) The top fifth of the world's people in the richest countries enjoy 82 per cent of the expanding export trade and 68 per cent of foreign direct investment, while the bottom fifth, barely more than 1 per cent.

(4) In 1960, 20 per cent of the world's people in the richest countries had 30 times the income of the poorest 20 per cent; in 1997, 74 times as much; and in 2015 it is estimated to be just 100 times.

(5) A few hundred millionaires now own as much wealth as the world's poorest 2.5 billion people.

(6) The combined wealth of the world's 200 richest people hit $1 trillion in 1999; the combined income of the 582 mil-lion people living in the 43 least developed- countries was $146 billion.

(7) As globalisation matures, the rate at which the rich people and countries become richer competes with and becomes directly proportional to the rate at which the poor people and poor countries become poorer.

The aspiration for winning civil and political rights which has primarily motivated the movement over all these years definitely remains. Without fully achieving economic, social and cultural rights, the above rights cannot be really achieved. Hence, the main emphasis should be given to these basic rights, i e, economic, social and cultural rights. Consequently, the human rights movement should now build a direct bridge with the ongoing people's movements as well as those that will surely arise in the near future, defending the basic interests of the labouring people. The implementation of globalisation policies led to the emergence of many such movements, like the Narmada Bachao Andolan of lakhs of evicted people, the anti-POSCO movement in Orissa, the farmers movement in Noida, Uttar Pradesh, etc, for safeguarding the living conditions of the marginalized poor.

6

Human Rights and Democracy

The language on human rights has been created within a revolutionary environment that called for a new social order and political governance. New identities were constructed and projected and new ideologies emerged in the context of the American Declaration of Independence and the French Revolution. Progressively one observed the emergence of a 'democratic' spectrum and democratic promise of a future society closer to justice, fairness, equality and freedom.

In this chapter we will explore the relationship between human rights and democracy contributing to the clarification of concepts and tasks ahead of us. Human rights and Democracy have the potential to go hand-in-hand and use each other's strengths to realize themselves. However, the relationship between democracy and human rights is not so obvious as one may tend to think. In fact, while instinctively one may want to believe that democracies must be committed to respect fundamental human rights, it is not clear how this is done. In this chapter we want to address the tension between democracy and human rights, particularly the role of human rights in democracies.

Contextualizing Human Rights Discourse

When we speak about 'human rights' we all intuitively know what the discourse is about there is a claim of universality, of trans-nationality, of moral content which is ultimately translated into legal and political forms or instantiations. Through a 'human rights' perspective one is able to condemn, criticize and analyze forms in which societies act and live, and although it is important to do so, as if the 'human rights discourse' would grant a criteria for evaluation of what individuals and states shouldn't do, it becomes more difficult to use this same reference to identify what individuals and states should do. i.e., while it is quite obvious when we are facing violations of human rights - like Guantanamo Bay or Muammar Gaddafi's war upon his own people - we should also have a set of measures that determine what should be done in order for these violations not find a space for insurgence.

This is important for at least two reasons: on the one hand, because when talking or living in a 'historical a priori' (to use a Foucauldian terminology) framed by a 'human rights discourse' it is important, necessary and useful to understand where this discourse comes from, in order to better understand where we are and what can we do with it; on the other hand, because only by having done this previous task can one be in a better position to understand and (re)define the relationship between human rights and democracy, identifying what is unique and distinct about it; therefore, to be able to answer the question: what are human rights and what is their role in democracies?

The expression 'human rights', as something analytically distinct from 'inalienable rights' or 'civil liberties', only started to be widely used after World War II. This was a term that was introduced with a new and stronger connotation with the Universal Declaration of Human Rights in 1948, Declaration which set the framework for all subsequent international and regional human rights treaties. If one looks at the circumstances that led to the drafting of the Universal Declaration of Human Rights (UDHR), one easily identifies the differences between its compelling motives versus the reasons that motivated other historically and politically important Declarations, such as the Enlightenment bills of rights - from the 1689 British Bill of Rights through to the French Declaration and American Bill of Rights. However, despite the differences they might have had – many of them expressing the different 'historical a priori' – a common thread can be identified, namely, the concern with defining and fulfilling the rights of man by defining conditions for republican government or democracy.

The Enlightenment movement introduced three new premises in the political discourse. First, it introduced a language of 'natural rights', associated to the concept of liberty, which would determine the scope of legitimacy of the government. Second, derived from the first and reflected in the concept and practice of citizenship within the republic, these natural rights were supported by the rights to free speech and protest. Third, by introducing 'individual rights' the role and characterization of the State as such needed to be revised – from now on, the State became no longer separated from the social body, as if it was the Hobbesian Leviathan. Instead, by acknowledging the importance of fair trails and due process, we observe a shift of paradigm where the State becomes an actor among other actors, with its specific rights and duties, accountable and responsible for its actions and therefore, liable to punishment if judged as 'criminal' or violator of natural rights of the individuals who belong to the Republic.

The circumstances that led to the drafting of the UDHR were quite different: after assuming that a language of 'natural rights' was a given, hypothetically accepted and recognized by citizens of a republican or democratic government as valid and legitimate, these 'natural rights' were crushed by genocidal events of World War II. Europe, supposedly an example of civilizational development, couldn't live up to its own principles and it was victim of its own poison. More recently, with the fall of the Soviet Union we observed many genocidal behaviors in Bosnia, Rwanda and Kosovo; we could even question the moral authority of Bush's attach on Iraq in 2003. We could also question the moral or legal authority of Obama's decision to kill Bin Laden in foreign territory.

Under this light, the drafting of the UDHR accomplished at least two things: first, it acknowledged that 'natural rights', 'individual rights' or 'human rights' could not simply be assumed as existing and being universally recognized by all; second, it spelled out the necessity of developing and materializing in writing a set of ethical values that could become standards for action and judgment at a global scale. By doing so, the UDHR translates a duplication of relations: on the one hand, it places the burden at the immanence level of the individual/ national state of meeting certain criteria in its relation to its citizens; on the other hand, it extends the boundaries of rights beyond the traditional frontiers of 'nation-states', moving to a global sphere were the state is an actor among other actors/states, and where individuals are defined in their relationship to a particular state as well as to the world in general, as a moral agent and legal enforcer.

What are Human Rights?

> "Natural rights is simple nonsense: natural and imprescriptible rights, rhetorical nonsense, nonsense upon stilts".
>
> – Bentham, *Anarchical Fallacies* (1791: 2)

Are human rights 'imaginary' or are they real? What role do they play in democracies? Tasioulas in his well know article "What is a human right?" says that when speaking of human rights one must have three things in mind: first, a concern with fidelity with history; second, the acknowledgment that there are moral issues and human rights issues, and that they not always overlap; finally, that one should be careful not be guilty of parochialism, thinking that human rights discourse is another way of promoting liberal western values only. Having said that, Tasioulas proceeds with an analysis of three different approaches to human rights, namely, the Reductive, the Orthodox and the Political View. The first one, the Reductive view, "reduces claims about human rights to claims about universal human interests." (2009: 940). Under this light, human rights are treated as a matter of universal human interests. Although one may easily agree on the claim that human rights are human interests which are transversal to all human beings, therefore, universal, by treating human rights via the lens of 'interests' two problems emerge: first, if human rights are a matter of evaluating, acknowledging and fighting for interests, what is so special about 'human rights discourse'? Does it make sense to have parallel terms if one is talking about one and the same thing? There must be something unique in this later in order to justify its existence. Second, by using a language of interests or of capabilities, like Nussbaum does, one is also creating the space for a virtually endless proliferation of rights and, to that extent, a loss of meaning. Like Tasioulas condends:

The idea of capabilities may well perform important work within a theory of the grounds, scope and normative implications of human rights, but it is not a promising candidate in terms of which to understand the very idea of a human right. Instead, we need to get beyond talk of interests, or any sub-set of interests, and conceive of human rights as an irreducibly moral notion (2009: 941).

According to the political view on human rights - a position which is defended by Raz or Rawls - human rights are rights that belong to a more general class of rights, generally equated with the Orthodox view. Common to the existing variations within this approach, Tasioulas claims that there is an immanent problem with this approach, namely, that "(t)hey make the very idea of human rights conceptually parasitic on the idea of a specific kind of political institution, whether it be the state (Beitz, Raz), state-like entities (Rawls' 'peoples'), or coercive institutional schemes (Pogge)." What bothers Tasioulas with this account, a discomfort, is that according to this specific approach to human rights one finds a criterion for legitimation of international response. For instance, given that Gaddafi openly violates human rights, international community is morally justified to respond against it - which is actually what happened with NATO intervention and the general moral condemnation of its action by the general public sphere - not only the institutional but also the people across the world.

The other approach to the human rights discourse identified by Tasioulas is the orthodox view. This view embodies the shift of paradigm from a human rights theory grounded on interests to a human rights theory grounded on morals. According to the orthodox view, "human rights are moral rights possessed by all human beings simply in virtue of their humanity." However, may this definition be deceptive? What does this really mean? First, there is a claim of morality - human rights are one kind among others of moral rights. It is the family to which they belong. Being a moral right implies that human rights are sources of duties or obligations: they are categorical, i.e, necessary; second, they are exclusionary; finally, they result in moral responses like blame or guilt, etc.

The second part of the definition, namely "possessed by all human beings" means that human rights - as specific moral rights - are fully transversal and global, applied to all, i.e., human rights are universal. Of course, one question could be raised, namely, are human rights applicable in all times of history, even in a 'pre-political' state of nature, or not? The answer to this question is 'no', because human rights, regardless of the universal application that derives from it, are moral rights that are experienced in particular contexts of time and space; therefore, I would be resistant to overlap human rights with natural rights tout court. On the other hand, this question could also be seen as a false question insofar if one adopts a Foucauldian position where we are conditioned by the 'historical a priori' within which we live in - an historical a priori that produces power relations, knowledge and proliferation of discourses - it simply doesn't make any sense to look for a transcendent link between different points in time.

Finally, the last expression of the orthodox definition, namely, "simply in virtue of their humanity" in all or certain generally specified socio-historical conditions simply in virtue of being human. We assume that this statement can be easily understood and accepted as straight forward – mainly because we don't think that for our particular purpose in this paper, it is relevant to engage in a discussion of meanings and contents of humanity.

In short, we affirm that a theory of human rights must be morally supported and defended. Human rights cannot be a matter of military intervention, or other forms of intervention only - mainly because one should give reasons in order to justify interventions, and these reasons are mostly grounded on same kind of moral arguments. On the other hand, a theory of human rights that in practice equates 'rights' to 'interests' is highly problematic when trying to define the order of priorities between rights. If rights are only a matter of interests, then, not only seems that the human rights discourse falls in redundancy, but also it lacks the substance to make itself a criteria for several forms of action - individually and collectively understood. Only a moral approach to human rights can be strong enough to make itself relevant in considering, evaluating, choosing and promoting certain forms of behavior, at individual, national and global levels.

The UDHR introduced new premises that re-shaped the human rights discourse and, indirectly, democratic theory and democratic discourse as well. These were the values of dignity, equality and community. After that, the human rights discourse started to work as expressing the articulation and relationship between these values and the traditional principles of liberty, democratic freedoms and justice.

After having set the framework in the Article 1, "All human beings are born free and equal in dignity and rights" - and equality here refers to a specific kind of equality, namely of dignity and of rights, - Article 22, which introduces the economic, social and cultural rights section of the Declaration, defines the relationship between dignity and rights, describing these rights as "indispensable for human dignity."

Article 22 of UDHR states: "Everyone, as a member of society, has the right to social security and is entitled to realization, through national effort and international co-operation and in accordance with the organization and resources of each State, of the economic, social and cultural rights indispensable for his dignity and the free development of his personality."

The premise of dignity places a new burden upon the State(s) and redefines the kind of relationship between State(s) and individuals. Not only must the state refrain from abusing individual liberties, but also, the State has the duty to take positive measures to respect individuals' inherent worth. The strength of the premise of dignity is reinforced by reading it in accordance to the premise of equality.

With equality, the drafters chose not just to stick with the Enlightenment formula of 'equality before the law'; instead, they also introduced the modern formulation that everyone is entitled to the rights in the Declaration "without distinction of any kind," such as race, colour, sex, religion, and so forth (Article 2). "Everyone is entitled to all the rights and freedoms set forth in this Declaration, without distinction of any kind, such as race, colour, sex, language, religion, political or other opinion, national or social origin, property, birth or other status. Furthermore, no distinction shall be made on the basis of the political, jurisdictional or international status of the country or territory to which a person belongs, whether it be independent, trust, non-self-governing or under any other limitation of sovereignty." Furthermore, "equal protection before the law" is reinforced by the "protection against any discrimination" – including "incitement to discrimination", as stated in Article 7. "All are equal before the law and are entitled without any discrimination to equal protection of the law. All are entitled to equal protection against any discrimination in violation of this Declaration and against any incitement to such discrimination." Article 7 UDHR.

Once it was accepted that human rights values require states to proactively take measures to root out discrimination then the concept of liberty was bound to change. Liberty could no longer mean be free to buy, to rent, to work; from the moment we introduce the premise of universality, where everyone's rights were to be secured, individual liberty had to be redefined and most likely, restrained.

The premise of community allows us to contextualize how the living of these rights can be accomplished. In article 29 the UDHR introduces the idea that 'everyone has duties to the community", with the explanation that it is only through the 'community' that "the full development" of an individual's personality" is possible.

Article 29 –

(1) Everyone has duties to the community in which alone the free and full development of his personality is possible.

(2) In the exercise of his rights and freedoms, everyone shall be subject only to such limitations as are determined by law solely for the purpose of securing due recognition and respect for the rights and freedoms of others and of meeting the just requirements of morality, public order and the general welfare in a democratic society.

(3) These rights and freedoms may in no case be exercised contrary to the purposes and principles of the United Nations.

From the UDHR onwards any limitations on fundamental rights must be lawful, proportionate and necessary to achieve a prescribed goal "in a democratic society." However, this 'democratic society' was never defined; it is always assumed but it is never spelled out what one means by it.

The introduction of the expression 'democratic society' in the human rights discourse - also in Article 29 - is revealing of something, namely, it provides the framework where one thinks human rights; but also, it announces something that goes much deeper, namely, that while human rights discourse can be analyzed from a functional perspective - and therefore, as providing certain necessary conditions for a democratic society - human rights discourse shape not only the process of democracy and for democratization as they also set the boundaries to the outcomes and goals of democracy. In other words, in human rights discourse the state is in fact obliged to "take preventive measures", in the stated view of the European Court of Human Rights "to protect an individual whose life is at risk from the criminal acts of another individual."

Democracy and Human Rights

A question must be raised at this point: what is the actual relationship between democracies and human rights? And what should it be? The implications of the previous insight are profound. If human beings do not just need freedom to flourish, but also a thriving community on which they depend, then it is inevitable that you have to redefine the limits on individual rights as well as the quality of relationship between individuals and community itself. These limits are necessary not only to ensure freedom for all but also to create the conditions for the 'common good', idea which is fully stated in the same Article 29 section 2.

This could also lead us to other levels of discussion, namely, what model of democracy is preferable? Which model should we choose in detriment of others? In order to fulfill human rights do democracies need to meet some previous political and institutional criteria or is it indifferent? From the moment one assumes 'community' as one of the conditions for the fulfillment of human rights, then, the way in which this community is conceived, imagined or experienced is going to matter. Therefore, 'democracy' as a vague and all encompassing concept is not sufficient to provide a concrete setting of what this 'community' should look like. It is necessary to define with more precision the kind of democratic instantiations that are more favorable to the fulfilling of human rights; and by doing so, it becomes equally clear that some other models of democracy do not necessarily entail a practical commitment to human rights theory and discourse.

Benjamin Barber's characterization of several types of democracy is supported by a particular interest about the relationship between the individual and the community. According to his approach, liberal democracy, for instance, is "thin" democracy because its values are "prudential" and "thus provisional, optional, and conditional – means to exclusively individualistic and private ends. From this precarious foundation, no firm theory of citizenship, participation, public goods, or civic virtue can be expected to arise" (2003:4).

Given that a liberal democracy is more concerned with the individual than the community, it first defends individual rights, and only after community ones. Within the liberal model of democracy, three tendencies can be identified according to Barber: the anarchist, the realist and the minimalist. A thin democracy is "instrumental, representative, in its three dispositions" (2003:117).

According to Barber's reading of "thin" democracy, a model like this can never really accomplish the democratic goals and ideals that the concept of democracy just by itself inspires. Quite the contrary, if one is inspired and committed to the democratic ideals of equality, justice and freedom, then one must introduce the variable of community in the democratic discourse. Democracy cannot mean only political democracy; it must also mean social and economic democracy. Under this light, the introduction of the community in the discourse marks a shift of paradigm, insofar society can no longer be defined from a egotistic and selfish point of view; quite the contrary, society must be redefined as encounter of individuals where the well being of all, or common good, must be regulative of individual actions and liberties. The perspective is complemented by the recognition of community's importance to individuals' flourishing, which in its turn will be reflected in the flourishing of the community as well.

Under the light brought by a reference to Barber's work, we want to clarify that in order for democracies to be closer to human rights theory and discourse it is important that democracies do not remain within a procedural level only, of reducing 'democracies' to the existence of elections in regular times. Also, it is not sufficient to underline individual rights only. Individuals must be seen in relation to the community they belong to. It is only through the analysis of this relationship, and the recognition of the institutional setting that supports it that a strong model of democracy can emerge.

So, what is a strong democracy? According to Barber, "strong democracy reuses on the idea of a selfgoverning community of citizens who are united less by homogeneous interests than by civic education and who are made capable of common purpose and mutual action by virtue of their civic attitudes and participatory institutions rather than their altruism or their good nature" (2003: 117). A democracy is as stronger at the level and quality of the participation and engagement of its citizens.

However, we want to stress out the idea that first, democracies that actually meet human rights criteria are strong democracies; second, the strength of a democracy should be measured through the levels of participation, civic engagement, but also institutional support and other measures that assure the correct implementation and practice of these rights, with the duties they entail. Third, a strong democracy cannot remain at the political level only; it must integrate the social, cultural, but also economic variables in order to articulate a fuller concept of community and citizenship. This is the greatest challenge contemporary democracies face today: how to integrate a discourse on human rights with economic premises within a democratic context?

To answer the question above one must acknowledge a fact, namely, that economics and the 'global economy' do have a great impact on the way democracies work - how they function, how the process of democratization is developed and how it is sustained - therefore, the economic premise must be taken into consideration when reflecting upon the relationship between human rights and democracy.

However, positions about the impact economics have in democracies and specially in they way it affects the conceptual promotion and practical implementation of human rights, vary. In one extreme, one finds those who argue that global economy is an advantage, i.e., a plus that can enhance the human rights cause. On the other extreme, one finds those who argue that the subsumption of democracies and other systems to economy makes us question the level of democracy itself, ultimately turning human rights discourse in an ideological instrument to advance economic goals. What can we say about this relationship?

For our purpose we will leave out the problems that authoritative states raise to the development of human rights. Let us focus on democratic states. Indeed, a question that emerges when we bring to discussion economy and human rights is the question to know what serves what: is the economy made to serve the good of society, or is the good of society made to serve the economy? Without relying in moral or metaphysical answers or assumptions, it should be the first case. Economy should be put to work in order to improve the human condition—our health, welfare, freedoms, and security. If one is committed to contribute to a safe and peaceful world, then, economy should be used in order to enhance these goals - and we know how economic measures can have a great impact in contributing to this achievement. As David Kinley (2009) argued that economic globalization has helped to lift millions of people out of abject poverty. It has helped to provide people with jobs, health care, housing, and education, as well as giving them voice, knowledge, and greater self-respect. In these respects it is a civilizing force. However, these benign effects have neither been universal nor uniform. And there are also casualties of globalization where its impact has been ineffective or negative– thus for every South Korea or Brazil, there is a Myanmar or Zimbabwe. The challenge in recognizing globalization as an instrument is to use it in ways that extend its beneficence and curtail its savagery. In other words, to civilize it.

Manuel Branco, on his turn, in an article entitled 'Economics against Human Rights' (2007) argues that the problem is that economics and human rights have difficulties in communicating - while the first speaks the language of needs, relying in the concept of 'capability', the second speaks the language of rights, relying in the concept of 'entitlement'. The direct implication of this is that each language and each paradigm give rise to a very different social and political landscape - while from an economic point of view it is conceivable to coexist with exclusion and inequality; from a human rights' perspective, equality and inclusion are a condition sine qua non, i.e., goods and services can be unequally distributed, while rights cannot. It is under this context that Manuel Branco argues that economics works against human rights.

Despite the different languages between economics and human rights discourse, Branco starts with the assumption that they share a similar goal, namely, to 'free' mankind - either from the constraints of needs, or the constraints of fear. However, the means to achieve this goal differ, and these differences become manifest in the discourse adopted by each of them. For instance, from an economic perspective, the goal is to satisfy needs and maximize utility. The economic dimension is constructed through the concepts of goods, exchange, money, value. Even from a Rawlsian perspective, economic inequality is compatible with social justice, as long as the minimum threshold is respected and the least well off are still better than in any other possible world. The human rights discourse, on the other hand, is grounded in the equalitarian premise, meaning that 'all' human beings have certain rights – all human beings are entitled to a set of rights, and no human being has more rights than other.

Apparently, one could think that at least for a while - encompassing the first and second generation of rights – these discourses didn't directly clash against each other. However, once 'economic' rights are introduced, economics was forced to deal with the dimension of rights, i.e., it was forced to think of a comprehensive way to deal with needs and rights. This revealed to be problematic; more so, in a democratic context where ideals not only have a regulative function; they also guide practical policy making and have direct repercussions in legislation and institutionalization.

Let us look at an example. It is a human right to have housing/ shelter or food. What are the implications economically speaking under a democratic umbrella? Governments would need to make sure that all of its citizens/ as human beings, have these goods; but how to assure that the (re) distribution is well made in order to fill out the gaps? The introduction and commitment to a discourse of human rights imposes a (moral) duty upon governments and States to take 'democracy' seriously - not only as a political, preferable, model, but also social and economic. The commitment to human rights discourse introduces and makes visible the responsibility and accountability at State level - ultimately, if a State does not fulfill the basic human rights list, can one say that the State is still 'democratic'?

The problem is that enhancing the economic goals sometimes openly conflict with enhancing the human rights cause. Let us take Article 23 of the Universal Declaration of Human Rights, which states that–

1. Everyone has the right to work, to free choice of employment, to just and favorable conditions of work and to protection against unemployment. (...)
2. Everyone who works has the right to just and favorable remuneration ensuring himself and his family an existence worthy of human dignity, and supplemented if necessary by other means of social protection.

Take the actual circumstances of Europe, from Greece to Ireland, Portugal, Spain, but also UK and others, where the unemployment rate increases every month, where people, who still have jobs, are invited to work much more for much less, where people live in constant fear of losing their income and therefore, falling in disgrace (because the State is cutting back the social supports and subsidies to unemployed). Is the actual economy contributing or opposing itself to the human rights cause, and with it, to democracy itself? If we read carefully these passages, what is written is that –

1. everyone has a right to work,
2. the job one has should be the result of a free choice by the employee,
3. one must have just and favorable conditions,
4. one must be protected against unemployment,
5. remuneration must be fair - and fairness or justice is here measured by the level of 'dignity' that it can assure to the employee and his/her family - if this remuneration is not sufficient to reach the minimum criteria of 'human dignity' then 6. the State is compelled to provide additional social protection.

Reality is quite different from the theoretical and normative claim brought by the discourse on human rights. We could analyze each of the items and refute them in practice; however, for the purpose of our argument. The quantitative, in the sense that 'all' human beings have a right to work, result from a free choice. The qualitative, in the sense that the job must meet certain criteria according to which 'human dignity' is assured. This criteria is vague and volatile, it has been the subject matter of legislators, who try to define the boundary between the just and unjust in the labor market, or between the sufficient or insufficient for living conditions and a certain well-being.

The relationship between economics and human rights is tense, but democracy cannot escape it. There are many other aspects that could be pointed out, exposing the tense relationship between the discourse on human rights and democracy. From a theoretical point of view it is important to spell out the forms that this tension between the discourse on human rights and democracy takes. That could happen through a comparative analysis between the adoption of the discourse on human rights, public policy making and actual institutionalization between different countries.

Second, this analysis would force us to conceive democracy differently, i.e., not as having the 'nation-state' figure as gravitational force; instead, by replacing it by democratic institutions. Only through an analysis of how democratic are democratic institutions can one measure the level of democracy of a society, and ultimately, account for its proximity to the discourse on human rights as regulative ideals and pragmatic goals.

Third, even if one shifts the focus from 'nation-state' to 'institution', still, it is necessary to complement that with an interdisciplinary approach. I.e., disciplines should research and act in concert, if we want to contribute to a better world.

Fourth, the inter-disciplinary is revealed in the dialogue between economics, political science, political philosophy and law. Having reflected upon the content and implication of concepts (philosophy task), and having studied and compared cases (political science), it is important to introduce the legal dimension and analyze the question of jurisdiction for human rights claims. For instance, if human rights are violated in Indonesia, in a factory that is owned by a Transnational corporation who has its headquarters in England or the U.S., then, it is important that a previous legal agreement exists between the countries involved in order to avoid these violations. Of course, this requires, and imposes a more demanding level of transparency of a) corporate law that defends economic interests and b) business decision-making that respects human rights as such, regardless of the country where the corporation acts. This assumes that corporations have the same measure of treatment of human beings regardless of the country where they are.

What would be the implications of this? If we want to promote the discourse and cause of human rights, it is necessary to reach an agreement, at global scale, on what the goal really is - is it to promote justice, fairness, equality, is it to provide conditions for an autonomous life and freedom or is it to maximize gains at the expense of human lives? It is important to spell it out and be clear on what the priorities are, in order to reveal the hypocrisy that has governed the world. If libertarian and liberal principles are more important than 'global justice' and human rights, then, democracies should redefine themselves and expose how the relationship between human rights and democracy is not as linear as it may seem. If, on the contrary, there is a recognition and agreement that, in order to talk about human rights we are acknowledging the existence or we are postulating a common good, then democracies just need to walk the talk.

7

Human Rights and Welfare

In a famous article, Herbert Hart (1995) argued that if there was one natural right, it was the equal right of all people to be free. This right is held by any adult human being capable of choice. Typical of many moral philosophers, this is presented as a universal rule, not mediated through membership in a society. Typically also, it glosses over the grounding of this rule on a particular conception of human nature.

Hart's theory, stated in reverse, runs something like this: the essence of being human is being moral. Morality cannot be imposed but is a product of autonomy and choice. Hence freedom is essential to morality. Therefore, in order to be human, to express one's human nature, every person has the right to be free.

A more general argument on Hart's lines is offered in precise detail by Gewirth. Identifying human rights with claim rights, Gewirth regards them as protective of the conditions of human action and justifies those conditions as necessary to fulfill the general needs of human agency. It is because human beings are prospective purposive agents that they can claim rights. Importantly, Gewirth goes beyond Hart's interest in freedom alone to maintain that, as a general proposition, all the human rights, those of well-being as well as those of freedom, have as their aim that each person have rational autonomy in the sense of being a self-controlling, self-developing agent who can relate to other persons on a basis of mutual respect and cooperation.

We propose instead a more general approach to a human right as a device, translatable into rules for social conduct, that relates to the things that human beings value most about themselves. It signals that special status and invulnerability should be accorded to those valuable goods, attributes, or acts that are considered essential to human and social well being. Specifically, to attach human rights to such values is to envelop them in a protective capsule. To do so is to assert that the realization of those values or interests which may be liberties, acts, conditions, powers is of particular importance to the rights-bearer and probably, at least indirectly, to the rights-guarantor. It suggests that a value attached to a right is so important that it must have priority over other values, though such priority may, it is frequently agreed, the prima facie rather than absolute. This means that it must be upheld at any reasonable cost and that failure to implement it requires powerful justification.

Philosophers will point out that, among living creatures, only human beings have moral properties. But this is not the same as saying that human beings are only moral entities. Demonstrably, they have other attributes as well, without which they cannot function as human beings. For example, they are capable of pain and suffering. The fact that cows too are capable of pain and suffering does not make this less of a human attribute. It simply means it is not an exclusively human attribute.

In sum, it is insufficient to assert, as does Gewirth, that human rights pertain to all humans by virtue of their nature as actual or prospective agents. It is also unnecessary and circuitous to suggest, as he does, that well-being merely services autonomy. It will certainly do so. But well-being may relate to augmenting one's sense of musical appreciation, or the enjoyment of companionship. Those are important human capacities independent of their contribution to agency and autonomy. Hence human rights also pertain to people directly by virtue of other facets of their nature for human beings comprise packages of physical, emotional, mental as well as moral properties. Each of these categories contains attributes of fundamental value to persons, without which they cannot function adequately. A theory of human rights must therefore consist of protective capsules for every one of these sets of attributes.

It is moreover of little utility to suggest that moral properties are superior to others. Each set of properties is essential to being human, so that a ranking order appears impossible without introducing further considerations that do not emanate from the nature of human attributes.

This flies against the tendency of many moral philosophers to regard agency and autonomy as the crowning glory of human existence, and the fulfilling of other human functions as mere corridors to that inner sanctum. On the alternative understanding proposed here, a theory and policy of human well-being must address themselves with equal impartiality to preventing mental torture, providing food, or obtaining the educational tools to make rational, or at least informed, choices.

Since the nineteenth century, in sharp contrast to the notions of seventeenth-century contract theory, it has been a commonplace to regard human nature as developmental, as moving from potential to actual, as a process of attributes teleologically unfolding to the point of their maturation. In other words, growth is seen as essential to human nature. Put conversely, the prevention, stunting, and possibly even some unnatural rechanneling of growth would be dehumanizing and detrimental to the performance of human functions.

Here again is the basis for a human right: the right to the unimpeded development of every human being. This can be contained by a liberty right, understood as the negative liberty of noninterference by others. The logic of the issue does not, however, point unequivocally in the direction of noninterference nor, indeed, in the direction of unrestrained interference. It points rather in the direction of ensuring that growth will continue unimpeded, whatever the impediment may be.

Negative-rights theorists regard the intervention of other individuals or bodies, even in the form of paternalistic do-gooding, as the main impediments to human development, and the sole impediments from which individuals deserve and may claim social protection. For those theorists, growth is either inevitable or self-determined. Intervention is thus permitted only in the actions of those other people, who would impede the development of an individual. The alternative theory of positive rights, often referred to as welfare rights, postulates that direct intervention in the life of the individual may be necessary to ensure her or his right to development and growth and that, further, intervention in the lives of others may be required to achieve that end. Its approach to human nature regards human growth as frequently, though not solely, dependent on external facilitation or cooperation.

One reason for this is that not all impediments to growth are caused by the intentional acts of other individuals and, hence, cannot be removed simply by prohibiting such acts. They are rather the products of unintentional acts of others, or defects of social organization, or nonhuman factors beyond individual control. Whereas negative-rights theorists may or may not be aware of these further factors, they do not apportion responsibility to any person or social body for their existence, and will not therefore insist on the right of individuals to be protected by others from those phenomena.

Positive-rights theorists, in contrast, recognize the need to cut through obstacles to human development no matter what their origin inasmuch as those obstacles are removable in principle and are deemed to interfere intolerably with human development. The notion of inherent growth allows them to extend rights from the minimal to the optimal without changing their nature. It is as if the protective capsule expanded together with the contents it was shielding.

We must now introduce yet another crucial dimension of human nature its dependence on social, historical, and behavioral contexts. Negative-rights theory adheres to a further assumption about human nature as axiomatic, when it is merely optional. It presents individuals as self-determining, as best capable of preserving their own interests, as indeed self-developing. This evokes a theory of human nature as self-sufficient, independent, and capable of rational pursuit of enlightened self-interest. It encourages an overly formal and abstract discussion of human rights. Its exponents not only believe in the absurd possibility of remaining neutral among competing conceptions of the good life, but they also bestow on that neutrality a high moral stance, arguing that each individual is the best judge of his or her development, or life-plan.

The idea of rights in the hands of those theorists becomes a highly ambiguous one, suggesting simultaneously that human beings are worthy entities deserving of respect and fair treatment, and yet indicating that they are also dangerous and mutually threatening creatures why otherwise would they need rights in order to protect themselves from their fellow humans?

This problem is partially, though not entirely, resolved by the introduction of a contrary view of human nature, conducive to a theory of positive rights. On this view, human beings are sympathetic and even naturally inclined to be sociable and cooperative. They can only function and give expression and reality to their abilities and features by means of other individuals. Interdependence becomes a fact of social organization; mutual concern becomes a fact of human psychology and disposition. On this account, the danger of individual to individual stressed by negative-rights theorists is greatly diminished. It is rejected as a rule, though acknowledged as an exception. As a consequence, rights cannot be grounded primarily on the protection of free action from the intervention of others, for such intervention may frequently be regarded as beneficial, desirable, indeed essential, to the expression of human qualities. On what, then, are rights grounded? Against whom or what are they directed?

A theory responding to these questions could, in an extreme form, place too high a premium on human sociability and mutate into a denial of the very necessity of individual rights, emphasizing instead the unlimited benevolence, rationality, and concern that human societies will evince for their members. This utopian or anarchist or alternatively totalitarian version is, however, far removed from the humanist, ethically tested modes of social conduct that have emerged out of the ideology of the welfare state.

Having proposed a view of human nature that is based both on growth and on sociability, we can now explore a further dimension of the divide between negative- and positive-rights theorists. Their differences derive not only from theories of human nature but also from theories of social structure. Of particular interest to a welfare theory of rights is an implied version of social structure that regards human beings as essentially interacting, so that the idea of the right to forbearance is neither absolute nor prima facie, but a restriction placed only upon such actions as will detract from the human ability to develop and flourish. That apart, intervention in others need be no intrusion, but a component of their capacity to function physically, mentally, emotionally, morality and a denial of their atomistic discreteness.

On this view, societies accept the responsibility for doing all they feasibly can to maintain their members well-being. They do so because to behave otherwise would ultimate dehumanize their members. They further do so because they recognize that many constraints operating on individual development are the product of social error, incompetence, and ineptitude. But they also do so, and accept responsibility or offer compensation for ills beyond individual or social control, such as a drought, because not to rectify them would harm society itself a prime beneficiary from the abilities and contributions of its members. Individual rights may serve social interests. A right then constitutes a claim that directly or indirectly enhances the quality of life in a community.

Theories concerning the relationship of individuals to society conform to two varieties. In the weaker sense, the emphasis remains on individuals, but human interdependence and membership in a community is perceived to be part of the human condition. In the stronger sense, society itself is seen as an actor and crucially a bearer of rights.

The weaker sense is the more common in current analyses of rights, but it is not a monolithic one. Its variations, though all very important to any understanding of rights, share the common feature that individuals alone are rights bearers. One version focuses on full membership in a society as defining the context within which the claims of individuals have their bearing. The status of citizenship may even be thought to confer the ethical right not to be treated worse than others by the state without a justicizing difference.

A second version stresses the social characteristics of human beings as deserving of special protection by means of individual rights. Welfare measures to improve individual lives are thus designed to encourage the development of socially desirable and socially supportive conduct. As T. Campbell (1983) has put it, reflecting a non-Marxist socialist conception of human nature, there has to be some selection of those forms of human interest and concerns which most fully express the ideal of cooperative, creative, and productive activities and enjoyments. In addition to most rights that liberals would advocate, an opportunity to participate in productive social life would entail that functional rights will have a central place in a socialist society.

A third version asserts that social cooperation and assistance are needed for any human right to be protected. Though a minimalist position, it is adopted by many rights theorists and merits, therefore, further consideration. It may again be illustrated through Gewirth (1982). For a person to have rights, he argues, is not only to demand that others not interfere with his having the necessary goods of action [but] that they also help him to attain those goods when he cannot do so by his own efforts. This will promote social solidarity and further a sense of common interest.

For Gewirth, as for many philosophers, any difficulty is ironed out by two further, but highly debatable, assumptions. The first states that human beings are all rational agents, at least as concerns themselves, and hence must concede that all individuals are entitled to the same liberty to pursue their good that each rational agent claims for her-or himself. Apart from the empirically less-than-perfect rationality of human beings in bringing themselves to agree to this postulate, it is a further variation on the neutral among different conceptions of the good position adhered to by negative libertarians, and many American liberal theorists. For though purposive action is necessary to agency, it is hardly likely that all purposive action by people would be desirable or beneficial for themselves or others. The right to act does not endorse the right to any action. Hence it will be necessary to bring in external standards to assess and direct individual purposive action. On alternative notions of human nature and social structure, as shall presently be argued, this may involve a role for social control.

The second assumption is one that Gewirth states explicitly: goods of well-being are generically the same for all agents. But whereas liberty, in its negative sense at least, can be plausibly universalized, this is not the case with well-being. True, there are components of well-being that are virtually universal, and they relate to basic biological and psychological needs: people can only survive in a specific range of temperatures, they need a minimum of calories in order to function, their experience of fear is detrimental to their happiness. Clearly, though, individuals are not only actors, as Gewirth prefers to see them, but enjoyers as well, and there is no known method of universalizing human enjoyment. By defining well-being goods as the truly grounded requirements of agency, Gewirth reduces well-being as well as freedom to an adjunct of a rational process, thus maintaining his ground by means of a circular approach to rights.

At best, Gewirth has offered an argument about the universal but vacuous existence of rights, but very little about ways to identify their content. One of Gewirth's more potent critics, Plant, advances successfully the case for the promotion of liberty and well-being through direct and continuous social intervention in supplying basic needs for education, food, and health (Plant 1988: 60-61). But he too is unwilling to extricate himself from the difficulty of arguing that societies must guarantee the right only to those goods that further the exercise of autonomous agency, rather than seeing them as providing for a whole range of human capabilities.

For all these reasons, adjudications among rights claims become inevitable, and the notions of community or society may play a crucial part in this process. For those who hold to the essential sociability of human beings, social membership affords crucial conditions for human functioning; social life confers much, though not all, value on human life and can therefore help determine what needsd protection by means of a right. Social agents may even stop an individual's behaviour harmful to him-or herself, in order to protect his or her own rights, let alone the rights of others. On this view, we cannot rule out the possibility that irrational or malicious individuals may threaten their own rights. Moreover, inasmuch as rights are linked to theories of intentionality, social arrangements and institutions may be causally and deliberately responsible for individual misfortunes. It has also been reasonably argued that societies have a duty to compensate individuals for foreseeable have a duty to compensate individuals for foreseeable but unintentional harm. It could even be held the societies have a duty to compensate individuals for misfortunes beyond human and social control, simply because societies are organized groups of individuals, mutually sustaining by nature, and such mutual sustenance is a fundamental feature of human nature that both explains and justifies on utilitarian as well as non- utilitarian ethical grounds the repairing of harm to their members.

The strong sense of social structure derived from influential nineteenth century social theories, which held that societies develop mechanisms of conscious collective self-regulation and control as part of the evolutionary process and that they become in themselves rational entities with interests, purposes, and characteristics of their own, that cannot be reduced to those of their members. Those organic theories suggested not only that the individual had rights against other individuals and against all groups, society included, but that society itself had rights that could be asserted against individuals. This extension of the concept of a rights bearer must necessarily extend the notion of a purposive agent in a form that individualistic moral philosophers dislike.

The issue was succinctly expressed by the liberal social philosopher L.T. Hobhouse: "A right is a basis upon which its possessor constructs his own course of action having therein a measure of initiative and free choice. The formula that liberty is limited by rights requires...the addendum that rights must include, in addition to the rights of individual members, the right of the community as a whole" (1922: 62-63). Considerations of social utility, ethical theories of the state, and social psychology combined to make a case for the interests of a society that had to be safeguarded, both in order to further its social good and for the benefit of its members. Hobhouse elaborated further: "Rights are elements in social welfare and deriving their authority therefrom. The individual has no moral rights which conflict with the social good" (ibid: 39-40). Thus, for example, a national health service can be justified in terms of the reduction of individual suffering and, in parallel, in terms of the adequate functioning of the community as an investment in the quality of labor power and creativity available to it. Society as a creator of values has a right to their protection, just as individuals do, so that forms of social property can be seen as satisfying social needs. Hobhouse again argues that the community, like the individual, performs certain functions which require their due return, apart from which they would be starved. Inevitably, social intervention in individual lives is justifiable when crucial social interests are at stake and where their preservation as an assertion of social rights is called for.

These theories were not however authoritarian or totalitarian. It was clearly understood that individual liberty, too, is in the social interest, for societies only flourish insofar as their individual parts do. Hence there was a defined limit on social intervention. It would always be in the social interest equipped with a wider perspective than that of individuals to encourage the wholesome development of its members, even if those members could not always perceive the social interest. Autonomy as individual self-determination was socially beneficial, provided such self-determination took into account both the individual's role in society and the common good. Constraint would operate in both directions the democratic procedure would safeguard individual rights from being harmed by careless or irresponsible agents of society; legislation and administration would ensure that social needs obtain due consideration and protection from irresponsible individuals. Personal and social rights were capable of harmonization. Hence the objection to a simplistic utilitarianism overriding individual welfare and rights did not apply. The entrenched protection of individual liberty was to be included in any formulation of the social interest.

We are now in a position to apply the rights strategy adumbrated here to a reassessment of the relationship between human rights and welfare rights. In particular, it seems possible to offer a stronger case for the latter than proposed by those welfare- rights theorists who remain restricted by the dictates of academic fashion to rights theories that are both in individualistic and autonomy-oriented in a reductionist manner.

By adopting an inclusionist approach to human capacities, utilizing developmental and communitarian perspective prevalent in social theory as well as offering a conception of social structure as plausible as an atomistic, separatist one, the debate over rights changes emphasis. First awareness of physiological and psychological human needs of individual but within a social context becomes a powerful source of welfare- right theory. The liberal welfare theorist J. A. Hobson identified the requirement necessary for the expenditure of vital energy and insisted on securing the physiological requisites of consumption as essential 'rights of property'. The further need to motivate human beings to socially useful and productive effort carved out a psychological requisite: without stimulating the human will neither the individual nor society would function. The provision of essential incentives to operating the will could therefore by claimed as a right. It was a vital human value that demanded protection on the basis of the psychological knowledge of the time.

But welfare rights are not predicated on need alone, for mental and moral development require the presence of opportunities. One way presenting this is to assert that, under conditions of disadvantage which would include relative deprivation, individuals have a right to a (arguably, full) share of the bounties their society has on offer, irrespective of need. Another is to argue in terms of a social need for individual creativity and experimentation. Both these arguments can be further enhanced through the recognition that individual development is a norm that ought to be attained, that a failure to attain it results in dehumanization, and that all reasonable actions by the community are justified that end. Dehumanization would relate to any avoidable or rectifiable shortfall in individual well-being, and reasonable actions would pursue individual well-being up to the point where that pursuit would begin dehumanizes others. Of course, the scarcity constraining the limited needs problem requires further communal determination of the external to which human rights, having been identified, can reasonably be maximized.

Most modern rights theory as has been recently demonstrated by Shapiro is an offshoot of the natural rights tradition (1986). From the perspective of developmental and communitarian thinking, the main defects of that tradition lie in its closed lists of rights, its static conception of human nature, and its all-or-nothing approach to the conferral of a right. The result is an optimal notion of a human right as a universal, absolute standard, from which backtracking to next-best lines of defense is inevitable.

However, rights that are predicated on a developing individual, whose needs and capacities may change too, and that are undetachable from social membership are neither absolute nor universal in any sharply defined sense. Some scholars, in fact, prefer to discard the concept of human rights and replace it with civic or social rights. But because some theories of human nature define is as essentially social, the difference would not seem a vital one. All human beings are born into societies and obtain rights by dint of that membership. Extreme relativism can be eschewed if we accept that many human needs are universal and that some requirements of human agency, such as freedom, may be universal too.

Beyond those a notion of rights that converges upon current knowledge and understanding of human faculties and upon ethically acceptable assessments of human conduct is a more workable one. Such knowledge and assessments derive from sciences that focus on the study of human beings as well as from definitions of human nature, purpose, and good that are rationally agreed on within the confines of particular cultures, though open to democratic molding. At any rate, the notion of universality is better regarded as a moderate gravitational force that orders and attracts the concept of rights, rather than a powerful black hole that swallows rights up and annihilates the concept altogether.

The strategy proposed here in defense of rights is a pluralist or multiple one, predicated on the fullest interpretation of human nature that current knowledge and arrangements can sustain. It accepts the denial of differences between negative and welfare rights, but remains dissatisfied with the agency-autonomy approach, an approach that may diminish the range of rights on offer. This analysis calls for an infrequently drawn distinction to be made between establishing that people have the right to the conditions directly necessary to their functioning as moral entities and establishing that it is moral to accord people rights

As for the distinction between welfare rights and human rights, it becomes superfluous. Wellman has argued a primary welfare right can be an autonomy right, hence there is no need to supplement autonomy rights with welfare rights (1982). It is so rights to enable whatever is necessary for human life to flourish. And it recognizes the community as the natural locus of human life and activity and, thus justifies the right to assistance from others in all aspects of essential human functioning. This constitutes a liberal, rather thus libertarian, approach to human rights.

HUMAN RIGHTS AND THE DEVELOPMENT

Again we are faced with two extremely rich, complex and, above all, evolving concepts. This time human rights and development are to be related to each other, and the agenda of the inquiry is, first, to look at the two ideas; second, to search for compatibilities and contradictions. A special warning against this kind of intellectual exercise should be given. Both concepts are evolving in concrete historical contexts, and will continue to do so. Consequently, there is a limit to how much can be obtained from a conceptual, logically orientated analysis. Typologies of human rights and development concepts can certainly be constructed and related to each other in the search for compatibilities and contradictions.

There are three sets of human rights discourses, sometimes called generations: Civil and Political Rights (CPRs); Economic, Social and Cultural Rights (ESCRs) and the possible rights to be, the Solidarity Rights (SRs). No doubt the first set is related to the interests of a bourgeoisie fighting its way out of feudal constraints; the second set to the interests of the working class and other groups marginalized and exploited, hurt and hit, by the emergence of that class as a dominant class; and the third set to the same kind of problems at the international level (development, peace and ecological balance), as an effort to overcome the contradictions created by international capitalism, private and state.

And the corresponding development concepts may be made to read like chapters in any book on Western history: the first set of development concepts is blue economic growth spearheaded by an entrepreneurial class unfettered by state control or initiative, guided by the market; the second set of development concepts is a reaction to this, red development economic growth controlled, even initiated, by a state bureaucracy, but spearheaded by the labor movement, codified in a plan; and the third set of concepts is a reaction to both of the former, green development, based more on the autonomy of the local level and the presumed beauty of the smaller economic cycles, also for world solidarity, and spearheaded by the new social movements. Think globally, act locally, in other words.

Much of the current development debate is concerned with whether one first has to suffer the contradictions of the blue to become red; and then the contradictions of either or both, stemming from the circumstance that they both lead to big systems, in order to become green. As many poor, Third World countries still are to a large extent traditional green (as opposed to post-modern green), could they possibly be better off strengthening that social formation, building on top of it only a relatively weak blue and red sector? And could the rich, first and second world, blue and once red, countries have done better building down their entrepreneurial and bureaucratic giants, at the same time strengthening old and new types of local communities? The sympathies of the author are in this general direction. But what happens right now seems to be red turning blue and blue turning even more blue, with more giantism (globalization) and more giant problems, with green opposition building up all over the world, and brown/black fascist frustration with the blue, yet anti-green, around the corner.

So both human rights and development concepts have their roots in, and are reflections of, Western history. It belongs to the picture that the West has a tendency to assume that Western history = universal history, meaning that not only human rights concepts but also development concepts are abstracted from Western history, universalized and exported to the rest of the world under the guise of modernization.

This gives us four styles of development; and there can be little doubt that so far what we have seen is mainly the macro-orientated, one-dimensional economic combination. There have been two basic models, liberal-capitalist and the Marxist-Socialist, both focusing on the economic dimension in its blue and red varieties, the former leading to growth without much control, the latter to control without much growth, exemplified by the two superpowers of the Cold War. The crisis of these two models, when exported to the Third World, is known today as the development crisis. Exacerbating the situation has been the fact that the two superpowers used to demand of their client states that they by and large adhere to the blue and red development models respectively.

At the other extreme, then, is the multi-dimensional, micro-orientated approach, often called human development and community development. This approach was very popular in the early decades of post-Second World War development practice. Characteristic of most theories and some practice in this tradition is a high level of local self-reliance, short economic cycles, informal/green economies, direct democracy, much participation, and much emphasis on human growth and personal development through health services and education. Many such communities, however, tend to focus on only one such aspect and hence become very imbalanced. And many countries, of course, focus not only on the economy but also on very much else and then become more balanced. All four combinations can be found empirically, but with a prevalence of the two mentioned.

Which is the correct style of development? One possible answer would be to say all of them, the answer preferred by the present author. However, as the current processes are so overwhelmingly of the macro-orientated, one- dimensional type a strong emphasis on the opposite type is needed today, not an exclusively green, but a greener approach, to obtain better balance. Real quality of life can probably best be experienced and obtained at the micro level. But the macro level is a rather strong reality and can both facilitate and impede this local quality of life dramatically. Moreover, we may praise holism, but total thinking and total practice may lead to inaction since everything becomes too complicated to make any first move, or to totalitarianism since everything has to be changed at once. The latter may not be so dangerous if only one small community is involved. But as a blueprint for a whole country, or for all communities, it can become very dangerous. Hence, starting in one corner, with one aspect, even introducing contradictions between the old and the new to get a process going, with much richer totalities in mind, may not be the worst approach. After all, imbalance can also have a very energizing impact to rectify the imbalance.

The basic needs approach is crucial as a guide in any development process. It is a protest movement: do not forget the human level; in all the efforts to build strong countries do not forget the purpose of it all, building strong human beings! The developmentalists of the blue and red varieties tried to co-opt the human needs movement by making it one-dimensional, focusing on the material human needs most clearly related to their economic growth and institution building. Precisely because of their success, e.g. in the UN organizations of the 1960s, 1970s and 1980s, dominated by the blue and the red together, micro-level development becomes even more important today to correct the course. But it has to cater to all kinds of human needs, material and non-material. No doubt, if the green movement with its anarchist overtones of "small is beautiful" mindless of the extent to which some big is necessary, were really successful there would be scope for a protest movement in favour of more macro-orientated approaches. Today the macro movements are more than sufficiently successful, and very deeply entrenched. No reason for that worry, so far. Thus, development is seen as a complex dialectic between the micro and macro levels, and between the one-dimensional and the more holistic approaches. Where, then, do the human rights fit into all of this?

Basic human rights share with basic human needs a universal concern for everybody, not only for the needs of the strong and the rights of the privileged. Precisely for that reason first priority should be for the needs of the most needy and the rights of those whose basic human rights have been most violated. In principle these are approaches from the bottom up, an indispensable corrective to the top-heaviness and the self- serving nature of so much of what elites put forward as development. But human rights differ from human needs in being institutionalized in the particular tripartite way, linking a norm- sender (principally the UN General Assembly), norm-receivers (the governments duty-bound to implement the norm), the norm-objects (the holders of the right, usually the individuals), and then there is also the norm-content (the substantive content of the norm).

Thus, there is little doubt that by its very structure the three- tier human rights tradition is more consonant with top-heavy, blue-red development ptotected, facilitated or initiated by the state, and less with development based on small, basic and autonomous units where the primordial beta-channel human rights tradition, the mutual rights and obligations, would fit better. Thus, there is the implicit stand pointed out in the chapter: the human rights tradition is an alpha-channel, macro approach coming to the rescue of the micro level, and in so doing increasing the legitimacy of the UN General Assembly, and the governments of states, at the expense of making the micro level more dependent. As rights multiply so would, the machineries to make them really justiciable: detection and reporting processes, adjudication processes, sanction processes, review processes. The more macro the system the more complex the machineries to make the rulers accountable to their subjects.

None of this should be considered more than warnings. As long as the basic human rights work in the interests of the most deprived the tradition is invaluable even if there are certain built-in limits to growth and dangers down the road. But it raises the question: could something between the codified, top-heavy human rights and the uncodified, bottom-level mutual rights and obligations be more compatible with green development, and hence something that in the present phase of human history should be encouraged? More explicit, more codified, but also more left to local processes of accountability, breaking the age-old tradition that the more terrible the crime, and the higher the status of the actors, the higher the level of the court till one ends up at the governmental and intergovernmental, supreme court and International Court of Justice levels, thereby sanctifying those levels?

What we are looking for is the consistent translation of human rights thinking into local normative culture, but then emphasizing the basic needs entitlement rther than the universality found, for instance, in the four components of the International Bill of Human Rights. Particular human rights, made specific to local culture and historical context, may be as significant as universal human rights. But one approach does not exclude the other.

Let us then turn to another dimension of human rights thinking of basic significance for the right to development, picking up the train of thought from the earlier discussion: is the right institution or structure-orientated? The meaning of this crucial distinction can be seen from a couple of examples:

> **In the field of food**: Is the focus on being fed, or on living in a structure able to produce sufficient food through the appropriate structural arrangements?
>
> **In the field of health**: Is the focus on access to institutions for somatic and mental health service, or on living in a structure that produces a maximum of somatic and mental health?
>
> **In the field of energy:** Is the focus on having access to energy conveniently converted, or on living in a structure able to obtain energy conversion?
>
> **In the field of participation**: Is the focus on access to a ballot box or on life in a participatory structure?

In the structural approach the basic idea is that certain goods and services are made available at a high level of automaticity, and that certain bads and disservices (famine, disease, pollution, and depletion) are avoided, also at a high level of automaticity. Example: pollution/depletion control is built into the structure when a farmer growing foodstuffs for subsistence is eco-conscious because he knows that he and his offspring will be the victims of the consequences of eco-imbalances. The transnational agro-business corporation does not have to take this into account as the consequences will be far away, and when they become too disastrous the TNC will, like nomads but less softly, move to other areas on which to prey. In the structural approach certain obstacles are removed by changing the structure. The approach is preventive rather than curative, like exercise and a healthy diet when the focus is on bads and disservices. Obviously they do not exclude each other.

All of this can also be obtained at the macro level, nationally and internationally, by governments and by intergovernmental organizations, but is more decision-dependent, less automatic. And there is one thing that cannot be obtained at the macro level: direct participation, a collectivity small enough to permit not only identification but direct participation so as to trigger off the mechanisms that ensure the automaticity, not only benign action from above, but the accumulated effect of myriads of actions below. The structural approach has as a condition at least an element of smallness. We say an element for those small communities could, of course, also be parts of something bigger, such as a confederation of basic social units, based both on the solidarity within and the solidarity among such communities. The key word is actually solidarity, and the key problem is how one builds a structure where solidarity is automatic.

Again, it is obvious that the thrust of the human rights approach has been at the macro rather than at the micro level, and institutional rather than structural. The first distinction reflects the personal interests of many people behind the human rights approach, more attracted by the glory of the macro level, governmental and/or intergovernmental, than the anonymity of the local level. The second distinction reflects their deep ideology, more actor-orientated than structure-orientated, and hence more geared towards institution-building than structural transformation. These people themselves will either deny the former, or deny that it has any significance other than positive; and they would be blind to the significance of the latter, seeing, like everybody, better the biases of others than of themselves.

HUMAN RIGHTS AND THE ECOLOGICAL BALANCE

How simple it would be if we could address the problem of ecological degradation in terms of polluters and depleters, establish universal norms of upper limits for pollution and depletion consonant with the concept of sustainable development, organize a world detection system for infraction of these norms, arraign those would infract them in a world court and then let the polluters (and depleters) pay, or even suffer imprisonment. Social evils would be conceived of in terms of evil acts, and behind evil acts the evil actors would be identified and punished, to change their evil ways or at least to frighten others with similar evil intentions. And as a result we could hand over to our children, or at least our grandchildren, the badly needed clean environment to which they would be entitled.

No doubt this paradigm captures something: the tip of the iceberg not only in the sense of being visible, but also in the sense that the most visible actors may also be the worst. But a structure consists of myriads of actions, including non-actions and acts of omission. They all somehow add up, or multiply, to the well-known problems of ecological deterioration today: decrease in bio-diversity, genetic erosion, ozone layer thinning, deforestation/desertification syndromes, global warming, toxic pollution, human overpopulation. By the logic of the actor-orientated paradigm the evil actor and the evil act are the cause. But an assumed cause should be proportionate to the magnitude of such consequences. No single act has such a grotesque consequence: the threat to all life on earth. Punishment, even the removal of some polluters and depleters from the economic cycles, seems inadequate to the task of protecting the needs of life in general and human life in particular.

Another deeper perspective has been added to depletion/pollution: decreasing diversity and decreasing symbiosis. The thinning of the ozone layer, deforestation and some of the toxic pollution threatening the symbiotic basis for life on earth: photosynthesis. In addition, human beings do not at present live symbiotically with the rest of nature, and ever more human beings ever less so. At the same time the diversity is decreased through erosion, flooding, and pollution. However we analyze the causes of eco-deterioration the effects hit deeply, thus underlining the urgency of the matter.

We obtain another perspective on eco-deterioration by asking why that problem is so important today. Tentative answer: because global industrialism has brought in its wake industrial and household waste high on inorganic and synthetic organic matter that is not biodegradable, and because global commercialism has brought in its wake economic cycles so world-encompassing and opaque that nobody really knows where a problem starts and where it ends. There are causes and effects all over the place and formulas such as the causes are local, the effects are global are misleading. The causes may be in a demand supply nexus connecting people in all parts of the world, and they may cause deterioration at some very local place somewhere. Or both cause and effect may be global. Or both local.

The process perspective, over time, would lead us to ask whether, if the root cause is ever-expanding global industrialism and commercialism, and the culture underlying this, the remedy might be a return to more organically based, local eco-cycles where enzymes can still handle production and consumption waste, and the distance from cause to effect is so short that people become aware of the negative consequences of actions located in their own neighborhood and easily identify the source of the problem.

HUMAN RIGHTS AND THE PEACE

Let us now try to apply this kind of reasoning to the problems of peace and war. Again the same situation: how simple it would be if all that was needed was to couch the problem in terms of aggressors and victims, establish norms for aggression, organize a world detection and adjudication machinery (again, the latter could be the International Court of Justice rather than the Security Council, in order to use legal rather than political criteria), and punish aggressors, partly to incapacitate them, partly to teach them a lesson and partly to teach others a lesson.

One single war may be said to be a phenomenon of the same order of magnitude as the country actors, usually governments, at the beginning of the causal chain. But the institution of war, throughout the centuries, even millennia, is of a higher order of magnitude, transcending any particular aggressor-victim system. There are deeper causes at work.

Nevertheless, it makes more sense to hold a country responsible for an attack on another than to hold some economic actors in manufacture and/or trade responsible for the calamities listed today as eco-catastrophes. In clear-cut cases economic actor A may be held responsible for some specific eco-deterioration. But such clear-cut cases are becoming increasingly rare: there are too complex cycles in space, too much accumulation over time. The economic actor can hide behind the structure.

Can the aggressor also hide behind a structure? There certainly is structural violence in the sense that unintended damage is done to individuals and countries, all over the world, at all times; the 40,000 children dying every day from avoidable causes (malnutrition, lack of hygiene) are a clear example. That violence should certainly be reduced, and that reduction of violence has been more or less identified with development earlier. As with ecology the point has been made that except in some clear-cut cases it may not make such sense to hold concrete actors responsible. Some perpetrators can use this, saying: what I do is nothing compared with what is going on every hour, every day, 365 days a year.

But the nagging question is not the relative size of the individual act and the total problem. The murder can also claim that his or her act is nothing compared to what else is going on. The problem is whether the aggressor is embedded in structures, with cultures leaving him or her no choice. And murderers, except at war as soldiers or when hired, cannot claim innocence as part of structures demanding their services, as can the polluters.

Of course aggression, like anything else, is caused, and of course some of those causes are structural, some cultural. Colonialism is such a structure, linking colony and colonial power. The former may revolt to become free, the latter may repress, before (pre-emption) or after the revolt (reaction). Do those causes justify the aggression, however, and, if not, did the aggressor have a choice; could he or she will non-aggression, or was will-power suspended by the causes?

Another approach would take as the point of departure the extent to which direct violence is rooted in structure and culture, and then remove the factors that seem to be conducive to violence. A conflict may be rooted in the structure, as between buyers and sellers of labor, or of raw materials, over the terms of exchange. Or a conflict can be seen as rooted in the state system itself, with its monopoly of violence vested in states that easily set a collision course over interests and values. If the conflicts are not solved creatively, and the (political) culture defines violence as legitimate in such situations, then structure implies conflict implies violence. But conflicts do not necessarily lead to violence; that depends more on the culture.

The road to peace goes through creative conflict resolution, which usually means transformation of some structures, and through the substitution of peace cultures for violence cultures, delegitimizing violence. The use of violence to punish the aggressor neither solves conflicts nor delegitimizes violence. On the contrary, it probably freezes the conflict and legitimizes violence. In other words, it is not only not productive of human rights implementation but even counterproductive, as though the fines imposed on polluters were themselves polluting (and the argument may be that indirectly they are: by pushing the costs on to the customers small consumers may be eliminated, making room for bigger consumers with more consumer waste).

The right to live in peace can be read as the right not to be a victim of aggression. But if we assume that aggression is not random but caused by structural and cultural factors between and within the actors, then the right to live in peace is the right to live in a social setting (in the words of article 28 of the Universal Declaration of Human Rights, a social and international order) where something is done about factors, not only actors. The difficulty of the legal tradition in handling them is not solved by arguing that structural and cultural changes are political rather than legal problems. Segregation in the Southern United States and apartheid in South Africa were structures upheld by cultures of arrogance; impeding human rights implementation. People were entitled to the removal of these obstacles. In the end not to remove them, an act of omission, became illegal. Hopefully, peace problems will also eventually graduate from actor-orientated only to include structure/ culture-orientated approaches.

8

Violation of Human Rights

Human rights violations occur when actions by state or non-state actors abuse, ignore, or deny basic human rights including civil, political, cultural, social, and economic rights. Furthermore, violations of human rights can occur when any state or non-state actor breaches any part of the UDHR treaty or other international human rights or humanitarian law. In regard to human rights violations of United Nations laws, Article 39 of the United Nations Charter designates the UN Security Council or an appointed authority as the only tribunal that may determine UN human rights violations.

Human rights abuses are monitored by United Nations committees, national institutions and governments and by many independent non-governmental organisations, such as Amnesty International, International Federation of Human Rights, Human Rights Watch, World Organisation Against Torture, Freedom House, International Freedom of Expression Exchange and Anti-Slavery International. These organisations collect evidence and documentation of alleged human rights abuses and apply pressure to enforce human rights laws.

Human rights advocates agree that, sixty years after its issue, the Universal Declaration of Human Rights is still more a dream than reality. Violations exist in every part of the world. For example, Amnesty International's 2009 World Report and other sources show that individuals are tortured or abused in at least 81 countries, face unfair trials in at least 54 countries and restricted in their freedom of expression in at least 77 countries.

Not only that, but women and children in particular are marginalized in numerous ways, the press is not free in many countries, and dissenters are silenced, too often permanently. While some gains have been made over the course of the last six decades, human rights violations still plague the world today. Wars of aggression, war crimes and crimes against humanity, including genocide, are breaches of International humanitarian law and represent the most serious of human rights violations.

In efforts to eliminate violations of human rights, building awareness and protesting inhumane treatment has often led to calls for action and sometimes improved conditions. The UN Security Council has interceded with peace keeping forces, and other states and treaties (NATO) have intervened in situations to protect human rights.

Right to Life

Every human being has the inherent right to life. This right shall be protected by law. No one shall be arbitrarily deprived of his life.

– Article 6.1 of the International Covenant on Civil and Political Rights

"Everyone has the right to life, liberty and security of person."

The right to life is the essential right that a human being has the right not to be killed by another human being. The concept of a right to life is central to debates on the issues of abortion, capital punishment, euthansia, self defense and war. According to many human rights activists, the death penalty violates this right. The United Nations has called on states retaining the death penalty to establish a moratorium on capital punishment with a view to its abolition. States which do not do so face considerable moral and political pressure.

An estimated 6,500 people were killed in 2007 in armed conflict in Afghanistan – nearly half being noncombatant civilian deaths at the hands of insurgents. Hundreds of civilians were also killed in suicide attacks by armed groups.

In Brazil in 2007, according to official figures, police killed at least 1,260 individuals – the highest total to date. All incidents were officially labeled "acts of resistance" and received little or no investigation.

In Uganda, 1,500 people die each week in the internally displaced person camps. According to the World Health Organization, 500,000 have died in these camps.

Vietnamese authorities forced at least 75,000 drug addicts and prostitutes into 71 over populated "rehab" camps, labeling the detainees at "high risk" of contracting HIV/AIDS but providing no treatment.

Freedom from Torture

> "No one shall be subjected to torture or to cruel, inhuman or degrading treatment or punishment."

Throughout history, torture has been used as a method of political re-education, interrogation, punishment, and coercion. In addition to state-sponsored torture, individuals or groups may be motivated to inflict torture on others for similar reasons to those of a state; however, the motive for torture can also be for the sadistic gratification of the torturer.

Since the mid-20th century, torture is prohibited under international law and the domestic laws of most countries. It is considered to be a violation of human rights, and is declared to be unacceptable by Article 5 of the UN Universal Declaration of Human Rights. Signatories of the Geneva Conventions of 1949 and the Additional Protocols I and II of June 8, 1977 officially agree not to torture captured persons in armed conflicts, whether international or internal. Torture is also prohibited by the United Nations Convention Against Torture, which has been ratified by 157 countries.

National and international legal prohibitions on torture derive from a consensus that torture and similar ill-treatment are immoral, as well as impractical. Despite these international conventions, organisations that monitor abuses of human rights (e.g., Amnesty International, the International Rehabilitation Council for Torture Victims) report widespread use condoned by states in many regions of the world. Amnesty International estimates that at least 81 world governments currently practice torture, some of them openly.

In 2008, US authorities continued to hold 270 prisoners in Guantánamo Bay, Cuba, without charge or trial, subjecting them to "water-boarding," torture that simulates drowning. Former-President George W. Bush authorized the CIA to continue secret detention and interrogation, despite its violation of international law.

In Darfur, violence, atrocities and abduction are rampant and outside aid all but cut off. Women in particular are the victims of unrestrained assault, with more than 200 rapes in the vicinity of a displaced persons camp in one five-week period, with no effort by authorities to punish the perpetrators.

In the Democratic Republic of the Congo, acts of torture and ill treatment are routinely committed by government security services and armed groups, including sustained beatings, stabbings and rapes of those in custody. Detainees are held incommunicado, sometimes in secret detention sites. In 2007, the Republican Guard (presidential guard) and Special Services police division in Kinshasa arbitrarily detained and tortured numerous individuals labeled as critics of the government.

Freedom from Slavery

> "No one shall be held in slavery or servitude; slavery and the slave trade shall be prohibited in all their forms."

Freedom from slavery is internationally recognised as a human right. Article 4 of the Universal Declaration of Human Rights states: "No one shall be held in slavery or servitude; slavery and the slave trade shall be prohibited in all their forms".

Despite this, the number of slaves today (in 2010) is higher than at any point in history, remaining as high as 12 million to 27 million, Most are debt slaves, largely in South Asia, who are under debt bondage incurred by lenders, sometimes even for generations. Human trafficking is primarily for prostituting women and children into sex industries.

Groups such as the American Anti-Slavery Group, Anti-Slavery International, Free the Slaves, the Anti-Slavery Society, and the Norwegian Anti-Slavery Society continue to campaign to rid the world of slavery.

In northern Uganda, the Lord's Resistance Army (LRA) guerrillas have kidnapped 20,000 children over the past twenty years and forced them into service as soldiers or sexual slaves for the army.

In Guinea-Bissau, children as young as five are trafficked out of the country to work in cotton fields in southern Senegal or as beggars in the capital city. In Ghana, children five to fourteen are tricked with false promises of education and future into dangerous, unpaid jobs in the fishing industry.

In Asia, Japan is the major destination country for trafficked women, especially women coming from the Philippines and Thailand. UNICEF estimates 60,000 child prostitutes in the Philippines.

The US State Department estimates 600,000 to 820,000 men, women and children are trafficked across international borders each year, half of whom are minors, including record numbers of women and girls fleeing from Iraq. In nearly all countries, including Canada, the US and the UK, deportation or harassment are the usual governmental responses, with no assistance services for the victims.

In the Dominican Republic, the operations of a trafficking ring led to the death by asphyxiation of 25 Haitian migrant workers. In 2007, two civilians and two military officers received lenient prison sentences for their part in the operation.

In Somalia in 2007, more than 1,400 displaced Somalis and Ethiopian nationals died at sea in trafficking operations.

Right to a Fair Trial

Everyone is entitled in full equality to a fair and public hearing by an independent and impartial tribunal, in the determination of his rights and obligations and of any criminal charge against him.

The right to a fair trial has been defined in numerous regional and international human rights instruments. It is one of the most extensive human rights and all international human rights instruments enshrine it in more than one article. The right to a fair trial is one of the most litigated human rights and substantial case law has been established on the interpretation of this human right. Despite variations in wording and placement of the various fair trial rights, international human rights instrument define the right to a fair trial in broadly the same terms. The aim of the right is to ensure the proper administration of justice. As a minimum the right to fair trial includes the following fair trial rights in civil and criminal proceedings:

- the right to be heard by a competent, independent and impartial tribunal,
- the right to a public hearing,
- the right to be heard within a reasonable time,

- the right to counsel,
- the right to interpretation.

Freedom of Speech

> "Everyone has the right to freedom of opinion and expression; this right includes freedom to hold opinions without interference and to seek, receive and impart information and ideas through any media and regardless of frontiers."

Freedom of speech is the freedom to speak freely without censorship. The term freedom of expression is sometimes used synonymously, but includes any act of seeking, receiving and imparting information or ideas, regardless of the medium used. In practice, the right to freedom of speech is not absolute in any country and the right is commonly subject to limitations, such as on libel, slander, obscenity, incitement to commit a crime, etc. The right to freedom of expression is recognised as a human right under Article 19 of the Universal Declaration of Human Rights and recognised in international human rights law in the International Covenant on Civil and Political Rights (ICCPR). Article 19 of the ICCPR states that "[e]veryone shall have the right to hold opinions without interference" and "everyone shall have the right to freedom of expression; this right shall include freedom to seek, receive and impart information and ideas of all kinds, regardless of frontiers, either orally, in writing or in print, in the form of art, or through any other media of his choice".

In Sudan, dozens of human rights defenders were arrested and tortured by national intelligence and security forces.

In Ethiopia, two prominent human rights defenders were convicted on false charges and sentenced to nearly three years in prison.

In Somalia, a prominent human rights defender was murdered.

In the Democratic Republic of the Congo, the government attacks and threatens human rights defenders and restricts freedom of expression and association. In 2007, provisions of the 2004 Press Act were used by the government to censor newspapers and limit freedom of expression.

Russia repressed political dissent, pressured or shut down independent media and harassed nongovernmental organizations. Peaceful public demonstrations were dispersed with force, and lawyers, human rights defenders and journalists were threatened and attacked. Since 2000, the murders of seventeen journalists, all critical of government policies and actions, remain unsolved.

In Iraq, at least thirty-seven Iraqi employees of media networks were killed in 2008, and a total of 235 since the invasion of March 2003, making Iraq the world's most dangerous place for journalists.

Freedom of Thought, Conscience and Religion

> Everyone has the right to freedom of thought, conscience and religion; this right includes freedom to change his religion or belief, and freedom, either alone or in community with others and in public or private, to manifest his religion or belief in teaching, practice, worship and observance.
>
> – *Article 18, The International Covenant on Civil and Political Rights*

Freedom of thought, conscience and religion are closely related rights that protect the freedom of an individual or community, in public or private, to think and freely hold conscientious beliefs and to manifest religion or belief in teaching, practice, worship, and observance; the concept is generally recognised also to include the freedom to change religion or not to follow any religion. The freedom to leave or discontinue membership in a religion or religious group – in religious terms called "apostasy" – is also a fundamental part of religious freedom, covered by Article 18 of the Universal Declaration of Human Rights.

Human rights groups such as Amnesty International organises campaigns to protect those arrested and or incarcerated as a prisoner of conscience because of their conscientious beliefs, particularly concerning intellectual, political and artistic freedom of expression and association. In legislation, a conscience clause is a provision in a statute that excuses a health professional from complying with the law (for example legalising surgical or pharmaceutical abortion) if it is incompatible with religious or conscientious beliefs.

In Myanmar, the military junta crushed peaceful demonstrations led by monks, raided and closed monasteries, confiscated and destroyed property, shot, beat and detained protesters, and harassed or held hostage the friends and family members of the protesters.

In China, Falun Gong practitioners were singled out for torture and other abuses while in detention. Christians were persecuted for practicing their religion outside state-sanctioned channels.

In Kazakhstan, local authorities in a community near Almaty authorized the destruction of twelve homes, all belonging to Hare Krishna members, falsely charging that the land on which the homes were built had been illegally acquired. Only homes belonging to members of the Hare Krishna community were destroyed.

Freedom of Movement

1. "Everyone has the right to freedom of movement and residence within the borders of each State.
2. "Everyone has the right to leave any country, including his own, and to return to his country."

Freedom of movement asserts that a citizen of a state in which that citizen is present has the liberty to travel, reside in, and/or work in any part of the state where one pleases within the limits of respect for the liberty and rights of others, and to leave that state and return at any time.

In Myanmar, thousands of citizens were detained, including 700 prisoners of conscience, most notably Nobel Laureate Daw Aung San Suu Kyi. In retaliation for her political activities, she has been imprisoned or under house arrest for twelve of the last eighteen years, and has refused government offers of release that would require her to leave the country.

In Algeria, refugees and asylum-seekers were frequent victims of detention, expulsion or ill treatment. Twenty-eight individuals from sub-Saharan African countries with official refugee status from the United Nations High Commissioner for Refugees (UNHCR) were deported to Mali after being falsely tried, without legal counsel or interpreters, on charges of entering Algeria illegally. They were dumped near a desert town where a Malian armed group was active, without food, water or medical aid.

In Kenya, authorities violated international refugee law when they closed the border to thousands of people fleeing armed conflict in Somalia.

Asylum-seekers were illegally detained at the Kenyan border without charge or trial and forcibly returned to Somalia.

In northern Uganda, 1.6 million citizens remained in displacement camps. In the Acholi subregion, the area most affected by armed conflict, 63 percent of the 1.1 million people displaced in 2005 were still living in camps in 2007, with only 7,000 returned permanently to their places of origin.

Right to Keep and Bear Arms

The right to keep and bear arms for defence is described in the philosophical and political writings of Aristotle, Cicero, John Locke, Machiavelli, the English Whigs and others. In countries with an English common law tradition, a long-standing common law right to keep and bear arms has long been recognised, as pre-existing in common law, prior even to the existence of national constitutions.

Future Generations

In 1997, UNESCO adopted the Declaration on the Responsibilities of the Present Generation Towards the Future Generation. The Declaration opens with the words:

> Mindful of the will of the peoples, set out solemnly in the Charter of the United Nations, to 'save succeeding generations from the scourge of war' and to safeguard the values and principles enshrined in the Universal Declaration of Human Rights, and all other relevant instruments of international law.

Article 1 of the declaration states "the present generations have the responsibility of ensuring that the needs and interests of present and future generations are fully safeguarded." The preamble to the declaration states that "at this point in history, the very existence of humankind and its environment are threatened" and the declaration covers a variety of issues including protection of the environment, the human genome, biodiversity, cultural heritage, peace, development, and education. The preamble recalls that the responsibilities of the present generations towards future generations has been referred to in various international instruments, including the Convention for the Protection of the World Cultural and

Natural Heritage (UNESCO 1972), the United Nations Framework Convention on Climate Change and the Convention on Biological Diversity (Rio de Janeiro, 1992), the Rio Declaration on Environment and Development (UN Conference on Environment and Development, 1992), the Vienna Declaration and Programme of Action (World Conference on Human Rights, 1993) and a number of UN General Assembly resolutions relating to the protection of the global climate for present and future generations adopted since 1990.

Sexual Orientation and Gender Identity

Sexual orientation and gender identity rights relate to the expression of sexual orientation and gender identity based on the right to respect for private life and the right not to be discriminated against on the ground of "other status" as defined in various human rights conventions, such as article 17 and 26 in the United Nations International Covenant on Civil and Political Rights and article 8 and article 14 in the European Convention on Human Rights.

As of 2011, homosexual behaviour is illegal in 76 countries and punishable by execution in seven countries. The criminalisation of private, consensual, adult sexual relations, especially in countries where corporal or capital punishment is involved, is one of the primary concerns of LGBT human rights advocates.

Other issues include: government recognition of same-sex relationships, LGBT adoption, sexual orientation and military service, immigration equality, anti-discrimination laws, hate crime laws regarding violence against LGBT people, sodomy laws, anti-lesbianism laws, and equal age of consent for same-sex activity.

A global charter for sexual orientation and gender identity rights has been proposed in the form of the 'Yogyakarta Principles', a set of 29 principles whose authors say they apply International Human Rights Law statutes and precedent to situations relevant to LGBT people's experience. The principles were presented at a United Nations event in New York on November 7, 2007, co-sponsored by Argentina, Brazil and Uruguay.

The principles have been acknowledged with influencing the French proposed UN declaration on sexual orientation and gender identity, which focuses on ending violence, criminalisation and capital punishment and does not include dialogue about same-sex marriage or right to start a family. The proposal was supported by 67 of the then 192 member countries of the United Nations, including all EU member states and the United States. An alternative statement opposing the proposal was initiated by Syria and signed by 57 member nations, including all 27 nations of the Arab League as well as Iran and North Korea.

Trade

Although both the Universal Declaration of Human Rights and the International Covenant on Economic, Social and Cultural Rights emphasise the importance of a right to work, neither of these documents explicitly mention free trade as a mechanism for ensuring this fundamental right.

Some experts argue that trade is inherent to human nature and that when governments inhibit international trade they directly inhibit the right to work and the other indirect benefits, like the right to education, that increased work and investment help accrue. Others have argued that the ability to trade does not affect everyone equally—often groups like the rural poor, indigenous groups and women are less likely to access the benefits of increased trade.

On the other hand, it can be argued that it is no longer primarily individuals but companies that trade, and therefore it cannot be guaranteed as a human right. Additionally, trying to fit too many concepts under the umbrella of what qualifies as a human right has the potential to dilute their importance. Finally, it is difficult to define a right to trade as either "fair" or "just" in that the current trade regime produces winners and losers but its reform is likely to produce different winners and losers.

Human Right to Water and Sanitation

The right to water has been recognised in a wide range of international documents, including treaties, declarations and other standards. For instance, the 1979 Convention on the Elimination of All Forms of Discrimination Against Women (CEDAW) requires State parties to ensure to women the right to "enjoy adequate living conditions, particularly in relation to water supply". The 1989 Convention on the Rights of the Child (CRC) requires States parties to combat disease and malnutrition "through the provision of adequate nutritious foods and clean drinking-water".

The most clear definition of the Human right to water has been issued by the UN Committee on Economic, Social and Cultural Rights. This treaty body interpreting legal obligations of State parties to the International Covenant on Economic, Social and Cultural Rights (ICESCR) issued in 2002 a non-binding interpretation affirming that access to water was a condition for the enjoyment of the right to an adequate standard of living and inextricably related to the right to the highest attainable standard of health and therefore a human right: The human right to water entitles everyone to sufficient, safe, acceptable, physically accessible and affordable water for personal and domestic uses.

On July 28, 2010, the United Nations General Assembly declared water and sanitation as human rights. Since then, all States have at least ratified one human rights convention which explicitly or implicitly recognises the right, and they all have signed at least one political declaration recognising this right.

Sexual and Reproductive Rights

Human rights include women's rights and sexual and reproductive rights. Sexual and reproductive rights are part of a continuum of human rights, which includes the rights to life, health and education, the rights to equality and non-discrimination, and the right to decide the timing, number and spacing of one's children.

Reproductive and sexual rights as part of human rights was affirmed internationally at the Programme of Action of the International Conference on Population and Development (ICPD) in Cairo in 1994. It was the first among international development frameworks to address issues related to sexuality, sexual and reproductive health, and reproductive rights.

The ICPD Programme of Action in paragraph 7.2 "defines an individual's sexual and reproductive health as complete well-being related to sexual activity and reproduction. Sexual and reproductive health and rights (SRHR) encompass both entitlements and freedoms. These are not a new set of rights but human rights in existing human rights instruments related to sexual and reproductive autonomy and the attainment of sexual and reproductive health. Additionally, the 1995 Beijing Platform for Action (PfA) expands this definition to cover both sexuality and reproduction by affirming in paragraph 96 the right to exercise control over and make decisions about one's sexuality, including sexual and reproductive health, free of coercion, discrimination and violence."

World Health Organisation

Reproductive rights were first established as a subset of human rights at the United Nations 1968 International Conference on Human Rights. The sixteenth article of the resulting Proclamation of Teheran states, "Parents have a basic human right to determine freely and responsibly the number and the spacing of their children."

Reproductive rights may include some or all of the following rights: the right to legal or safe abortion, the right to control one's reproductive functions, the right to quality reproductive healthcare, and the right to education and access in order to make reproductive choices free from coercion, discrimination, and violence.

Reproductive rights may also be understood to include education about contraception and sexually transmitted infections, and freedom from coerced sterilisation and contraception, protection from gender-based practices such as Female Genital Cutting (FGC) and Male Genital Mutilation (MGM).

Right to Internet Access and Digital Rights

In October 2009, Finland's Ministry of Transport and Communications announced that every person in Finland would have the legal right to Internet access. Since July 2010, the government has legally obligated telecommunications companies to offer broadband Internet access to every permanent residence and office. The connection must be "reasonably priced" and have a downstream rate of at least 1 Mbit/s.

In March 2010, the BBC, having commissioned an opinion poll, reported that "almost four in five people around the world believe that access to the internet is a fundamental right." (BBC 2011) The poll, conducted by the polling company Globe Scan for the BBC World Service, collated the answers of 27,973 adult citizens across 26 countries to find that 79 per cent of adults either strongly agreed or somewhat agreed with the statement: "access to the internet should be a fundamental right of all people" (OHCHR 1951).

Right to Non-Refoulement vs. Right to Asylum

Non-refoulement is the right not to be returned to a place of persecution and is the foundation for international refugee law, as outlined in the 1951 Convention Relating to the Status of Refugees. Both the right to non-refoulement and the right to asylum have taken centre stage in recent debates over the treatment of refugees. A central worry about the right to asylum is that it can limit a states power to handle a mass influx of refugees. Processing asylum applications can take a considerable amount of time, and this amount rises with the amount of refugees applying. This creates an incentive for more refugees to apply, since they are allowed to stay in the country during the application process. One potential solution to the problem of mass influx is proposed by U.S.based political philosopher Andy Lamey. Lamey proposes a portable procedural model that focuses on the right to non-refoulement. Crucially, the procedural rights defended by this model can be applied outside national borders, within any rights respecting country; this allows the burden of mass influx to be shared by a plurality of countries without violating the procedural rights of the refugee.

Right to Democracy

1. "Everyone has the right to take part in the government of his country, directly or through freely chosen representatives."
2. "Everyone has the right to equal access to public service in his country."
3. "The will of the people shall be the basis of the authority of government; this will shall be expressed in periodic and genuine elections which shall be by universal and equal suffrage and shall be held by secret vote or by equivalent free voting procedures."

In Zimbabwe, hundreds of human rights defenders and members of the main opposition party, the Movement for Democratic Change (MDC), were arrested for participating in peaceful gatherings.

In Pakistan, thousands of lawyers, journalists, human rights defenders and political activists were arrested for demanding democracy, the rule of law and an independent judiciary.

In Cuba, at the end of 2007, sixty two prisoners of conscience remained incarcerated for their nonviolent political views or activities.

Conclusion

In conclusion we can say that human rights exist, as embodied in the Universal Declaration of Human Rights and the entire body of international human rights law. They are recognized, at least in principle, by most nations and form the heart of many national constitutions. Yet the actual situation in the world is far distant from the ideals envisioned in the Declaration.

Many are skeptical about the full realization of human rights as a remote and unattainable goal. Even international human rights laws are difficult to enforce and pursuing a complaint can take years and a great deal of money. These international laws serve as a restraining function but are insufficient to provide adequate human rights protection, as evidenced by the stark reality of abuses perpetrated daily.

Discrimination is rampant throughout the world. Thousands are in prison for speaking their minds. Torture and politically motivated imprisonment, often without trial, are commonplace, condoned and practiced even in some democratic countries.

Conclusion

The Universal Declaration of Human Rights speaks of the equal and inalienable rights of all members of the human family and goes on to provide a long list of norms that allegedly fall within this category. These include:

(1) due process rights such as rights to a fair trial or to freedom from arbitrary arrest;

(2) rights of personal security and autonomy such as rights to protection from crime, to freedom of movement, to privacy, and to freedom of thought and religion;

(3) rights of political participation such as rights to vote and to express one's political opinions;

(4) equality rights such as rights to freedom from discrimination and to equality before the law; and

(5) economic and social rights such as rights to a decent standard of living, education, and medical care.

In effect the Universal Declaration asserts that all humans have inalienable rights to the freedoms and benefits that are enjoyed in the most developed and humane democracies. Its assertion is not merely that providing these things to all is a desirable goal or ideal; it is rather the much stronger claim that making these things available to all is obligatory. Many people, including ones who are sympathetic to the general idea of human rights, have worried that the claims of the Universal Declaration are utopian. Its list of rights is a long one, and the implementation of those rights requires resources that many countries lack at present. These rights are said to be universal and inalienable, but little or nothing is said about the severely retarded, aliens, and those convicted of serious crimes. The rights declared tend to be defined in broad terms, and their weight or priority in competition with each other or with other values or norms is not specified. Further, the world in which these rights must be implemented is culturally and politically diverse, unstable and subject to conflict, and limited in its resources for satisfying human desires and dreams. Thus it is hard to resist the conclusion that the Universal Declaration is unrealistic and utopian, that it is poorly suited to the world in which most humans live. And it is also hard to resist the worry that insistence on respect everywhere for all of the rights in the Universal Declaration may rule out trade-offs that are essential to the progress of many countries. We want to argue, however, that human rights are not inherently utopian. Our thesis is that it is possible to revise the Universal Declaration's conception of human rights so as to avoid the charge of utopianism while preserving much of its content.

To focus our discussion it will be helpful to have in mind some examples of the kinds of conflicts that an extensive list of broadly phrased rights can generate. First, there is the case where one person's right to "A" conflicts with another person's right to "A". For example, Asim's exercise of his right to a fair trial may reveal information and generate publicity that makes it difficult or impossible to satisfy Amiya's right to a fair trial. Second, there is the case where one person's right to "A" conflicts with another person's right to "B". For example, Asim's exercise of his right to a fair trial may require an infringement of Amiya's right to privacy. A variant of this occurs when implementing an effective right to someone uses up the only resources that could have been used to implement an effective right to others. Providing the personnel to conduct fair criminal trials may use resources without which it is impossible to implement a right to education. A third type of conflict involving rights occurs when one person's right to something conflicts with the interests of other persons. For example, some people's exercise of their right to freedom of religion in proselytizing new converts may conflict with the interest of parents in preventing their children from being captured by bizarre religious sects.

To understand the ways in which conflicts between rights and other norms can be avoided or relieved, it is useful to analyze in detail the components of a fully specified right. First, rights identify a certain status that gives one the right, that makes one the right holder. These conditions of possession may be narrow enough to apply to only one person (for example, the person named in a will) or broad enough to include the whole human race. Procedures for permanently alienating a right, such as selling it, repudiating it, or forfeiting it, can also be specified in its conditions of possession.

Second, many rights can only be brought into play in specified circumstances. A right to a trial by jury, for example, can only be activated when one has been charged with a crime. Many rights generated obligations only when they are invoked or claimed in appropriate circumstances. These conditions of engagement are different from conditions of possession because the fact that one has not been charged with a crime does not imply that one does not, as a general matter of say, constitutional law, have a right to a trial by jury. When an operable right is successfully claimed or invoked it can be said to be engaged. To waive or refuse to exercise one's right in a case in which it is operable often prevents the right from being engaged. Some rights, however, seem to be continuously engaged. A person's right not to be tortured would be engaged and would generate obligations not to torture even though the person being tortured was too weak to involve that right.

Third, the weight of a right involves the specification of its rank of importance in relation to other norms. Weight pertains to whether a right can sometimes be overridden by other considerations in cases of conflict. A prima facie right is a non absolute right whose weight in competition with other considerations is not fully specified.

Fourth, the addressees of a right are the parties who bear obligation or other normative burdens such as liabilities or disabilities in regard to making available the prescribed freedom of benefit. Conflicts that arise here if the addressees of a right are unable to comply while satisfying their higher priority obligations.

Finally, the scope of a right specifies what freedom or benefit must be made available under what circumstances to the right holder. A right's scope specifies what it is to. If, for example, the right to freedom of speech does not include protection for speeches made from the visitor's gallery during sessions of Lok Sabha, then this exception would be specified in, or be a consequence of, the right's scope.

Suppose that Asim's right to be fair conflicts with Amiya's right to privacy in the following way: Amiya is an essential witness in case, but in order to serve as a witness he will have to reveal some information about himself that he would rather keep private. One way to resolve this conflict would be to decide that at least one of these rights is not a right at all and to remove it from one's catalog of rights. Other ways of resolving this conflict are suggested by the distinctions just drawn. First, we could change the conditions of possession of one of these rights so that Amiya or Asim ceased to be a right holder. Here one might allege, for example, that Amiya had forfeited his right to privacy by some earlier criminal act. But if one wanted to preserve the idea that the right to privacy is inalienable then this option would be unattractive. Second, one could resolve the conflict by getting one of the parties to waive or not exercise his or her right. Third, the conflict could be resolved by holding that one right was of higher priority than the other and thus overrides it. Fourth, the conflict could be ended or at least be suspended temporarily by a breakdown of government making it impossible to proceed with any trials. Finally, the conflict could be resolved by a change in the scope of one of the rights. It might be decided, for example, that the scope of Amiya's right to privacy is limited in such a way that it does not protect his right to privacy in cases where that would interfere with providing due process in a criminal case.

It is clear from this that there are at least five ways of resolving conflicts of rights and that there are five corresponding ways in which one can fail to have a right. Thus talk about not having or alienating a right can mean a number of different things. When we say that a right is inalienable we may not mean to rule out all of the ways in which a right can fail to dictate a result in a case.

If a right is universal and inalienable, this is an aspect of its conditions of possession. The Universal Declaration asserts that human rights are both universal and inalienable, and these strong claims are attractive in our egalitarian age because they ensure that no one is left without human rights. We assert that human rights are universal to avoid leaving the oppressed noncitizen, minority group member or social outcaste without rights to appeal to. And we assert that human rights are inalienable to avoid giving oppressive governments the option of saying that their subjects' rights have been forfeited or voluntarily given up.

It seems that these claims are plausible in regard to some but not all of the norms that we now take to be human rights. The right to freedom from torture, for example, seems to be universal and inalienable. All humans including persons who lived long ago, young children, the retarded, and the senile can plausibly be said to have this right, and there is no objection to the idea that this is a right that people cannot permanently give up or forfeit. To the objection that the right not to be tortured is alienable because we can imagine extreme cases in which torturing someone would be justifiable because it is the only way of saving the human race. The assertion that a right is inalienable does not imply that it cannot be overridden in some cases by more important considerations. It should also be emphasized that the claim that a right is inalienable does not imply that it cannot be waived in particular cases or that its scope contains no exceptions.

Although strong claims of universality and inalienability may be true of some rights, they are not true of many other rights. Some of the rights declared in the Universal Declaration cannot be universal in the strong sense of applying to all humans at all times because they assert that people are entitled to services that presuppose contemporary or at least relatively recent social and political institutions. Due process rights presuppose modern legal systems and the institutional safeguards they provide. Social and economic rights presuppose modern relations of production and the institutions of the twentieth-century welfare or socialist state. Our point here is not merely that people living 10,000 years ago would not have thought to demand these rights; it is rather that the scope of these rights can only be defined by reference to institutions that have emerged relatively recently in human history. Trans historical rights would have to be formulated in much broader terms. Perhaps some of these rights could be reformulated so as to avoid this objection, but the result would be very abstract rights that are subject to a variety of interpretations and hence less useful in political criticism.

Another problem about universality concerns humans of severely limited mental capacities. Here the issue is whether humans who are very young, severely retarded, comatose, or senile are included when we assert that all humans have these rights. That we would want to say that these humans have some human rights, such as the right to life, to due process, and to freedom from torture, but we doubt that we would want to say that these humans have the right to vote, to run for political office, to found a family, or to freedom of movement. These rights presuppose a greater degree of rationality and autonomy than these humans possess. One way of drawing the boundary here would be to distinguish between the rights of humans and the rights of persons.

A third problem about universality concerns the rights of noncitizens. Although aliens in a country should have most of the same rights that citizens do, it is not wrong to deny aliens some political rights such as the right to vote or to hold public office. The Universal Declaration implicitly recognizes this when the right of political participation is phrased as a right of everyone to participate directly or indirectly in the government of his country (Article 21). The Covenant on Civil and Political Rights makes this explicit by formulating political rights as rights of citizens rather than of everyone.

These three problems suggest that claims about the universality of human rights need to be understood as containing some qualifications. Similar problems arise in regard to the claim that human rights are inalienable. Inalienable means that a right cannot be forfeited or voluntarily given up. If a person has an inalienable right to A, this implies that an attempt to repudiate permanently one's own right to A or an attempt by others to take away one's right to A would be without moral effect. If everyone lacks the power to eliminate permanently a right of his or her own or of others, the right is immune to elimination and thus inalienable. Since the right cannot be eliminated, other persons who act as if it had been eliminated may violate it.

The first problem with the claim that human rights are inalienable is found in the fact that some of the rights in the Universal Declaration are forfeitable in many legal systems by the commission of serious crimes. In the United States, for example, one's right to vote can be forfeited by the conviction of a felony and we cannot see that taking the vote away from felons violates a still-existing moral right to political participation. If a person's moral right to vote could survive the revocation of his or her legal right to vote as an inalienable right would then subsequent failure to grant and honor the legal right would constitute a prima facie wrong as a violation of a moral right. But no such prima facie wrong seems to be involved in denying convicted felons the right to vote. Hence this right seems to be alienable.

The idea that one cannot permanently repudiate one's rights is also problematic in some cases. The reason why some eighteenth century theorists wanted to assert the inalienability of natural rights was that they wanted to counter the Hobbesian claim that people had agreed to give up all of their natural rights when they left the state of nature and entered civil society. Perhaps selling oneself into slavery would amount to a permanent alienation of one's liberty, and perhaps we can agree that the right to liberty is inalienable and hence that individuals lack the moral power to do this. We doubt, however, that it is plausible to say that all human rights are immune to repudiation. Suppose that a public official repudiated his moral and legal rights to privacy so that his life would be an open book. This might be a foolish thing to do, but it is not clear that individuals lack the power to do this or that other persons would act wrongly if they acted in accordance with this repudiation. A more realistic example involves agreeing to accept certain permanent limits on what one can say and publish in order to receive a security clearance for government intelligence work.

Even if rights cannot be alienated in the sense of permanently given up it does not follow that one cannot waive or refrain from exercising them in particular cases. If one could not waive or refrain from exercising one's right to emigrate, one would have to be constantly moving from country to country. A claim that human rights can neither be given up permanently nor waived temporarily would have very paternalistic overtones since it amounts to an assertion that one must keep and use on every possible opportunity all of one's human rights.

One way of preserving the claim that human rights are universal and inalienable in a very strong sense of these terms is to reduce drastically the number of rights that one takes to be human rights. Scholars have taken this approach to its logical extreme by arguing that inalienable rights to be rights that cannot be forfeited, given up, waived, or overridden, and that can never be rendered moot by the fact that the parties obligated by them are unable to meet their obligations. Having given this extremely strong definition of what an inalienable right is, we are is forced to the conclusion that there is only one such right, a vague and general right to protection.

This is an unconditional and inalienable right to institutions which provide general protection to all high-order goods and permit each individual member of the community to place the burden of proof upon those who would deny him his good or interfere with his pursuit of it.

It may be useful to try to identify some basic human rights that are universal and inalienable in some strong sense. Part of our objection here is that very abstract rights such as a right to protection or a right to equal consideration admit of radically different interpretations and hence are not of much use in political criticism. For this purpose one needs more specific norms like those of the Universal Declaration that make reference to particular problems and institutions.

Two reasons for saying that the Universal Declaration is utopian are that the rights it contains are stated in broad terms with few qualifications and that no ranking is provided for these rights even though it is obvious that they can conflict. Our project of bringing human rights down to earth is by arguing that most of them must be understood to contain exceptions or qualifications and that few of them are absolute in competition with each other or with other considerations such as the preservation of international peace.

Scope, it will be recalled, concerns what a right is to, the freedoms it benefits that the right prescribes to the rightholder when it is engaged. For our purposes here we will not need a sharp boundary between conditions of operability, which pertain to when a right can be brought into play, and scope. Weight, it will be recalled, concerns the ranking or priority of a right when it conflicts with other considerations.

We would probably be willing to treat the matter as one of scope, and one might hope that all conflicts of norms could be dealt with by redrawing boundaries and inserting exceptions. Eventually norms would have their boundaries drawn in ways that minimize or eliminate the possibility of conflicts, and the relative priority of deferent norms would be reflected in the expansion or retraction of their boundaries when they cover contiguous areas. But there are at least three barriers standing in the way of this program. One is that we can not anticipate all conflicts of rights with each other and with other considerations, and we are often uncertain about what we should do in the cases that we can imagine. The second barrier is that a right containing sufficient qualifications and exceptions to avoid all possible conflicts would probably be too complex to be teachable to humans. Finally, the third barrier is that relieving a conflict by building in an exception will sometimes have the incorrect implication that the overridden right did not really apply in the case and hence that we need feel no regret about our treatment of the person whose right was overridden. If moral tragedy is possible then there may be conflicts not only at the edges of rights and other norms but between their very centers. Furthermore, adding exceptions to cover such cases may cause us to misunderstand what is happening as nontragic. Retaining the vocabulary of weight and overriding may help us to preserve the possibility of recognizing moral tragedy when it occurs.

The utopian character of the Universal Declaration was remedied in part when a number of the nations of Western Europe undertook to rewrite it into a treaty that would create an international law of human rights among the signatories. The result was the European Convention on Human Rights, and the rights it declares are much more qualified than those of the Universal Declaration. In comparison with the Universal Declaration's simple right to life, the European Convention's characterization of that right is so cautious as to seem excessively qualified.

1. Everyone's right to life shall be protected by law. No one shall be deprived of his life intentionally save in the execution of a sentence of a court following his conviction of a crime for which this is provided by law.
2. Deprivation of life shall not be regarded as inflicted in contravention of this article when it results from the use of force which is no more than absolutely necessary;
   (a) in defense of any person from unlawful violence;
   (b) in order to effect a lawful arrest or to prevent the escape of a person lawfully detained;
   (c) in action lawfully taken for the purpose of quelling a riot or insurrection.

Although these qualifications greatly reduce the potential for conflicts between the right to life and other considerations, they do not entirely eliminate the possibility of such conflicts. Thus the European Convention also offers a partial ranking of the rights it declares. It allows countries to derogate from their obligations under the Convention during time of war or other public emergency threatening the life of the nation. But any restrictions on people's rights that are imposed under such circumstances must be publicly declared and must be only those that are strictly required by the exigencies of the situation.

And no derogations are allowed in regard to the right to life, the right not to be tortured, the right to freedom from slavery, and the right against being convicted for violating retroactive criminal laws. Similar provisions are found in the International Covenant on Civil and Political Rights. The effect of these provisions is to forbid states to murder, torture, or enslave during an emergency while permitting them to suspend freedom of expression and due process of law.

Thus the view of the international human rights movement is that rights not to be murdered, tortured, or enslaved are absolute or near absolute, and that is a view that we can heartily endorse and defend. But many other rights, particularly political rights, are far from absolute.

Many of the obligations that human rights generate for government are expensive to comply with, and many governments today have very limited resources with which to meet people's needs and to provide for the protection of their rights. One of the great inadequacies of the Universal Declaration is that it does not speak to this problem, it does not say which rights are to be implemented when resources are insufficient to implement them all. Further, it postulates a number of economic and social rights that are extremely expensive to implement.

A number of writers have suggested that the main way to deal with this problem is to delete economic and social rights from our lists of human rights. Maurice Cranston (1967, 1973), for example, fears that if welfare rights are counted as human rights, the impossibility of realizing them at present will cause many people to think that human rights are mere ideals or aspirations and thus devalue the language of rights. Although welfare rights are obviously expensive to implement, Cranston believes that civil and political rights are easily implemented in any country: Since those rights are for the most part rights against interference, a large part of the legislation needed has to do no more than restrain the government's own executive arm.

This contrast is greatly oversimplified. Human rights require governments not only to respect them but also to protect them against violations by others. One's right to life or liberty can be violated by individuals as well as by states, and the state is obligated to provide effective protections for these rights. If we remove from the human rights roster all of the rights that, say, Bangladesh cannot effectively implement now, there will be much more than just economic and social rights missing from that list. Weak governments often have little control over regional officials and hence are often powerless to keep those officials from violating people's rights.

When one attempts to formulate human rights standards for the whole world one must assume some representative level of resources and institutional adequacy. To use Rawls's stages for illustration, international human rights would be formulated at a stage intermediate between the original position; where one formulates very abstract principles of justice and some very basic rights, and the constitutional stage, where one is designing institutions for a particular country in a particular era. As relatively specific international guides to what should be included in national constitutions and institutions, international human rights must assume the available institutions of a particular era and a level of resources that is typical of countries in that era. If too high a level of resources is assumed, the rights formulated will be very demanding and are therefore vulnerable to charges of utopianism whereas if too low a level is chosen the list will be rather undemanding for many countries and hence not useful in political criticism.

The level of resources chosen by the authors of the Universal Declaration was probably too high; it corresponds to what the most developed nations are capable of doing. But this admission does not require one to assume that the appropriate level is one that the poorest nations could satisfy or that economic and social rights must be removed entirely from the list. Perhaps the levels of resources now available to most countries would at least allow one to assert rights to satisfaction of people's basic physical needs.

In opposition to this point of view Charles Frankel argued that assertions of human rights are nonsensical when those who are obligated by those rights are not all able to comply. It would be nonsense to say that a non swimmer has a moral duty to swim to the help of a drowning man. This argument, which is designed to show that claims about human rights have dangerously utopian overtones, fails to take into account the difference between attributing duties to individuals in particular cases and attributing general duties to whole classes of people. The ascription of a duty to a whole class of people is not rendered nonsensical by the fact that in some cases people with the duty will be unable to comply. Otherwise many general duties (for example, the duty to take good care of one's children) would be nonsensical since there are often a few people who are unable to comply with such norms for financial or psychological reasons. For a general norm to be realistic it is only required that most people be able to comply. Like many other critics of rights, Frankel construed a right as a simpler and more absolute category than it actually is. An exaggeration of the power of claims about rights can be seen in the following argument:

> If someone said that it would be good if all school children had not lunches at public expense...we would ask about its cost, compare that cost to implementing other proposals on the public agenda, and determine whether, if we adopted it, we would be sacrificing things we thought more valuable. But if someone says that all school children have a right to hot lunches, such questions are out of order. If it is a right, then it has to be implemented. So long as rights are rights, they are priority items on the public agenda. They lie outside the range of everyday political decision.

It is true that rights are priority items on the public agenda and that if a decision is governed by a right then ordinary cost-benefiting balancing is not appropriate. But this does not turn rights into absolutes that demand implementation no matter what. The recognition of a person's right to something against government does not mean that government officials cannot ask whether supplying that person with that thing at a particular time is compatible with meeting all of that government's obligations that are of high priority. Recognition of a right in a context where the resources for its implementation are nearly available places it on the political agenda and identifies its realization as a mandatory object of struggle. But it does not imply that we must immediately implement that right at the cost of sacrificing things that are of higher priority.

The complex ways in which rights are related to implementing social and political practices can also be seen in the fact that rights can be implemented both in a group's morality and in its law. This fact has important implications for questions about whether it is pointless to assert the existence of human rights when resources for implementing them as effective legal rights are limited or unavailable. Suppose, for example, that a government lacks the financial and human resources needed for creating a social security system that will satisfy in the most effective manner a human right to assistance during periods of illness and disability. It does not follow from this that such a right to assistance is irrelevant to this country or that it should not be recognized. First, it can be implemented as a moral right in the sense that people recognize as part of their morality the legitimacy of calling upon government and other people to assist one during illness and disability. This means, for example, that the importance of providing for the sick and disabled is recognized, that people criticizing those who call for such assistance are likely to be rebuked, and that governmental officials who deny any responsibility to work towards providing for such assistance are criticized. Implementation of a right in a group's morality can be a factor in promoting social and political change.

Second, a moral right to assistance during disability falls upon individuals when government lacks the resources to provide an appropriate system for implementing the right. A norm that is firmly enough grounded in considerations of human dignity, autonomy, and welfare to qualify as a human right will not just disappear when it is impossible to comply with it in the standard way. In a country where resources are insufficient to implement through governmental action a legal right to assistance during disability and illness, a number of implications could have an obligation to use the resources available, once higher priority obligations are met, to implement this right as a legal right. Another implication could be that government officials have obligations to promote the growth of resources that will make full implementation of this right possible, and citizens may have obligations to cooperate with these efforts. Still another possible implication is that governments with surplus resources have obligations to assist in making available or generating the resources that are required for the implementation of this and other rights. Finally, residents of the country may have obligations to use their own resources, time, and energies to provide informally or through organized charities the assistance that sick and disabled people need. In this kind of situation families may incur a special obligation to help their members during sickness and disability; a charity system might then be used to provide for those without families. Thus traditional forms of family support and charity assistance can be seen as modes of implementing peoples rights to assistance during disability and illness under circumstances where more formal governmental systems are unavailable.

Having defended briefly the usefulness and intelligibility of recognizing human rights even in circumstances where they cannot be fully implemented immediately, we now want to indicate some points of agreement with such writers as Cranston and Frankel. One point of agreement is that it is important to preserve the distinction between such benefits as hot school lunches or holidays with pay that are merely good things and benefits and freedoms whose availability is of such paramount importance that it is appropriate to view them as rights.

Another point of agreement is that the authors of the Universal Declaration were too expansive in the rights they declared. Some of these lack the requisite importance, and others are perhaps too far from implementation given the resources and knowledge available today. But we do not agree that the appropriate way to shorten the list is to eliminate all welfare rights. The line of overreaching by the authors of contemporary rights documents need not be viewed as the line between civil and political rights and welfare rights.

A final point of agreement is that the expectations of people in developing countries should not be raised so high that their revolutionary demands make impossible the degree of national and international stability that the growth of human productivity requires. Without the growth of such productivity and increase in our ability to distribute fairly its rewards, the chances of improved conditions in regard to basic rights are slim. But this should not be taken as a condemnation of the rhetoric of rights since the role of that rhetoric in creating such expectations is small, especially in comparison to that of communications devices that permit people everywhere to see how well most Europeans and Americans live. Nor should this concern be allowed to turn into a mere endorsement of the international status quo. A demand that society and production be organized in such a way that all people can find the means to satisfy at least their most basic needs and have protections for their most basic rights is not unreasonable, even if the consequences of this demand by people all over the earth make difficult such domestic and international politics. It is important to distinguish a legitimate concern that people's demands not exceed human capacities to produce from a reactionary concern to keep people's expectations low so that they won't rock the boat.

We are not attacking, for instance, the right of free speech or any of the other specific rights listed in the U.S. Constitution's Bill of Rights or the United Nations' Charter. We are rather, attacking any specific right's being called a 'human right'. Such designation is not only fraudulent but, in case anyone might want to say that there can be noble lies, grossly wicked, amounting indeed to genocide.

In the past, for instance, it was commonly argued that God endowed all human beings with certain inalienable rights. One can see why it would be appropriate to call the rights in question 'human rights'. In the present, one can imagine utilitarians arguing that certain rights when adhered to naturally conduce to the greatest happiness of the greatest numbers of human beings and that these may therefore be designated human rights.

Both these arguments are, however, incomplete as stated and have to draw on external resources in order to arrive at their conclusions, namely, that such-and-such things are human rights. For example, where in fact do we find God decreeing that the inalienable rights of the Declaration of Independence are rights, much less rights belonging to all human beings? Certainly not in the Bible. Nor, so far as we are aware, in any other collection of purported divine revelations. Plainly, they have had their actual origin in other places and arguments: to be specific, in the intuitively valid arguments. And when the utilitarian says 'naturally conduce to the greatest happiness of the greatest number of human beings' we are certainly entitled to ask what he means by saying 'naturally' and he will have to say, 'Because of what human nature is'.

In saying this the utilitarian takes us to the intuitively valid argument for human rights that we have been referring to: that argument which mirrors in propositional form the actual causal genesis of subjective rights in whatever communities profess them and that seems alone to provide an objective foundation for asserting the existence of natural human rights or, more briefly, human rights.

The argument we have been speaking of has been rooted historically in the peculiarly Grecian-Western conflation of man's nature into reason: illustrated in Plato's identification, in *The Republic*, of the rational part of the tripartite soul with a man; in Aristotle, in the definition of man as rational animal, but with man's excellence said to lie in his reason; and in modern exponents of the argument for example, Tibor Machan in his recent article, 'Towards a Theory of Individual Human Rights' in what amounts to a definition of man as simply reason. On the basis, then, of the persuasive premise that the kind of a thing that a thing is determined its good, it is argued again, for example, by Machan that the good for man, including even his moral good, is living a rational life or exercising his reason. Continuing, this argument goes on to maintain that since rights are essentially a means for allowing an individual to exercise his will in social situations without interference from others, the proper role of rights, in view of the good for man, has to be as a means for allowing the free exercise and development of the individual's reason. What appears to follow, therefore, is that, devolving from man's essential nature, these rights for example, the rights of free speech and inquiry are inherent or natural human rights, thus rights extant whatever may be the awareness or conventions of a particular society.

Since, though, it is apparently possible to select any consistent set of components at all of human nature to praise or dispraise, just as it is possible to select any joinable set of sounds at all in the development of a language, one selection being as causally arbitrary as another, every community will naturally differ in its code of rights, just as it differs in its language. In actual fact, therefore, there are no such things as 'human rights'. There are the rights of Indians, the rights of Englishmen, the rights of Americans, the rights of Mexicans, the rights of Japanese, and so on.

If our analysis of the relationship between human nature and the existence of subjective rights is correct it is easy to see why the advocacy of human rights has to be wicked and even genocidal. Say that a certain politician, Reagen let us say, demands that human rights be everywhere adhered to and enforced. What he is in fact demanding, of course, is that his own community's code of rights be imposed upon all other communities and thus that their own different codes of rights be eradicated. That is a bit like performing cultural surgery upon a people and according to one of the clauses of its standard definition that constitutes genocide. Since, in addition, the very notion of a human right is fraudulent, the surgery in question has to constitute simple malpractice. It cannot be excused on the ground that one is improving the population in question's code of rights or some such thing. Analogously, Reagan might claim that English is the human language and so demand that all other languages be replaced by English. The perniciousness of any such case is transparent. But to the extent that notions of justice and rights are as vital to and cherished by their possessors as their language, equally pernicious and indeed vicious has to be the case implicitly contained in the modification of the noun, 'rights', by the adjective 'human'. We propose, therefore, that by any sound-thinking indeed, any morally concerned person must *rethink* about human rights, if not be *against* human rights.

Human Rights in the Global Society

Our foregoing discussions have hinted at the fact that "human rights" are discursive and utopian in nature. Yet, human rights are inevitable in this age of globalization and violence. Therefore, the debate over the impact of globalization has raised profound questions for students and proponents of human rights. Have globalization theorists been proven right in their prognosis that globalization would improve the prospects for human rights in political communities across the world? Does globalization presage a power shift from national governments to evolving systems of regional and global governance that will give more effective protection to human rights? The answers to these questions lie in part in the nature of the globalization process itself and partly in the changed structural context in which globalizing forces operate. To the extent that globalization embodies a broad range of competing and often contradictory values no conceptual framework or theoretical position can be either fully adopted or entirely dismissed. Understanding the complex relations between globalization and human rights requires an examination of the contemporary context of the post-Cold War order within which such relations occur. Whether globalization is the defining feature of this order remains a subject of debate.

A broad consensus, however, holds that globalization both contributed to the demise of the Cold War and is a basic feature for contemporary order. A study of the post-Cold War period, however, yields mixed results. It demonstrates flaws in overly optimistic theories of globalization, but also underscores the rise and importance of transnational cooperation and global civil society.

The post-Cold War era has not brought the global peace and stability that many observers hoped for. History did not, as optimists expected, "end". Instead, it has given rise to surprising turbulence, shocking violence, and intense controversy that have damaged human rights. The optimists were correct to foresee that globalization would intensify, if we measure its expansion by faster communications, greater interdependence within the world economy, and accelerate flows of people, goods, and ideas across borders. They were also right to foresee the expansion of international regimes intended to regulate finance and trade, migration, aviation, weapons proliferation, and of course human rights, among many other issues. These two developments—intensified technical, economic, and social globalization, and the expansion of prodemocracy interstate regimes were precisely the sorts of trends toward a more secure and prosperous world that many human rights advocates in the West (and some elsewhere) looked forward to as the Cold War ended.

Yet both developments have by now revealed darker sides that even their proponents must acknowledge. Although some economists argue that globalization has reduced global inequality, others contend that globalization has worsened inequality and increased the vulnerability of large populations to economic instability. The debate turns on how global inequality is conceptualized. David Dollar and Aart Kraay are probably correct that the rapid economic growth of large and formerly poor countries like China, India, and Vietnam has diminished inequality measured as the distribution of income among individuals worldwide. The critics argue, however, that it is equally true that inequality has increased when measured both country-to-country and within developing countries individual-to-individual. Moreover, as shown by surging inequality within China and India, just because economic growth raises the income of the poor does not mean that it lessens inequality. This apparent contradiction is explained by the fact that China and India are so huge demographically that their growth has brought hundreds of millions of individuals out of property at the same time that a wealth gap has widened between those persons living at the poverty line and entrepreneurs at the top of the wealth pyramid.

Also at the same time, poverty has deepened in the countries that have adapted less well to globalization, but since they are demographically smaller, their problems are not reflected in Dollar and Kraay's aggregate findings. Dani Rodrik points out that the best results - economically , and even more so socially and politically - have been generated by countries that refused to play by globalization's purported rules and that instead' implemented strong defensive policies to mitigate and control its effects. In short, the early faith has dissipated that deep, rapid trade and monetary liberalization would deliver both fast and fair economic growth. Aside from its pure economic effects, it is clear that globalization has generated profound social disruption and cultural resistance, and has at least indirectly contributed to some of the devastating outbreaks of inter-state war, civil war, terrorism, refugee flows and illegal migration, and even genocide that have marred the post-Cold War period. In the era of globalization, states find themselves more vulnerable than ever to the impacts of one another's internal economic, social, political, and even cultural instabilities. This has produced stronger motives for mutual intervention, thus fundamentally challenging the relatively stable old-world order of formally equal sovereign states. In addition, the increasing reach under globalization of such international financial institutions as the World Bank and the International Monetary Fund, and of international legal regimes for trade and investment like the World Trade Organization, has created new dilemmas of fairness – whose interests should these regimes serve? – and new struggles over the ability to control international trade standards and regimes.

As recounted in the introduction to this book, the move toward a more robust international human rights regime has been one of the most striking developments of the post-Cold War era. In its relations with globalization, the human rights regime typifies the complex dynamics and multilayered ethical implications of the new era. Interdependence has created stronger motives for states to try collectively to regulate some aspects of one another's internal behavior, while at the same time globalization has enlarged the information base for the international community to take an interest in the internal affairs of states. The rise of regimes in other functional areas, especially those relating to economic interactions, has made it seem more natural and even more necessary that states should also join conventions and treaties relating to human rights. And if globalization has helped to spread and legitimize the human rights idea, so too the human rights idea with its impulse to level differences and open markets has helped prepare the ground for globalization.

Despite its often benevolent effects, the growth of the international human rights regime has not been exempt from the dilemmas and paradoxes that attend other aspects of globalization and international regime formation. While the same reactions against cultural subversion and the devaluation of local identities that confront human rights also confront other features of globalization, the same ethical questions that confront the human rights regime also confront other international regimes.

Rather than leading to the harmonious cosmopolitan order envisioned by the drafters of the Universal Declaration of Human Rights (UDHR), the notion of universal rights stimulates conflict and generates its own opposition. Often this notion is framed in correspondingly universal terms and institutions, claiming universal validity. Although their advocates might often argue that their validity stems from a universally true foundation of ontological givens, we see these ideas and institutions, rather, as constructed approaches. Competing approaches do not need to rest on axiomatic foundational transcultural truths; rather, they draw their power from the specific cultural and political contexts in which they are constructed.

Our investigations suggest that these are key issues that the human rights community must confront honestly in constructing human rights in the age of the globalization. First, the emerging international human rights regime is linked to and conspicuously serves the interests of dominant Western liberal states. Second, it is associated largely with Western culture and identity. Third, promoting human rights also tends to promote the conditions for globalization writ large. In making these points, we are not suggesting that the idea does not serve the interests of the weak and poor whom it is ostensibly designed to protect. No doubt it frequently does so. Our intervention is a friendly one, aimed at helping the regime stabilize itself ethically and politically in the stormier atmosphere that it confronts today. Proponents of the international human rights regime cannot credibly claim that it is purely altruistic or that it is neutral as regards economic, political, and more controversially social and cultural, systems. Stronger legitimation and broader effectiveness must be built on a foundation of intellectual honesty. Facing such challenges, in what ways will human rights – as an idea, and as an institutional system – have to change to remain relevant and to grow in authority? One answer to the challenge of strengthening the human rights regime focuses on culture and values, and has been widely vetted in recent years. This is the idea that the human rights idea needs to break the bonds of cultural particularity of its rootedness in the Western tradition needs to regroup itself on a multicultural basis, or even on several overlapping multicultural bases. On the other hand, certain complexities confront this program. One is that the struggle between globalizers and Iocalizers, both claiming roots in local traditions and both, paradoxically, claiming some kind of universal validity for their positions, will be fought out over a long period of time.

The problem of how to construct human rights in the age of globalization has been to insist that human rights are no longer grounded in any particular cultural setting but have shifted to a basis in international positive law. This is not to deny that the idea of human rights originated in the West. But by now, the obligations of states to comply with international human rights norms are rooted in a series of treaties and conventions that they have signed, most notably the International Covenant on Civil and Political Rights and the International Covenant on Economic, Social, and Cultural Rights. This is a crucial growth frontier for human rights in the current age. As human rights become entrenched in international and domestic law, institutions arise designed to support and promote it. Even if these are relatively weak, they command certain personnel and resources, they create relentless pressure at both the international and national levels for human rights improvements, and they have the potential to grow in influence. The struggles over intellectual property as human rights in many developing world have argued that traditional and communal modes of ownership can serve as the best safeguards against transnational corporations controlling intellectual property in seeds, genetic information, and agricultural techniques. Further, more and more of what has historically been considered basically human or part of a common heritage of mankind is now treated as the intellectual property of individual authors. The advocates of people's rights challenge the foundational premises of intellectual private property. While private property is forcefully installed around the world as part of economic globalization, communal and collective forms of ownership establish themselves in response to that process. The ownership of culture as such appears to be less amenable to the norm of universality than it is presumed under the Universal Declaration of Human Rights. Likewise, as Kavita Philip argues, when a product patent increases the price of a resource that was previously free and integral to the life of a villager, political ecologists would argue that we cannot separate economic rights from environmental rights, nor analyze human rights in isolation from the context of the global power differentials within which transnationals operate in dispersed locations and with scattered accountability. Faced with competing conception of human rights – that is, civil – political rights and socioeconomic and cultural rights – the authors of the UDHR edged more toward a liberal than a socialist conception of the rights.

Moreover, because the declaration had a nonbinding character, many states voted in favor of the UN General Assembly resolution, despite their strong ideological objections to and profound disagreement with its content. They were seemingly convinced that it would not create obligations for them in the future. In the end, although the draft attempted to combine aspects of liberalism and social democracy, its balance as a whole was unmistakably Western. Michael Ignatieff, albeit from a different perspective, argues that the moral consensus, which sustained the Universal Declaration in 1948, has over time increasingly splintered. There is no evidence that economic globalization entails moral globalization. In fact, as economies have integrated their business practices, ownership, languages, and networks of communication, a countermovement has developed to maintain the integrity of national communities, national cultures, religions, and indigenous ways of life.

The end of the Cold War and the processes of globalization in the sense of post-1989 developments have accelerated that process of transformation. The processes of struggle we are describing, struggle over globalization within the human rights terrain, are by no means equal. Surely conspicuous among the losers – or those who benefit less, who are less able to use the human lights lingo to serve their ends – are small indigenous populations as well as the large populations of the poor and the powerless. Thus in building the new legal order, we need to be more attentive to the unintended consequences. Whose interests are really served? Which forces are taking advantage?

Despite the advance of globalization, we are still constructing human rights. The task in a sense has become harder than before because the stronger the regime, the more complex the political and normative struggles among the many interests who would make use of it to their own ends. In human rights as in globalization the liberal/capitalist Western society stands to gain more than the rest.

Likewise the various forms of global and regional fundamentalism can arguably exploit different aspects and problems associated with globalization, including the disillusionment resulting from the prevailing identity crisis, poverty, and social injustice. In a world where certain forms of injustice are progressively worsening, human rights continue to be just one of the instruments of amelioration. Human rights must be continuously rethought and reconstructed in response to emerging global transformations if they are to be a cure for rather than a cause of discord among and within different societies and cultures. It may be the case that no simple or coherent blueprint can serve to construct the best human rights regime for the age of globalization. In confronting this conundrum, we hope, however, the value of eschewing grand theory in favor of close attention to the particular impacts of the human rights regime in local settings.

In a quick overview, we offered a sketch of the history of the concept of human (natural) rights. We discussed the nature of human rights as understood within the context of a human community and the history of thought about such communities. Next we provided the moral justification for the political principles that were identified as man's rights, by defending the view that human excellence consists in the sustained choice to be rational to the degree of one's individual capacity. Next we argued that this notion, and the idea of human nature involved, support the conclusion that in a social context each person possesses certain rights by virtue of being a human being. From here we moved on to a consideration of the role and function of government, if any, in a human community the legal system of which is based on human rights; argued that proper government consists of those institutions designed by members of some human community for purposes of protecting and preserving a system in accord with human rights. Next we considered some of the implications of the overall theory for purposes of evaluating the real politik of our present society, indicating that most of the laws and institutions and the policies flowing from these constitute violations of human rights, although exceptions exist in America more than elsewhere known to me. Then we examined some features of the theory that have come under reasonable criticism, trying to answer both relevant and in some cases less compelling but still prevalent objections. Last we considered the prospects for the implementation of the human rights given the present intellectual and political climate are not favorable.

In this conclusion, we want to recapitulate our ideas of human rights utopianism. After one has proposed and argued for a theory, it is wise and reasonable to ask, can it be realized at all, or is it, like some others that have gained prominence in history, a mere unattainable (although to some appealing) idea? Then we also wish to make a point about the persuasive character of theories and books in the field of ethics and politics.

It has not been our task to argue for ideals that are unreachable. Although there is a respected tradition which holds that political philosophy should propose ideal systems of that sort, we consider this approach wrongheaded and dangerous-but mostly unjustifiable when dealing with human affairs. In making plans for one's life or for the institutions in one's society many forget about those for whom the plans are devised, namely human beings. This produces means unsuited for what people can achieve. Guiding oneself in life by impossible goals must involve going against reality-it would be like knowingly increasing the buoyancy of a submarine when trying to have it descend further. As mistakes or close enough approximations high aspirations may not be harmful. Then one is still admitting that further knowledge would make the task a more realistic one. But when one knows that some goals are impossible, it is criminal to sell people methods suited to their achievement. Goals such as perfect competition, full employment, guaranteed happiness, perfect ecological balance, free medical care for all, peace forever, and the like have guided both personal and political conduct often enough with horrible consequences for almost everyone involved. They ought to teach the lesson well: avoid utopianism. It encourages irresponsible hypothesizing of conditions for the future and leads to policies for moving from the present toward what could not even exist. Meanwhile real solutions, which may be far more modest, are neglected and, eventually, people grow cynical about all attempts to solve problems.

The present theory does not admit of the value of utopianism. Impossible dreams no, difficult to achieve goals yes! If they are worth it.

But to convince people that some goal is worthy of pursuit is not a process with only one participant. There is no way that even the best argument can make someone move out to reach for the best goals in life. There are many personal and cultural factors that enter into the process of persuasion, even if the thesis of which someone is to be persuaded is sound and the arguments are all in order. People sometimes like to just continue with old ideas-it does take a hell of a lot of effort to go through most of one's implicit and explicit beliefs and see if they will hold up against challenge. What if in the end the challenger really had nothing to offer? Why waste time? Who is he to tread on the views one has lived with for years and gotten by with comfortably enough?

We can only hope that there is some common ground on which trust has been established, however harsh some of our views may be for those who thinks differently. Obviously, if all of the reader's views were alien to the author communication could not even begin. But we are in a world we are capable of understanding quite well, provided we give it our attention. So we are already together on some issues, simply by living and doing whatever we are doing. And surely one of the merits of our case is that it claims no special status for those who can understand it. Moreover, it is supposed to be, if the homework has been done, fully consistent with the facts anyone may know who exerts the effort to look and think, facts that face everyone everywhere. So long as these are kept in view and the present work is understood clearly enough, the theory we have developed will, if correct, integrate well with the rest of one's knowledge.

There is no reasonable doubt that the free society is the soundest and best possible human society. As such it may appear utopian. And for that reason alone many will turn away from it, even leave the arguments unexamined. But every person owes himself the acknowledgment that present society could be better than what it is-even if it could be much worse. And he also owes himself the confidence in man and in the individual person that he/she is to undertake some effort to improve his political circumstances. There are many other matters to be taken care of, and we have not tried to promise solutions for them. Others have done fine work in medicine, building construction, nutrition, plastics, chemistry, movie making, and so on, so that political thinkers need not bother with that. Yet everyone owes himself some attention to political matters, and our last appeal is for such attention. There is evidence to prove that people have made a mess of things in the world politically, but that they can make the reparations as well. And today there is need for even more than reparations. A radical reconsideration of the prominent political attitudes and ideals in our culture is fully in order.

The Future of Human Rights

A person who has read the foregoing account of human rights law may wonder whether all the work that has gone into its creation and implementation has made any difference. If so much international human rights law exists, why is the world such a mess? A simple answer with much truth in it is that the world's human rights problems are large and deeply entrenched, and that human rights law and organizations are, by comparison, not very strong – particularly within the United Nations. Some of the countries that have the worst human rights records do not participate in the UN human rights system, and many others participate in a formal and hypocritical way. Regional systems, particularly in Europe and the Americas, do somewhat better. They have their own human rights courts, are more powerful, and enjoy more serious and sincere participation by many of their members.

The first 50 years of the human rights movement were handicapped by the Cold War. With that handicap removed, the 1990s were a period of growth and improvement in human rights law and institutions. The period since 2001 has seen a preoccupation with terrorism that has taken much attention and energy away from other human rights problems. Success in promoting human rights requires monumental success in other areas including building more capable, responsive, efficient, and non-corrupt governments, dealing with failed states, increasing economic productivity, improving the power and status of women, improving education, and managing international tensions and conflicts. Realizing human rights worldwide is a project for centuries, not decades. This is not to say, however, that progress cannot proceed at a faster pace than it currently does. Still, human rights are more widely accepted than they have ever been. They have become part of the currency of international relations, and most countries participate in the human rights system. Treaty arrangements help encourage and pressure countries to deal with their human rights problems. The human rights project continues and has not failed. It has captured our popular imagination.

Documents

1

THE MAGNA CARTA

The Great Charter

Abuses by King John caused a revolt by nobles who compelled him to execute this recognition of rights for both noblemen and ordinary Englishmen. It established the principle that no one, including the king or a lawmaker, is above the law.

Preamble: John, by the grace of God, king of England, lord of Ireland, duke of Normandy and Aquitaine, and count of Anjou, to the archbishop, bishops, abbots, earls, barons, justiciaries, foresters, sheriffs, stewards, servants, and to all his bailiffs and liege subjects, greetings. Know that, having regard to God and for the salvation of our soul, and those of all our ancestors and heirs, and unto the honor of God and the advancement of his holy Church and for the rectifying of our realm, we have granted as underwritten by advice of our venerable fathers, Stephen, archbishop of Canterbury, primate of all England and cardinal of the holy Roman Church, Henry, archbishop of Dublin, William of London, Peter of Winchester, Jocelyn of Bath and Glastonbury, Hugh of Lincoln, Walter of Worcester, William of Coventry, Benedict of Rochester, bishops; of Master Pandulf, subdeacon and member of the household of our lord the Pope, of brother Aymeric (master of the Knights of the Temple in England), and of the illustrious men William Marshal, earl of Pembroke, William, earl of Salisbury, William, earl of Warenne, William, earl of Arundel, Alan of

Galloway (constable of Scotland), Waren Fitz Gerold, Peter Fitz Herbert, Hubert De Burgh (seneschal of Poitou), Hugh de Neville, Matthew Fitz Herbert, Thomas Basset, Alan Basset, Philip d'Aubigny, Robert of Roppesley, John Marshal, John Fitz Hugh, and others, our liegemen.

1. In the first place we have granted to God, and by this our present charter confirmed for us and our heirs forever that the English Church shall be free, and shall have her rights entire, and her liberties inviolate; and we will that it be thus observed; which is apparent from this that the freedom of elections, which is reckoned most important and very essential to the English Church, we, of our pure and unconstrained will, did grant, and did by our charter confirm and did obtain the ratification of the same from our lord, Pope Innocent III, before the quarrel arose between us and our barons: and this we will observe, and our will is that it be observed in good faith by our heirs forever. We have also granted to all freemen of our kingdom, for us and our heirs forever, all the underwritten liberties, to be had and held by them and their heirs, of us and our heirs forever.

2. If any of our earls or barons, or others holding of us in chief by military service shall have died, and at the time of his death his heir shall be full of age and owe "relief", he shall have his inheritance by the old relief, to wit, the heir or heirs of an earl, for the whole barony of an earl by £100; the heir or heirs of a baron, £100 for a whole barony; the heir or heirs of a knight, 100s, at most, and whoever owes less let him give less, according to the ancient custom of fees.

3. If, however, the heir of any one of the aforesaid has been under age and in wardship, let him have his inheritance without relief and without fine when he comes of age.

4. The guardian of the land of an heir who is thus under age, shall take from the land of the heir nothing but reasonable produce, reasonable customs, and reasonable services, and that without destruction or waste of men or goods; and if we have committed the wardship of the lands of any such minor to the sheriff, or to any other who is responsible to us for its issues, and he has made destruction or waster of what he holds in wardship, we will take of him amends, and the land shall be committed to two lawful and discreet men of that fee, who shall be responsible for the issues to us or to him to whom we shall assign them; and if we have given or sold the

wardship of any such land to anyone and he has therein made destruction or waste, he shall lose that wardship, and it shall be transferred to two lawful and discreet men of that fief, who shall be responsible to us in like manner as aforesaid.

5. The guardian, moreover, so long as he has the wardship of the land, shall keep up the houses, parks, fishponds, stanks, mills, and other things pertaining to the land, out of the issues of the same land; and he shall restore to the heir, when he has come to full age, all his land, stocked with ploughs and wainage, according as the season of husbandry shall require, and the issues of the land can reasonable bear.

6. Heirs shall be married without disparagement, yet so that before the marriage takes place the nearest in blood to that heir shall have notice.

7. A widow, after the death of her husband, shall forthwith and without difficulty have her marriage portion and inheritance; nor shall she give anything for her dower, or for her marriage portion, or for the inheritance which her husband and she held on the day of the death of that husband; and she may remain in the house of her husband for forty days after his death, within which time her dower shall be assigned to her.

8. No widow shall be compelled to marry, so long as she prefers to live without a husband; provided always that she gives security not to marry without our consent, if she holds of us, or without the consent of the lord of whom she holds, if she holds of another.

9. Neither we nor our bailiffs will seize any land or rent for any debt, as long as the chattels of the debtor are sufficient to repay the debt; nor shall the sureties of the debtor be distrained so long as the principal debtor is able to satisfy the debt; and if the principal debtor shall fail to pay the debt, having nothing wherewith to pay it, then the sureties shall answer for the debt; and let them have the lands and rents of the debtor, if they desire them, until they are indemnified for the debt which they have paid for him, unless the principal debtor can show proof that he is discharged thereof as against the said sureties.

10. If one who has borrowed from the Jews any sum, great or small, die before that loan be repaid, the debt shall not bear interest while the heir is under age, of whomsoever he may hold; and if the debt fall into our

hands, we will not take anything except the principal sum contained in the bond.

11. And if anyone die indebted to the Jews, his wife shall have her dower and pay nothing of that debt; and if any children of the deceased are left under age, necessaries shall be provided for them in keeping with the holding of the deceased; and out of the residue the debt shall be paid, reserving, however, service due to feudal lords; in like manner let it be done touching debts due to others than Jews.

12. No scutage not aid shall be imposed on our kingdom, unless by common counsel of our kingdom, except for ransoming our person, for making our eldest son a knight, and for once marrying our eldest daughter; and for these there shall not be levied more than a reasonable aid. In like manner it shall be done concerning aids from the city of London.

13. And the city of London shall have all it ancient liberties and free customs, as well by land as by water; furthermore, we decree and grant that all other cities, boroughs, towns, and ports shall have all their liberties and free customs.

14. And for obtaining the common counsel of the kingdom anent the assessing of an aid (except in the three cases aforesaid) or of a scutage, we will cause to be summoned the archbishops, bishops, abbots, earls, and greater barons, severally by our letters; and we will moveover cause to be summoned generally, through our sheriffs and bailiffs, and others who hold of us in chief, for a fixed date, namely, after the expiry of at least forty days, and at a fixed place; and in all letters of such summons we will specify the reason of the summons. And when the summons has thus been made, the business shall proceed on the day appointed, according to the counsel of such as are present, although not all who were summoned have come.

15. We will not for the future grant to anyone license to take an aid from his own free tenants, except to ransom his person, to make his eldest son a knight, and once to marry his eldest daughter; and on each of these occasions there shall be levied only a reasonable aid.

16. No one shall be distrained for performance of greater service for a knight's fee, or for any other free tenement, than is due therefrom.

17. Common pleas shall not follow our court, but shall be held in some fixed place.

18. Inquests of novel disseisin, of mort d'ancestor, and of darrein presentment shall not be held elsewhere than in their own county courts, and that in manner following; We, or, if we should be out of the realm, our chief justiciar, will send two justiciaries through every county four times a year, who shall alone with four knights of the county chosen by the county, hold the said assizes in the county court, on the day and in the place of meeting of that court.

19. And if any of the said assizes cannot be taken on the day of the county court, let there remain of the knights and freeholders, who were present at the county court on that day, as many as may be required for the efficient making of judgments, according as the business be more or less.

20. A freeman shall not be amerced for a slight offense, except in accordance with the degree of the offense; and for a grave offense he shall be amerced in accordance with the gravity of the offense, yet saving always his "contentment"; and a merchant in the same way, saving his "merchandise"; and a villein shall be amerced in the same way, saving his "wainage" if they have fallen into our mercy: and none of the aforesaid amercements shall be imposed except by the oath of honest men of the neighborhood.

21. Earls and barons shall not be amerced except through their peers, and only in accordance with the degree of the offense.

22. A clerk shall not be amerced in respect of his lay holding except after the manner of the others aforesaid; further, he shall not be amerced in accordance with the extent of his ecclesiastical benefice.

23. No village or individual shall be compelled to make bridges at river banks, except those who from of old were legally bound to do so.

24. No sheriff, constable, coroners, or others of our bailiffs, shall hold pleas of our Crown.

25. All counties, hundred, wapentakes, and trithings (except our demesne manors) shall remain at the old rents, and without any additional payment.

26. If anyone holding of us a lay fief shall die, and our sheriff or bailiff shall exhibit our letters patent of summons for a debt which the deceased owed us, it shall be lawful for our sheriff or bailiff to attach and enroll the chattels of the deceased, found upon the lay fief, to the value of that debt, at the sight of law worthy men, provided always that nothing whatever be thence removed until the debt which is evident shall be fully paid to us; and the residue shall be left to the executors to fulfill the will of the deceased; and if there be nothing due from him to us, all the chattels shall go to the deceased, saving to his wife and children their reasonable shares.

27. If any freeman shall die intestate, his chattels shall be distributed by the hands of his nearest kinsfolk and friends, under supervision of the Church, saving to everyone the debts which the deceased owed to him.

28. No constable or other bailiff of ours shall take corn or other provisions from anyone without immediately tendering money therefor, unless he can have postponement thereof by permission of the seller.

29. No constable shall compel any knight to give money in lieu of castle-guard, when he is willing to perform it in his own person, or (if he himself cannot do it from any reasonable cause) then by another responsible man. Further, if we have led or sent him upon military service, he shall be relieved from guard in proportion to the time during which he has been on service because of us.

30. No sheriff or bailiff of ours, or other person, shall take the horses or carts of any freeman for transport duty, against the will of the said freeman.

31. Neither we nor our bailiffs shall take, for our castles or for any other work of ours, wood which is not ours, against the will of the owner of that wood.

32. We will not retain beyond one year and one day, the lands those who have been convicted of felony, and the lands shall thereafter be handed over to the lords of the fiefs.

33. All kydells for the future shall be removed altogether from Thames and Medway, and throughout all England, except upon the seashore.

34. The writ which is called praecipe shall not for the future be issued to anyone, regarding any tenement whereby a freeman may lose his court.

35. Let there be one measure of wine throughout our whole realm; and one measure of ale; and one measure of corn, to wit, "the London quarter"; and one width of cloth (whether dyed, or russet, or "halberget"), to wit, two ells within the selvedges; of weights also let it be as of measures.

36. Nothing in future shall be given or taken for a writ of inquisition of life or limbs, but freely it shall be granted, and never denied.

37. If anyone holds of us by fee-farm, either by socage or by burage, or of any other land by knight's service, we will not (by reason of that fee-farm, socage, or burgage), have the wardship of the heir, or of such land of his as if of the fief of that other; nor shall we have wardship of that fee-farm, socage, or burgage, unless such fee-farm owes knight's service. We will not by reason of any small serjeancy which anyone may hold of us by the service of rendering to us knives, arrows, or the like, have wardship of his heir or of the land which he holds of another lord by knight's service.

38. No bailiff for the future shall, upon his own unsupported complaint, put anyone to his "law", without credible witnesses brought for this purposes.

39. No freemen shall be taken or imprisoned or disseised or exiled or in any way destroyed, nor will we go upon him nor send upon him, except by the lawful judgment of his peers or by the law of the land.

40. To no one will we sell, to no one will we refuse or delay, right or justice.

41. All merchants shall have safe and secure exit from England, and entry to England, with the right to tarry there and to move about as well by land as by water, for buying and selling by the ancient and right customs, quit from all evil tolls, except (in time of war) such merchants as are of the land at war with us. And if such are found in our land at the beginning of the war, they shall be detained, without injury to their bodies or goods, until information be received by us, or by our chief justiciar, how the merchants of our land found in the land at war with us are treated; and if our men are safe there, the others shall be safe in our land.

42. It shall be lawful in future for anyone (excepting always those imprisoned or outlawed in accordance with the law of the kingdom, and natives of any country at war with us, and merchants, who shall be treated

as if above provided) to leave our kingdom and to return, safe and secure by land and water, except for a short period in time of war, on grounds of public policy-reserving always the allegiance due to us.

43. If anyone holding of some escheat (such as the honor of Wallingford, Nottingham, Boulogne, Lancaster, or of other escheats which are in our hands and are baronies) shall die, his heir shall give no other relief, and perform no other service to us than he would have done to the baron if that barony had been in the baron's hand; and we shall hold it in the same manner in which the baron held it.

44. Men who dwell without the forest need not henceforth come before our justiciaries of the forest upon a general summons, unless they are in plea, or sureties of one or more, who are attached for the forest.

45. We will appoint as justices, constables, sheriffs, or bailiffs only such as know the law of the realm and mean to observe it well.

46. All barons who have founded abbeys, concerning which they hold charters from the kings of England, or of which they have long continued possession, shall have the wardship of them, when vacant, as they ought to have.

47. All forests that have been made such in our time shall forthwith be disafforsted; and a similar course shall be followed with regard to river banks that have been placed "in defense" by us in our time.

48. All evil customs connected with forests and warrens, foresters and warreners, sheriffs and their officers, river banks and their wardens, shall immediately by inquired into in each county by twelve sworn knights of the same county chosen by the honest men of the same county, and shall, within forty days of the said inquest, be utterly abolished, so as never to be restored, provided always that we previously have intimation thereof, or our justiciar, if we should not be in England.

49. We will immediately restore all hostages and charters delivered to us by Englishmen, as sureties of the peace of faithful service.

50. We will entirely remove from their bailiwicks, the relations of Gerard of Athee (so that in future they shall have no bailiwick in England); namely, Engelard of Cigogne, Peter, Guy, and Andrew of Chanceaux, Guy of Cigogne, Geoffrey of Martigny with his brothers, Philip Mark with his brothers and his nephew Geoffrey, and the whole brood of the same.

51. As soon as peace is restored, we will banish from the kingdom all foreign born knights, crossbowmen, serjeants, and mercenary soldiers who have come with horses and arms to the kingdom's hurt.

52. If anyone has been dispossessed or removed by us, without the legal judgment of his peers, from his lands, castles, franchises, or from his right, we will immediately restore them to him; and if a dispute arise over this, then let it be decided by the five and twenty barons of whom mention is made below in the clause for securing the peace. Moreover, for all those possessions, from which anyone has, without the lawful judgment of his peers, been disseised or removed, by our father, King Henry, or by our brother, King Richard, and which we retain in our hand (or which as possessed by others, to whom we are bound to warrant them) we shall have respite until the usual term of crusaders; excepting those things about which a plea has been raised, or an inquest made by our order, before our taking of the cross; but as soon as we return from the expedition, we will immediately grant full justice therein.

53. We shall have, moreover, the same respite and in the same manner in rendering justice concerning the disafforestation or retention of those forests which Henry our father and Richard our brother afforested, and concerning the wardship of lands which are of the fief of another (namely, such wardships as we have hitherto had by reason of a fief which anyone held of us by knight's service), and concerning abbeys founded on other fiefs than our own, in which the lord of the fee claims to have right; and when we have returned, or if we desist from our expedition, we will immediately grant full justice to all who complain of such things.

54. No one shall be arrested or imprisoned upon the appeal of a woman, for the death of any other than her husband.

55. All fines made with us unjustly and against the law of the land, and all amercements, imposed unjustly and against the law of the land, shall be entirely remitted, or else it shall be done concerning them according to the decision of the five and twenty barons whom mention is made below in the clause for securing the pease, or according to the judgment of the majority of the same, along with the aforesaid Stephen, archbishop of Canterbury, if he can be present, and such others as he may wish to bring with him for this purpose, and if he cannot be present the business shall

nevertheless proceed without him, provided always that if any one or more of the aforesaid five and twenty barons are in a similar suit, they shall be removed as far as concerns this particular judgment, others being substituted in their places after having been selected by the rest of the same five and twenty for this purpose only, and after having been sworn.

56. If we have disseised or removed Welshmen from lands or liberties, or other things, without the legal judgment of their peers in England or in Wales, they shall be immediately restored to them; and if a dispute arise over this, then let it be decided in the marches by the judgment of their peers; for the tenements in England according to the law of England, for tenements in Wales according to the law of Wales, and for tenements in the marches according to the law of the marches. Welshmen shall do the same to us and ours.

57. Further, for all those possessions from which any Welshman has, without the lawful judgment of his peers, been disseised or removed by King Henry our father, or King Richard our brother, and which we retain in our hand (or which are possessed by others, and which we ought to warrant), we will have respite until the usual term of crusaders; excepting those things about which a plea has been raised or an inquest made by our order before we took the cross; but as soon as we return (or if perchance we desist from our expedition), we will immediately grant full justice in accordance with the laws of the Welsh and in relation to the foresaid regions.

58. We will immediately give up the son of Llywelyn and all the hostages of Wales, and the charters delivered to us as security for the peace.

59. We will do towards Alexander, king of Scots, concerning the return of his sisters and his hostages, and concerning his franchises, and his right, in the same manner as we shall do towards our owher barons of England, unless it ought to be otherwise according to the charters which we hold from William his father, formerly king of Scots; and this shall be according to the judgment of his peers in our court.

60. Moreover, all these aforesaid customs and liberties, the observances of which we have granted in our kingdom as far as pertains to us towards our men, shall be observed b all of our kingdom, as well clergy as laymen, as far as pertains to them towards their men.

61. Since, moreover, for God and the amendment of our kingdom and for the better allaying of the quarrel that has arisen between us and our barons, we have granted all these concessions, desirous that they should enjoy them in complete and firm endurance forever, we give and grant to them the underwritten security, namely, that the barons choose five and twenty barons of the kingdom, whomsoever they will, who shall be bound with all their might, to observe and hold, and cause to be observed, the peace and liberties we have granted and confirmed to them by this our present Charter, so that if we, or our justiciar, or our bailiffs or any one of our officers, shall in anything be at fault towards anyone, or shall have broken any one of the articles of this peace or of this security, and the offense be notified to four barons of the foresaid five and twenty, the said four barons shall repair to us (or our justiciar, if we are out of the realm) and, laying the transgression before us, petition to have that transgression redressed without delay. And if we shall not have corrected the transgression (or, in the event of our being out of the realm, if our justiciar shall not have corrected it) within forty days, reckoning from the time it has been intimated to us (or to our justiciar, if we should be out of the realm), the four barons aforesaid shall refer that matter to the rest of the five and twenty barons, and those five and twenty barons shall, together with the community of the whole realm, distrain and distress us in all possible ways, namely, by seizing our castles, lands, possessions, and in any other way they can, until redress has been obtained as they deem fit, saving harmless our own person, and the persons of our queen and children; and when redress has been obtained, they shall resume their old relations towards us. And let whoever in the country desires it, swear to obey the orders of the said five and twenty barons for the execution of all the aforesaid matters, and along with them, to molest us to the utmost of his power; and we publicly and freely grant leave to everyone who wishes to swear, and we shall never forbid anyone to swear. All those, moreover, in the land who of themselves and of their own accord are unwilling to swear to the twenty five to help them in constraining and molesting us, we shall by our command compel the same to swear to the effect foresaid. And if any one of the five and twenty barons shall have died or departed from the land, or be incapacitated in any other manner which would prevent the foresaid provisions being carried out, those of the said twenty five barons who are left shall choose another in

his place according to their own judgment, and he shall be sworn in the same way as the others. Further, in all matters, the execution of which is entrusted, to these twenty five barons, if perchance these twenty five are present and disagree about anything, or if some of them, after being summoned, are unwilling or unable to be present, that which the majority of those present ordain or command shall be held as fixed and established, exactly as if the whole twenty five had concurred in this; and the said twenty five shall swear that they will faithfully observe all that is aforesaid, and cause it to be observed with all their might. And we shall procure nothing from anyone, directly or indirectly, whereby any part of these concessions and liberties might be revoked or diminished; and if any such things has been procured, let it be void and null, and we shall never use it personally or by another.

62. And all the will, hatreds, and bitterness that have arisen between us and our men, clergy and lay, from the date of the quarrel, we have completely remitted and pardoned to everyone. Moreover, all trespasses occasioned by the said quarrel, from Easter in the sixteenth year of our reign till the restoration of peace, we have fully remitted to all, both clergy and laymen, and completely forgiven, as far as pertains to us. And on this head, we have caused to be made for them letters testimonial patent of the lord Stephen, archbishop of Canterbury, of the lord Henry, archbishop of Dublin, of the bishops aforesaid, and of Master Pandu if as touching this security and the concessions aforesaid.

63. Wherefore we will and firmly order that the English Church be free, and that the men in our kingdom have and hold all the aforesaid liberties, rights, and concessions, well and peaceably, freely and quietly, fully and wholly, for themselves and their heirs, of us and our heirs, in all respects and in all places forever, as is aforesaid. An oath, moreover, has been taken, as well on our part as on the art of the barons, that all these conditions aforesaid shall be kept in good faith and without evil intent.

Given under our hand - the above named and many others being witnesses - in the meadow which is called Runnymede, between Windsor and Staines, on the fifteenth day of June, in the seventeenth year of our reign.

2

THE UNITED STATES DECLARATION OF INDEPENDENCE IN CONGRESS, JULY 4, 1776.

The unanimous Declaration of the thirteen united States of America

When in the Course of human events, it becomes necessary for one people to dissolve the political bands which have connected them with another, and to assume among the powers of the earth, the separate and equal station to which the Laws of Nature and of Nature's God entitle them, a decent respect to the opinions of mankind requires that they should declare the causes which impel them to the separation.

We hold these truths to be self-evident, that all men are created equal, that they are endowed by their Creator with certain unalienable Rights, that among these are Life, Liberty and the pursuit of Happiness.— That to secure these rights, Governments are instituted among Men, deriving their just powers from the consent of the governed,— That whenever any Form of Government becomes destructive of these ends, it is the Right of the People to alter or to abolish it, and to institute new Government, laying its foundation on such principles and organizing its powers in such form, as to them shall seem most likely to effect their Safety and Happiness. Prudence, indeed, will dictate that Governments long established should not be changed for light and transient causes; and accordingly all experience hath shewn, that mankind are more disposed to suffer, while evils are sufferable, than to right themselves by abolishing the forms to which they are accustomed. But when a long train of abuses and usurpations, pursuing invariably the same Object evinces a design to reduce them under absolute Despotism, it is their right, it is their duty, to throw off such Government, and to provide new Guards for their future security.— Such has been the patient sufferance of these Colonies; and such is now the necessity which constrains them to alter their former Systems of Government. The history of the present King of Great Britain is a history of repeated injuries and usurpations, all having in direct object the establishment of an absolute Tyranny over these States. To prove this, let facts be submitted to a candid world.

He has refused his Assent to Laws, the most wholesome and necessary for the public good.

He has forbidden his Governors to pass Laws of immediate and pressing importance, unless suspended in their operation till his Assent should be obtained; and when so suspended, he has utterly neglected to attend to them.

He has refused to pass other Laws for the accommodation of large districts of people, unless those people would relinquish the right of Representation in the Legislature, a right inestimable to them and formidable to tyrants only.

He has called together legislative bodies at places unusual, uncomfortable, and distant from the depository of their public Records, for the sole purpose of fatiguing them into compliance with his measures.

He has dissolved Representative Houses repeatedly, for opposing with manly firmness his invasions on the rights of the people.

He has refused for a long time, after such dissolutions, to cause others to be elected; whereby the Legislative powers, incapable of Annihilation, have returned to the People at large for their exercise; the State remaining in the mean time exposed to all the dangers of invasion from without, and convulsions within.

He has endeavoured to prevent the population of these States; for that purpose obstructing the Laws for Naturalization of Foreigners; refusing to pass others to encourage their migrations hither, and raising the conditions of new Appropriations of Lands.

He has obstructed the Administration of Justice, by refusing his Assent to Laws for establishing Judiciary powers.

He has made Judges dependent on his Will alone, for the tenure of their offices, and the amount and payment of their salaries.

He has erected a multitude of New Offices, and sent hither swarms of Officers to harass our people, and eat out their substance.

He has kept among us, in times of peace, Standing Armies without the Consent of our legislatures.

He has affected to render the Military independent of and superior to the Civil power.

He has combined with others to subject us to a jurisdiction foreign to our constitution, and unacknowledged by our laws; giving his Assent to their Acts of pretended Legislation:

For Quartering large bodies of armed troops among us:

For protecting them, by a mock Trial, from punishment for any Murders which they should commit on the Inhabitants of these States:

For cutting off our Trade with all parts of the world:

For imposing Taxes on us without our Consent: For depriving us in many cases, of the benefits of Trial by Jury:

For transporting us beyond Seas to be tried for pretended offences

For abolishing the free System of English Laws in a neighbouring Province, establishing therein an arbitrary government, and enlarging its Boundaries so as to render it at once an example and fit instrument for introducing the same absolute rule into these Colonies:

For taking away our Charters, abolishing our most valuable Laws, and altering fundamentally the Forms of our Governments:

For suspending our own Legislatures, and declaring themselves invested with power to legislate for us in all cases whatsoever.

He has abdicated Government here, by declaring us out of his Protection and waging War against us.

He has plundered our seas, ravaged our Coasts, burnt our towns, and destroyed the lives of our people.

He is at this time transporting large Armies of foreign Mercenaries to complete the works of death, desolation and tyranny, already begun with circumstances of Cruelty & perfidy scarcely paralleled in the most barbarous ages, and totally unworthy of the Head of a civilized nation.

He has constrained our fellow Citizens taken Captive on the high Seas to bear Arms against their Country, to become the executioners of their friends and Brethren, or to fall themselves by their Hands.

He has excited domestic insurrections amongst us, and has endeavoured to bring on the inhabitants of our frontiers, the merciless Indian Savages, whose known rule of warfare, is an undistinguished destruction of all ages, sexes and conditions.

In every stage of these oppressions we have petitioned for redress in the most humble terms: Our repeated petitions have been answered only by repeated injury. A Prince whose character is thus marked by every act which may define a Tyrant, is unfit to be the ruler of a free people. Nor have we been wanting in attentions to our British brethren. We have warned them from time to time of attempts by their legislature to extend an unwarrantable jurisdiction over us. We have reminded them of the circumstances of our emigration and settlement here. We have appealed to their native justice and magnanimity, and we have conjured them by the ties of our common kindred to disavow these usurpations, which, would inevitably interrupt our connections and correspondence. They too have been deaf to the voice of justice and of consanguinity. We must, therefore, acquiesce in the necessity, which denounces our Separation, and hold them, as we hold the rest of mankind, Enemies in War, in Peace Friends.

We, therefore, the representatives of the united States of America, in General Congress, Assembled, appealing to the Supreme Judge of the world for the rectitude of our intentions, do, in the Name, and by Authority of the good People of these Colonies, solemnly publish and declare, That these United Colonies are, and of Right ought to be Free and Independent States; that they are Absolved from all Allegiance to the British Crown, and that all political connection

between them and the State of Great Britain, is and ought to be totally dissolved; and that as Free and Independent States, they have full Power to levy War, conclude Peace, contract Alliances, establish Commerce, and to do all other Acts and Things which Independent States may of right do. And for the support of this Declaration, with a firm reliance on the protection of divine Providence, we mutually pledge to each other our Lives, our Fortunes and our sacred Honor.

[*The 56 signatures on the Declaration were arranged in six columns:*]

3

DECLARATION OF THE RIGHTS OF MAN AND CITIZEN

Approved by the National Assembly of France, August 26, 1789

The representatives of the French people, organized as a National Assembly, believing that the ignorance, neglect, or contempt of the rights of man are the sole cause of public calamities and of the corruption of governments, have determined to set forth in a solemn declaration the natural, unalienable, and sacred rights of man, in order that this declaration, being constantly before all the members of the Social body, shall remind them continually of their rights and duties; in order that the acts of the legislative power, as well as those of the executive power, may be compared at any moment with the objects and purposes of all political institutions and may thus be more respected, and, lastly, in order that the grievances of the citizens, based hereafter upon simple and incontestable principles, shall tend to the maintenance of the constitution and redound to the happiness of all. Therefore the National Assembly recognizes and proclaims, in the presence and under the auspices of the Supreme Being, the following rights of man and of the citizen:

Article 1

Men are born and remain free and equal in rights. Social distinctions may be founded only upon the general good.

Article 2

The aim of all political association is the preservation of the natural and imprescriptible rights of man. These rights are liberty, property, security, and resistance to oppression.

Article 3

The principle of all sovereignty resides essentially in the nation. No body nor individual may exercise any authority which does not proceed directly from the nation.

Article 4

Liberty consists in the freedom to do everything which injures no one else; hence the exercise of the natural rights of each man has no limits except those which assure to the other members of the society the enjoyment of the same rights. These limits can only be determined by law.

Article 5

Law can only prohibit such actions as are hurtful to society. Nothing may be prevented which is not forbidden by law, and no one may be forced to do anything not provided for by law.

Article 6

Law is the expression of the general will. Every citizen has a right to participate personally, or through his representative, in its foundation. It must be the same for all, whether it protects or punishes. All citizens, being equal in the eyes of the law, are equally eligible to all dignities and to all public positions and occupations, according to their abilities, and without distinction except that of their virtues and talents.

Article 7

No person shall be accused, arrested, or imprisoned except in the cases and according to the forms prescribed by law. Any one soliciting, transmitting, executing, or causing to be executed, any arbitrary order, shall be punished. But any citizen summoned or arrested in virtue of the law shall submit without delay, as resistance constitutes an offense.

Article 8

The law shall provide for such punishments only as are strictly and obviously necessary, and no one shall suffer punishment except it be legally inflicted in virtue of a law passed and promulgated before the commission of the offense.

Article 9

As all persons are held innocent until they shall have been declared guilty, if arrest shall be deemed indispensable, all harshness not essential to the securing of the prisoner's person shall be severely repressed by law.

Article 10

No one shall be disquieted on account of his opinions, including his religious views, provided their manifestation does not disturb the public order established by law.

Article 11

The free communication of ideas and opinions is one of the most precious of the rights of man. Every citizen may, accordingly, speak, write, and print with freedom, but shall be responsible for such abuses of this freedom as shall be defined by law.

Article 12

The security of the rights of man and of the citizen requires public military forces. These forces are, therefore, established for the good of all and not for the personal advantage of those to whom they shall be entrusted.

Article 13

A common contribution is essential for the maintenance of the public forces and for the cost of administration. This should be equitably distributed among all the citizens in proportion to their means.

Article 14

All the citizens have a right to decide, either personally or by their representatives, as to the necessity of the public contribution; to grant this freely; to know to what uses it is put; and to fix the proportion, the mode of assessment and of collection and the duration of the taxes.

Article 15

Society has the right to require of every public agent an account of his administration.

Article 16

A society in which the observance of the law is not assured, nor the separation of powers defined, has no constitution at all.

Article 17

Since property is an inviolable and sacred right, no one shall be deprived thereof except where public necessity, legally determined, shall clearly demand it, and then only on condition that the owner shall have been previously and equitably indemnified.

4

THE UNITED STATES BILL OF RIGHTS

On September 25, 1789, Congress transmitted to the state Legislatures twelve proposed amendments to the Constitution. Numbers three through twelve were adopted by the states to become the United States (U.S.) Bill of Rights, effective December 15, 1791.

James Madison proposed the U.S. Bill of Rights. It largely responded to the Constitution's influential opponents, including prominent Founding Fathers, who argued that the Constitution should not be ratified because it failed to protect the basic principles of human liberty. The U.S. Bill of Rights was influenced by George Mason's 1776 Virginia Declaration of Rights, the 1689 English Bill of Rights, works of the Age of Enlightenment pertaining to natural rights, and earlier English political documents such as the Magna Carta (1215).

Two additional articles were proposed to the States; only the final ten articles were ratified quickly and correspond to the First through Tenth Amendments to the Constitution. The first Article, dealing with the number and apportionment of U.S. Representatives, never became part of the Constitution. The second Article, limiting the ability of Congress to increase the salaries of its members, was ratified two centuries later as the 27th Amendment. Though they are incorporated into the document known as the "Bill of Rights", neither article establishes a right as that term is used today. For that reason, and also because the term had been applied to the first ten amendments long before the 27th Amendment was ratified, the term "Bill of Rights" in modern U.S. usage means only the ten amendments ratified in 1791.

The United States Bill of Rights plays a central role in American law and government, and remains a fundamental symbol of the freedoms and culture of the nation. One of the original fourteen copies of the U.S. Bill of Rights is on public display at the National Archives in Washington, D.C.

Amendment I (1): *Freedom of religion, speech, and the press; rights of assembly and petition*

Congress shall make no law respecting an establishment of religion, or prohibiting the free exercise thereof; or abridging the freedom of speech, or of the press, or the right of the people peaceably to assemble, and to petition the Government for a redress of grievances.

Amendment II (2): *Right to bear arms*

A well regulated Militia, being necessary to the security of a free State, the right of the people to keep and bear Arms, shall not be infringed.

Amendment III (3): *Housing of soldiers*

No Soldier shall, in time of peace be quartered in any house, without the consent of the Owner, nor in time of war, but in a manner to be prescribed by law.

Amendment IV (4): *Search and arrest warrants*

The right of the people to be secure in their persons, houses, papers, and effects, against unreasonable searches and seizures, shall not be violated, and no Warrants shall issue, but upon probable cause, supported by Oath or affirmation, and particularly describing the place to be searched, and the persons or things to be seized.

Amendment V (5): *Rights in criminal cases*

No person shall be held to answer for a capital, or otherwise infamous crime, unless on a presentment or indictment of a Grand Jury, except in cases arising in the land or naval forces, or in the Militia, when in actual service in time of War or public danger; nor shall any person be subject for the same offence to be twice put in jeopardy of life or limb, nor shall be compelled in any criminal case to be a witness against himself, nor be deprived of life, liberty, or property, without due process of law; nor shall private property be taken for public use without just compensation.

Amendment VI (6): *Rights to a fair trial*

In all criminal prosecutions, the accused shall enjoy the right to a speedy and public trial, by an impartial jury of the State and district wherein the crime shall have been committed; which district shall have been previously ascertained by law, and to be informed of the nature and cause of the accusation; to be confronted with the witnesses against him; to have compulsory process for obtaining witnesses in his favour, and to have the assistance of counsel for his defence.

Amendment VII (7): *Rights in civil cases*

In Suits at common law, where the value in controversy shall exceed twenty dollars, the right of trial by jury shall be preserved, and no fact tried by a jury shall be otherwise re-examined in any Court of the United States, than according to the rules of the common law.

Amendment VIII (8): *Bails, fines, and punishments*

Excessive bail shall not be required, nor excessive fines imposed, nor cruel and unusual punishments inflicted.

Amendment IX (9): *Rights retained by the people*

The enumeration in the Constitution of certain rights shall not be construed to deny or disparage others retained by the people.

Amendment X (10): *Powers retained by the states and the people*

The powers not delegated to the United States by the Constitution, nor prohibited by it to the States, are reserved to the States respectively, or to the people.

5

AMELIORATION OF THE CONDITION OF THE WOUNDED ON THE FIELD OF BATTLE (RED CROSS CONVENTION)

Convention signed at Geneva August 22, 1864

Ratifications exchanged at Geneva June 22, 1865

Declaration of accession signed by the President of the United States March 1, 1882 .

Senate advice and consent to accession March 16, 1882

Accession of the United States accepted by Switzerland June 9, 1882 *Entered into force June* 22, 1865; *for the United States June* 9, 1882 *Proclaimed by the President of the United States July* 26, 1882 *Superseded by conventions of July 6,1906/ July* 27,1929,2 *and August*

12, 1949,8 *as between contracting parties to the later conventions in each instance*

22 Stat. 940; Treaty Series 377

The Swiss Confederation; His Royal Highness the Grand Duke of Baden; His Majesty the King of the Belgians; His Majesty the King of Denmark; Her Majesty the Queen of Spain; His Majesty the Emperor of the French; His Royal Highness the Grand Duke of Hesse; HiS Majesty the King of Italy; His Majesty the King of the Netherlands; His Majesty the King of Portugal and of the Algarves; His Majesty the King of Prussia; His Majesty the King of Wiirtemberg, being equally animated with the desire to soften, as much as depends on them, the evils of warfare, to suppress its useless hardships and improve the fate of wounded soldiers on the field of battle, have resolved to conclude a convention to that effect, and have named for their plenipotentiaries, viz:

The Swiss Confederation:

Guillaume Henri Dufour, Grand Officer of the Imperial Order of the Legion of Honor, General in Chief of the federal army, Member of the Council of the States,

Gustave Moynier, President of the International Relief Committee for wounded soldiers and of the Geneva Society of Public Utility, and Samuel

Lehmann, federal Colonel, Doctor in Chief of the federal army, Member of the National Council;

His Royal Highness the Grand Duke of Baden:

Robert Volz, Knight of the Order of the Lion of Zrehringen, M. D., Medi-cal Councillor at the Direction of Medical Affairs, and Adolphe Steiner, Knight of the Order of the Lion of Zrehringen, Chief Staff Physician;

His Majesty the King of the Belgians:

Auguste Visschers, Officer of the Order of Leopold, Councillor at the Council of Mines;

His Majesty the King of Denmark:

Charles-Emile Fenger, Commander of the Order of Danebrog, decorated with the silver cross of the same Order, Grand Cross of the Order of Leopold of Belgium, etc. etc., His Councillor of State;

Her Majesty the Queen of Spain:

Don Jose Heriberto Garcia de Quevedo, Gentleman of Her Chamber on active service, Knight of the Grand Cross of Isabella the Catholic, Numerary Commander of the Order of Charles III, Knight of the first class of the Royal and Military Order of St. Ferdinand, Officer of the Legion of Honor of France, Her Minister Resident to the Swiss Confederation;

His Majesty the Emperor of the French:

Georges-Charles J agerschmidt, Officer of the Imperial Order of the Legion of Honor, Officer of the Order of Leopold of Belgium, Knight of the Order of the Red Eagle of Prussia of the third class, etc. etc., Sub-Director at the Ministry of Foreign Affairs;

Henri Eugene Seguineau de Preval, Knight of the Imperial Order of the Legion of Honor, decorated with the Imperial Order of the Medjidie of fourth class, Knight of the Order of Saints Maurice and Lazarus of Italy, etc. etc., military Sub-Commissioner of first class; and Martin Francois Boudier, Officer of the Imperial Order of the Legion of Honor, decorated with the Imperial Order of the Medjidie of the fourth class, decorated with the medal of Military Valor of Italy, etc. etc., doctor in chief of second class;

His Royal Highness the Grand Duke of Hesse:

Charles Auguste Brodruck, Knight of the Order of Philip the Magnanimous, of the Order of St. Michael of Bavaria, Officer of the Royal Order of the Holy Savior, etc., Chief of Battalion, Staff Officer;

His Majesty the King of Italy:

Jean Capello, Knight of the Order of Saints Maurice and Lazarus, His Consul General Switzerland, and Felix Baroffio, Knight of the Order of Saints Maurice and Lazarus, Doctor in Chief of medical division;

His Majesty the King of the Netherlands:

Bernard Ortuinus Theodore Henri Westenberg, Officer of His Order of the Crown of Oak, Knight of the Orders of Charles III of Spain, of the Crown of Prussia, of Adolphe of Nassau, L. D., His Secretary of Legation at Frankfort;

His Majesty the King of Portugal and of the Algarves:Jose Antonio Marques, Knight of the Order of Christ, of Our Lady of the Conception of Villa-Vi~osa, of Saint Benedict of Aviz, of Leopold of Belgium, etc., M. D., Surgeon of Brigade, Sub-Chief of the Department of Health at the Ministry of War;

His Majesty the King of Prussia:

Charles Albert de Kamptz, Knight of the Order of the Red. Eagle of second class, etc. etc. etc., His Envoy Extraordinary and Minister Plenipotentiary to the Swiss Confederation, Private Councillor of Legation,

Godefroi Frederic Fran~ois Lreffier, Knight of the Order of the Red Eagle of third class, etc. etc., M. D., Physician in Chief of the fourth Army Corps;

Georges Hermann Jules Ritter, Knight of the Order of the Crown of third class, etc. etc., Private Councillor at the Ministry of War;

His Majesty the King of Wiirtemberg:

Christophe Ulric Hahn, Knight of the Order of Saints Maurice and Lazarus, etc., Doctor of Philosophy and Theology, Member of the Central Royal Direction for Charitable Institutions:

Who, after having exchanged their powers, and found them in good and due form, agreed to the following articles:

Article 1

Ambulances and military hospitals shall be acknowledged to be neuter, and, as such, shall be protected and respected by belligerents so long as any sick or wounded may be therein.

Such neutrality shall cease if the ambulances or hospitals should be held by a military force.

Article 2

Persons employed in hospitals and ambulances, comprising the staff for superintendence, medical service, administration, transport of wounded, as well as chaplains, shall participate in the benefit of neutrality, whilst so employed, and so long as there remaln any wounded to bring in or to succor.

Article 3

The persons designated in the preceding article may, even after occupation by the enemy, continue to fulfil their duties in the hospital or ambulance which they serve, or may withdraw in order to rejoin the corps to which they belong.

Under such circumstances, when these persons shall cease from their functions, they shall be delivered by the occupying army to the outposts of the enemy.

Article 4

As the equipment of military hospitals remains subject to the laws of war, persons attached to such hospitals cannot, in withdrawing, carry away any articles but such as are their private property.

Under the same circumstances an ambulance shall, on the contrary, retain its equipment.

Article 5

Inhabitants of the country who may bring help to the wounded shall be respected, and shall remain free. The generals of the belligerent Powers shall make it their care to inform the inhabitants of the appeal addressed to their humanity, and of the neutrality which will be the consequence of it.

Any wounded man entertained and taken care of in a house shall be con-sidered as a protection thereto. Any inhabitant who shall have entertained wounded men in his house shall be exempted from the quartering of troops, as well as from a part of the contributions of war which may be imposed.

Article 6

Wounded or sick soldiers shall be entertained and taken care of, to whatever nation they may belong.

Commanders-in-chief shall have the power to deliver immediately to the outposts of the enemy soldiers who have been wounded in an engagement, when circumstances permit this to be done, and with the consent of both parties.

Those who are recognized, after their wounds are healed, as incapable of serving, shall be sent back to their country.

The others may also be sent back, on condition of not again bearing arms during the continuance of the war.

Evacuations, together with the persons under whose directions they take place, shall be protected by an absolute neutrality.

Article 7

A distinctive and uniform flag shall be adopted for hospitals, ambulances and evacuations. It must, on every occasion, be accompanied by the national flag. An arm-badge (brassard) shall also be allowed for individuals neutralized, but the delivery thereof shall be left to military authority.

The flag and the arm-badge shall bear a red cross on a white ground.

Article 8

The details of execution of the present convention shall be regulated by the commander-in-chief of belligerent armies, according to the instructions of their respective governments, and in conformity with the general principles laid down in this convention.

Article 9

The high contracting Powers have agreed to communicate the present convention to those Governments which have not found it convenient to send plenipotentiaries to the International Conference at Geneva, with an invitation to accede thereto; the protocol is for that purpose left open.

Article 10

The present convention shall be ratified, and the ratifications shall be exchanged at Berne, in four months, or sooner, if possible.

In faith whereof the respective Plenipotentiaries have signed it and have affixed their seals thereto.

Done at Geneva, the twenty-second day of the month of August of the year one thousand eight hundred and sixty-four.

6

UNITED NATIONS UNIVERSAL DECLARATION OF HUMAN RIGHTS 1948

Adopted and proclaimed by General Assembly resolution 217 A (III) of 10 December 1948

Preamble

Whereas recognition of the inherent dignity and of the equal and inalienable rights of all members of the human family is the foundation of freedom, justice and peace in the world,

Whereas recognition of the inherent dignity and of the equal and inalienable rights of all members of the human family is the foundation of freedom, justice and peace in the world,

Whereas disregard and contempt for human rights have resulted in barbarous acts which have outraged the conscience of mankind, and the advent of a world in which human beings shall enjoy freedom of speech and belief and freedom from fear and want has been proclaimed as the highest aspiration of the common people.

Whereas it is essential, if man is not to be compelled to have recourse, as a last resort, to rebellion against tyranny and oppression, that human rights should be protected by the rule of law,

Whereas it is essential to promote the development of friendly relations between nations, Whereas the peoples of the United Nations have in the Charter reaffirmed their faith in fundamental human rights, in the dignity and worth of the human person and in the equal rights of men and women and have determined to promote social progress and better standards of life in larger freedom,

Whereas Member States have pledged themselves to achieve, in co-operation with the United Nations, the promotion of universal respect for and observance of human rights and fundamental freedoms,

Whereas a common understanding of these rights and freedoms is of the greatest importance for the full realization of this pledge,

Now, Therefore,

THE GENERAL ASSEMBLY proclaims THIS UNIVERSAL DECLARATION OF HUMAN RIGHTS as a common standard of achievement for all peoples and all nations, to the end that every individual and every organ of society, keeping this Dec-laration constantly in mind, shall strive by teaching and education to promote respect for these rights and freedoms and by progressive measures, national and international, to secure their universal and effective recognition and observance, both among the peoples of Member States themselves and among the peoples of territories under their jurisdiction.

Article 1

All human beings are born free and equal in dignity and rights. They are endowed with reason and conscience and should act towards one another in a spirit of brotherhood.

Article 2

Everyone is entitled to all the rights and freedoms set forth in this Declaration, without distinction of any kind, such as race, colour, sex, language, religion, political or other opinion, national or social origin, property, birth or other status.

Furthermore, no distinction shall be made on the basis of the political, jurisdictional or international status of the country or territory to which a person belongs, whether it be independent, trust, non-self-governing or under any other limitation of sovereignty.

Article 3

Everyone has the right to life, liberty and security of person.

Article 4

No one shall be held in slavery or servitude; slavery and the slave trade shall be pro-hibited in all their forms.

Article 5

No one shall be subjected to torture or to cruel, inhuman or degrading treatment or punishment.

Article 6

Everyone has the right to recognition everywhere as a person before the law.

Article 7

All are equal before the law and are entitled without any discrimination to equal protec-tion of the law. All are entitled to equal protection against any discrimination in violation of this Declaration and against any incitement to such discrimination.

Article 8

Everyone has the right to an effective remedy by the competent national tribunals for acts violating the fundamental rights granted him by the constitution or by law.

Article 9

No one shall be subjected to arbitrary arrest, detention or exile.

Article 10

Everyone is entitled in full equality to a fair and public hearing by an independent and impartial tribunal, in the determination of his rights and obligations and of any criminal charge against him.

Article 11

1. Everyone charged with a penal offence has the right to be presumed innocent until proved guilty according to law in a public trial at which he has had all the guarantees necessary for his defence.

2. No one shall be held guilty of any penal offence on account of any act or omission which did not constitute a penal offence, under national or international law, at the time when it was committed. Nor shall a heavier penalty be imposed than the one that was applicable at the time the penal offence was committed.

Article 12

No one shall be subjected to arbitrary interference with his privacy, family, home or correspondence, nor to attacks upon his honour and reputation. Everyone has the right to the protection of the law against such interference or attacks.

Article 13

1. Everyone has the right to freedom of movement and residence within the borders of each state.

2. Everyone has the right to leave any country, including his own, and to return to his country.

Article 14

1. Everyone has the right to seek and to enjoy in other countries asylum from persecution.

2. This right may not be invoked in the case of prosecutions genuinely arising from non-political crimes or from acts contrary to the purposes and principles of the United Nations.

Article 15

1. Everyone has the right to a nationality.

2. No one shall be arbitrarily deprived of his nationality nor denied the right to change his nationality.

Article 16

1. Men and women of full age, without any limitation due to race, nationality or religion, have the right to marry and to found a family. They are entitled to equal rights as to marriage, during marriage and at its dissolution.

2. Marriage shall be entered into only with the free and full consent of the intending spouses.

3. The family is the natural and fundamental group unit of society and is entitled to protection by society and the State.

Article 17

1. Everyone has the right to own property alone as well as in association with others.

2. No one shall be arbitrarily deprived of his property.

Article 18

Everyone has the right to freedom of thought, conscience and religion; this right includes freedom to change his religion or belief, and freedom, either alone or in community with others and in public or private, to manifest his religion or belief in teaching, practice, worship and observance.

Article 19

Everyone has the right to freedom of opinion and expression; this right includes freedom to hold opinions without interference and to seek, receive and impart information and ideas through any media and regardless of frontiers.

Article 20

1. Everyone has the right to freedom of peaceful assembly and association.

2. No one may be compelled to belong to an association.

Article 21

1. Everyone has the right to take part in the government of his country, directly or through freely chosen representatives.

2. Everyone has the right of equal access to public service in his country.

3. The will of the people shall be the basis of the authority of government; this will shall be expressed in periodic and genuine elections which shall be by universal and equal suffrage and shall be held by secret vote or by equivalent free voting procedures.

Article 22

Everyone, as a member of society, has the right to social security and is entitled to realization, through national effort and international co-operation and in accordance with the organization and resources of each State, of the economic, social and cultural rights indispensable for his dignity and the free development of his personality.

Article 23

1. Everyone has the right to work, to free choice of employment, to just and favourable conditions of work and to protection against unemployment.

2. Everyone, without any discrimination, has the right to equal pay for equal work.

3. Everyone who works has the right to just and favourable remuneration ensuring for himself and his family an existence worthy of human dignity, and supplemented, if necessary, by other means of social protection.

4. Everyone has the right to form and to join trade unions for the protection of his interests.

Article 24

Everyone has the right to rest and leisure, including reasonable limitation of working hours and periodic holidays with pay.

Article 25

1. Everyone has the right to a standard of living adequate for the health and well being of himself and of his family, including food, clothing, housing and medical care and necessary social services, and the right to security in the event of unemployment, sickness, disability, widowhood, old age or other lack of livelihood in circumstances beyond his control.

2. Motherhood and childhood are entitled to special care and assistance. All children, whether born in or out of wedlock, shall enjoy the same social protection.

Article 26

1. Everyone has the right to education. Education shall be free, at least in the elementary and fundamental stages. Elementary education shall be compulsory. Technical and professional education shall be made generally available and higher education shall be equally accessible to all on the basis of merit.

2. Education shall be directed to the full development of the human

personality and to the strengthening of respect for human rights and fundamental freedoms. It shall promote understanding, tolerance and friendship among all nations, racial or religious groups, and shall further the activities of the United Nations for the maintenance of peace.

3. Parents have a prior right to choose the kind of education that shall be given to their children.

Article 27

1. Everyone has the right freely to participate in the cultural life of the community, to enjoy the arts and to share in scientific advancement and its benefits.

2. Everyone has the right to the protection of the moral and material interests resulting from any scientific, literary or artistic production of which he is the author.

Article 28

Everyone is entitled to a social and international order in which the rights and freedoms set forth in this Declaration can be fully realized.

Article 29

1. Everyone has duties to the community in which alone the free and full development of his personality is possible.

2. In the exercise of his rights and freedoms, everyone shall be subject only to such limitations as are determined by law solely for the purpose of securing due recognition and respect for the rights and freedoms of others and of meeting the just requirements of morality, public order and the general welfare in a democratic society.

3. These rights and freedoms may in no case be exercised contrary to the purposes and principles of the United Nations.

Article 30

Nothing in this Declaration may be interpreted as implying for any State, group or person any right to engage in any activity or to perform any act aimed at the destruction of any of the rights and freedoms set forth herein.

7

INTERNATIONAL COVENANT ON ECONOMIC, SOCIAL AND CULTURAL RIGHTS

Adopted and opened for signature, ratification and accession by General Assembly resolution 2200 A (XXI) of 16 December 1966

ENTRY INTO FORCE: 3 JANUARY 1976, IN ACCORDANCE WITH ARTICLE 27

PREAMBLE

The States Parties to the present Covenant,

Considering that, in accordance with the principles proclaimed in the Charter of the United Nations, recognition of the inherent dignity and of the equal and inalienable rights of all members of the human family is the foundation of freedom, justice and peace in the world,

Recognizing that these rights derive from the inherent dignity of the human person,

Recognizing that, in accordance with the Universal Declaration of Human Rights, the ideal of free human beings enjoying freedom from fear and want can only be achieved if conditions are created whereby everyone may enjoy his economic, social and cultural rights, as well as his civil and political rights,

Considering the obligation of States under the Charter of the United Nations to promote universal respect for, and observance of, human rights and freedoms,

Realizing that the individual, having duties to other individuals and to the community to which he belongs, is under a responsibility to strive for the promotion and observance of the rights recognized in the present Covenant,

Agree upon the following articles:

PART I

Article 1

1. All peoples have the right of self-determination. By virtue of that

right they freely determine their political status and freely pursue their economic, social and cultural development.

2. All peoples may, for their own ends, freely dispose of their natural wealth and resources without prejudice to any obligations arising out of international economic co-operation, based upon the principle of mutual benefit, and international law. In no case may a people be deprived of its own means of subsistence.

3. The States Parties to the present Covenant, including those having responsibility for the administration of Non-Self-Governing and Trust Territories, shall promote the realization of the right of self-determination, and shall respect that right, in conformity with the provisions of the Charter of the United Nations.

PART II

Article 2

1. Each State Party to the present Covenant undertakes to take steps, individually and through international assistance and co-operation, especially economic and technical, to the maximum of its available resources, with a view to achieving progressively the full realization of the rights recognized in the present Covenant by all appropriate means, including particularly the adoption of legislative measures.

2. The States Parties to the present Covenant undertake to guarantee that the rights enunciated in the present Covenant will be exercised without discrimination of any kind as to race, colour, sex, language, religion, political or other opinion, national or social origin, property, birth or other status.

3. Developing countries, with due regard to human rights and their national economy, may determine to what extent they would guarantee the economic rights recognized in the present Covenant to non-nationals.

Article 3

The States Parties to the present Covenant undertake to ensure the equal right of men and women to the enjoyment of all economic, social and cultural rights set forth in the present Covenant.

Article 4

The States Parties to the present Covenant recognize that, in the enjoyment of those rights provided by the State in conformity with the present Covenant, the State may subject such rights only to such limitations as are determined by law only in so far as this may be compatible with the nature of these rights and solely for the purpose of promoting the general welfare in a democratic society.

Article 5

1. Nothing in the present Covenant may be interpreted as implying for any State, group or person any right to engage in any activity or to perform any act aimed at the destruction of any of the rights or freedoms recognized herein, or at their limitation to a greater extent than is provided for in the present Covenant.

2. No restriction upon or derogation from any of the fundamental human rights recognized or existing in any country in virtue of law, conventions, regulations or custom shall be admitted on the pretext that the present Covenant does not recognize such rights or that it recognizes them to a lesser extent.

PART III

Article 6

1. The States Parties to the present Covenant recognize the right to work, which includes the right of everyone to the opportunity to gain his living by work which he freely chooses or accepts, and will take appropriate steps to safeguard this right.

2. The steps to be taken by a State Party to the present Covenant to achieve the full realization of this right shall include technical and vocational guidance and training programmes, policies and techniques to achieve steady economic, social and cultural development and full and productive employment under conditions safeguarding fundamental political and economic freedoms to the individual.

Article 7

The States Parties to the present Covenant recognize the right of everyone to the enjoyment of just and favourable conditions of work which ensure, in particular:

(*a*) Remuneration which provides all workers, as a minimum, with:

(i) Fair wages and equal remuneration for work of equal value without distinction of any kind, in particular women being guaranteed conditions of work not inferior to those enjoyed by men, with equal pay for equal work;

(ii) A decent living for themselves and their families in accordance with the provisions of the present Covenant;

(*b*) Safe and healthy working conditions;

(*c*) Equal opportunity for everyone to be promoted in his employment to an appropriate higher level, subject to no considerations other than those of seniority and competence;

(*d*) Rest, leisure and reasonable limitation of working hours and periodic holidays with pay, as well as remuneration for public holidays.

Article 8

1. The States Parties to the present Covenant undertake to ensure:

(*a*) The right of everyone to form trade unions and join the trade union of his choice, subject only to the rules of the organization concerned, for the promotion and protection of his economic and social interests. No restrictions may be placed on the exercise of this right other than those prescribed by law and which are necessary in a democratic society in the interests of national security or public order or for the protection of the rights and freedoms of others;

(*b*) The right of trade unions to establish national federations or confederations and the right of the latter to form or join international trade-union organizations;

(*c*) The right of trade unions to function freely subject to no limitations other than those prescribed by law and which are necessary in a democratic society in the interests of national security or public order or for the protection of the rights and freedoms of others;

(*d*) The right to strike, provided that it is exercised in conformity with the laws of the particular country.

2. This article shall not prevent the imposition of lawful restrictions on the exercise of these rights by members of the armed forces or of the police or of the administration of the State.

3. Nothing in this article shall authorize States Parties to the International Labour Organisation Convention of 1948 concerning Freedom of Association and Protection of the Right to Organise to take legislative measures which would prejudice, or apply the law in such a manner as would prejudice, the guarantees provided for in that Convention.

Article 9

The States Parties to the present Covenant recognize the right of everyone to social security, including social insurance.

Article 10

The States Parties to the present Covenant recognize that:

1. The widest possible protection and assistance should be accorded to the family, which is the natural and fundamental group unit of society, particularly for its establishment and while it is responsible for the care and education of dependent children. Marriage must be entered into with the free consent of the intending spouses.

2. Special protection should be accorded to mothers during a reasonable period before and after childbirth. During such period working mothers should be accorded paid leave or leave with adequate social security benefits.

3. Special measures of protection and assistance should be taken on behalf of all children and young persons without any discrimination for reasons of parentage or other conditions. Children and young persons should be protected from economic and social exploitation. Their employment in work harmful to their morals or health or dangerous to life or likely to hamper their normal development should be punishable by law. States should also set age limits below which the paid employment of child labour should be prohibited and punishable by law.

Article 11

1. The States Parties to the present Covenant recognize the right of

everyone to an adequate standard of living for himself and his family, including adequate food, clothing and housing, and to the continuous improvement of living conditions. The States Parties will take appropriate steps to ensure the realization of this right, recognizing to this effect the essential importance of international co-operation based on free consent.

2. The States Parties to the present Covenant, recognizing the fundamental right of everyone to be free from hunger, shall take, individually and through international co-operation, the measures, including specific programmes, which are needed:

(*a*) To improve methods of production, conservation and distribution of food by making full use of technical and scientific knowledge, by disseminating knowledge of the principles of nutrition and by developing or reforming agrarian systems in such a way as to achieve the most efficient development and utilization of natural resources;

(*b*) Taking into account the problems of both food-importing and food-exporting countries, to ensure an equitable distribution of world food supplies in relation to need.

Article 12

1. The States Parties to the present Covenant recognize the right of everyone to the enjoyment of the highest attainable standard of physical and mental health.

2. The steps to be taken by the States Parties to the present Covenant to achieve the full realization of this right shall include those necessary for:

(*a*) The provision for the reduction of the stillbirth-rate and of infant mortality and for the healthy development of the child;

(*b*) The improvement of all aspects of environmental and industrial hygiene;

(*c*) The prevention, treatment and control of epidemic, endemic, occupational and other diseases;

(*d*) The creation of conditions which would assure to all medical service and medical attention in the event of sickness.

Article 13

1. The States Parties to the present Covenant recognize the right of everyone to education. They agree that education shall be directed to the full development of the human personality and the sense of its dignity, and shall strengthen the respect for human rights and fundamental freedoms. They further agree that education shall enable all persons to participate effectively in a free society, promote understanding, tolerance and friendship among all nations and all racial, ethnic or religious groups, and further the activities of the United Nations for the maintenance of peace.

2. The States Parties to the present Covenant recognize that, with a view to achieving the full realization of this right:

(*a*) Primary education shall be compulsory and available free to all;

(*b*) Secondary education in its different forms, including technical and vocational secondary education, shall be made generally available and accessible to all by every appropriate means, and in particular by the progressive introduction of free education;

(*c*) Higher education shall be made equally accessible to all, on the basis of capacity, by every appropriate means, and in particular by the progressive introduction of free education;

(*d*) Fundamental education shall be encouraged or intensified as far as possible for those persons who have not received or completed the whole period of their primary education;

(*e*) The development of a system of schools at all levels shall be actively pursued, an adequate fellowship system shall be established, and the material conditions of teaching staff shall be continuously improved.

3. The States Parties to the present Covenant undertake to have respect for the liberty of parents and, when applicable, legal guardians to choose for their children schools, other than those established by the public authorities, which conform to such minimum educational standards as may be laid down or approved by the State and to ensure the religious and moral education of their children in conformity with their own convictions.

4. No part of this article shall be construed so as to interfere with the liberty of individuals and bodies to establish and direct educational institutions, subject always to the observance of the principles set forth in

paragraph 1 of this article and to the requirement that the education given in such institutions shall conform to such minimum standards as may be laid down by the State.

Article 14

Each State Party to the present Covenant which, at the time of becoming a Party, has not been able to secure in its metropolitan territory or other territories under its jurisdiction compulsory primary education, free of charge, undertakes, within two years, to work out and adopt a detailed plan of action for the progressive implementation, within a reasonable number of years, to be fixed in the plan, of the principle of compulsory education free of charge for all.

Article 15

1. The States Parties to the present Covenant recognize the right of everyone:

(*a*) To take part in cultural life;

(*b*) To enjoy the benefits of scientific progress and its applications;

(*c*) To benefit from the protection of the moral and material interests resulting from any scientific, literary or artistic production of which he is the author.

2. The steps to be taken by the States Parties to the present Covenant to achieve the full realization of this right shall include those necessary for the conservation, the development and the diffusion of science and culture.

3. The States Parties to the present Covenant undertake to respect the freedom indispensable for scientific research and creative activity.

4. The States Parties to the present Covenant recognize the benefits to be derived from the encouragement and development of international contacts and cooperation in the scientific and cultural fields.

PART IV

Article 16

1. The States Parties to the present Covenant undertake to submit in conformity with this part of the Covenant reports on the measures which

they have adopted and the progress made in achieving the observance of the rights recognized herein.

2. (*a*) All reports shall be submitted to the Secretary-General of the United Nations, who shall transmit copies to the Economic and Social Council for consideration in accordance with the provisions of the present Covenant;

(*b*) The Secretary-General of the United Nations shall also transmit to the specialized agencies copies of the reports, or any relevant parts therefrom, from States Parties to the present Covenant which are also members of these specialized agencies in so far as these reports, or parts therefrom, relate to any matters which fall within the responsibilities of the said agencies in accordance with their constitutional instruments.

Article 17

1. The States Parties to the present Covenant shall furnish their reports in stages, in accordance with a programme to be established by the Economic and Social Council within one year of the entry into force of the present Covenant after consultation with the States Parties and the specialized agencies concerned.

2. Reports may indicate factors and difficulties affecting the degree of fulfillment of obligations under the present Covenant.

3. Where relevant information has previously been furnished to the United Nations or to any specialized agency by any State Party to the present Covenant, it will not be necessary to reproduce that information, but a precise reference to the information so furnished will suffice.

Article 18

Pursuant to its responsibilities under the Charter of the United Nations in the field of human rights and fundamental freedoms, the Economic and Social Council may make arrangements with the specialized agencies in respect of their reporting to it on the progress made in achieving the observance of the provisions of the present Covenant falling within the scope of their activities. These reports may include particulars of decisions and recommendations on such implementation adopted by their competent organs.

Article 19

The Economic and Social Council may transmit to the Commission on Human Rights for study and general recommendation or, as appropriate, for information the reports concerning human rights submitted by States in accordance with articles 16 and 17, and those concerning human rights submitted by the specialized agencies in accordance with article 18.

Article 20

The States Parties to the present Covenant and the specialized agencies concerned may submit comments to the Economic and Social Council on any general recommendation under article 19 or reference to such general recommendation in any report of the Commission on Human Rights or any documentation referred to therein.

Article 21

The Economic and Social Council may submit from time to time to the General Assembly reports with recommendations of a general nature and a summary of the information received from the States Parties to the present Covenant and the specialized agencies on the measures taken and the progress made in achieving general observance of the rights recognized in the present Covenant.

Article 22

The Economic and Social Council may bring to the attention of other organs of the United Nations, their subsidiary organs and specialized agencies concerned with furnishing technical assistance any matters arising out of the reports referred to in this part of the present Covenant which may assist such bodies in deciding, each within its field of competence, on the advisability of international measures likely to contribute to the effective progressive implementation of the present Covenant.

Article 23

The States Parties to the present Covenant agree that international action for the achievement of the rights recognized in the present Covenant includes such methods as the conclusion of conventions, the adoption of recommendations, the furnishing of technical assistance and the holding of regional meetings and technical meetings for the purpose of consultation and study organized in conjunction with the Governments concerned.

Article 24

Nothing in the present Covenant shall be interpreted as impairing the provisions of the Charter of the United Nations and of the constitutions of the specialized agencies which define the respective responsibilities of the various organs of the United Nations and of the specialized agencies in regard to the matters dealt with in the present Covenant.

Article 25

Nothing in the present Covenant shall be interpreted as impairing the inherent right of all peoples to enjoy and utilize fully and freely their natural wealth and resources.

PART V

Article 26

1. The present Covenant is open for signature by any State Member of the United Nations or member of any of its specialized agencies, by any State Party to the Statute of the International Court of Justice, and by any other State which has been invited by the General Assembly of the United Nations to become a party to the present Covenant.

2. The present Covenant is subject to ratification. Instruments of ratification shall be deposited with the Secretary-General of the United Nations.

3. The present Covenant shall be open to accession by any State referred to in paragraph 1 of this article.

4. Accession shall be effected by the deposit of an instrument of accession with the Secretary-General of the United Nations.

5. The Secretary-General of the United Nations shall inform all States which have signed the present Covenant or acceded to it of the deposit of each instrument of ratification or accession.

Article 27

1. The present Covenant shall enter into force three months after the date of the deposit with the Secretary-General of the United Nations of the thirty-fifth instrument of ratification or instrument of accession.

2. For each State ratifying the present Covenant or acceding to it after the deposit of the thirty-fifth instrument of ratification or instrument of accession, the present Covenant shall enter into force three months after the date of the deposit of its own instrument of ratification or instrument of accession.

Article 28

The provisions of the present Covenant shall extend to all parts of federal States without any limitations or exceptions.

Article 29

1. Any State Party to the present Covenant may propose an amendment and file it with the Secretary-General of the United Nations. The Secretary-General shall thereupon communicate any proposed amendments to the States Parties to the present Covenant with a request that they notify him whether they favour a conference of States Parties for the purpose of considering and voting upon the proposals.

In the event that at least one third of the States Parties favours such a conference, the Secretary-General shall convene the conference under the auspices of the United Nations. Any amendment adopted by a majority of the States Parties present and voting at the conference shall be submitted to the General Assembly of the United Nations for approval.

2. Amendments shall come into force when they have been approved by the General Assembly of the United Nations and accepted by a two-thirds majority of the States Parties to the present Covenant in accordance with their respective constitutional processes.

3. When amendments come into force they shall be binding on those States Parties which have accepted them, other States Parties still being bound by the provisions of the present Covenant and any earlier amendment which they have accepted.

Article 30

Irrespective of the notifications made under article 26, paragraph 5, the Secretary-General of the United Nations shall inform all States referred to in paragraph 1 of the same article of the following particulars:

(*a*) Signatures, ratifications and accessions under article 26;

(*b*) The date of the entry into force of the present Covenant under article 27 and the date of the entry into force of any amendments under article 29.

Article 31

1. The present Covenant, of which the Chinese, English, French, Russian and Spanish texts are equally authentic, shall be deposited in the archives of the United Nations.

2. The Secretary-General of the United Nations shall transmit certified copies of the present Covenant to all States referred to in article 26.

8

INTERNATIONAL COVENANT ON CIVIL AND POLITICAL RIGHTS

Adopted and opened for signature, ratification and accession byGeneral Assembly resolution 2200 A (XXI) of 16 December 1966

ENTRY INTO FORCE: 23 MARCH 1976, IN ACCORDANCE WITH ARTICLE 49

PREAMBLE

The States Parties to the present Covenant,

Considering that, in accordance with the principles proclaimed in the Charter of the United Nations, recognition of the inherent dignity and of the equal and inalienable rights of all members of the human family is the foundation of freedom, justice and peace in the world,

Recognizing that these rights derive from the inherent dignity of the human person,

Recognizing that, in accordance with the Universal Declaration of Human Rights, the ideal of free human beings enjoying civil and political freedom and freedom from fear and want can only be achieved if conditions are created whereby everyone may enjoy his civil and political rights, as well as his economic, social and cultural rights,

Considering the obligation of States under the Charter of the United Nations to promote universal respect for, and observance of, human rights and freedoms,

Realizing that the individual, having duties to other individuals and to the community to which he belongs, is under a responsibility to strive for the promotion and observance of the rights recognized in the present Covenant,

Agree upon the following articles:

PART I

Article 1

1. All peoples have the right of self-determination. By virtue of that right they freely determine their political status and freely pursue their economic, social and cultural development.

2. All peoples may, for their own ends, freely dispose of their natural wealth and resources without prejudice to any obligations arising out of international economic co-operation, based upon the principle of mutual benefit, and international law. In no case may a people be deprived of its own means of subsistence.

3. The States Parties to the present Covenant, including those having responsibility for the administration of Non-Self-Governing and Trust Territories, shall promote the realization of the right of self-determination, and shall respect that right, in conformity with the provisions of the Charter of the United Nations.

PART II

Article 2

1. Each State Party to the present Covenant undertakes to respect and to ensure to all individuals within its territory and subject to its jurisdiction the rights recognized in the present Covenant, without distinction of any kind, such as race, colour, sex, language, religion, political or other opinion, national or social origin, property, birth or other status.

2. Where not already provided for by existing legislative or other measures, each State Party to the present Covenant undertakes to take the necessary steps, in accordance with its constitutional processes and with the provisions of the present Covenant, to adopt such legislative or other measures as may be necessary to give effect to the rights recognized in the present Covenant.

3. Each State Party to the present Covenant undertakes:

(*a*) To ensure that any person whose rights or freedoms as herein recognized are violated shall have an effective remedy, notwithstanding that the violation has been committed by persons acting in an official capacity;

(*b*) To ensure that any person claiming such a remedy shall have his right thereto determined by competent judicial, administrative or legislative authorities, or by any other competent authority provided for by the legal system of the State, and to develop the possibilities of judicial remedy;

(*c*) To ensure that the competent authorities shall enforce such remedies when granted.

Article 3

The States Parties to the present Covenant undertake to ensure the equal right of men and women to the enjoyment of all civil and political rights set forth in the present Covenant.

Article 4

1. In time of public emergency which threatens the life of the nation and the existence of which is officially proclaimed, the States Parties to the present Covenant may take measures derogating from their obligations under the present Covenant to the extent strictly required by the exigencies of the situation, provided that such measures are not inconsistent with their other obligations under international law and do not involve discrimination solely on the ground of race, colour, sex, language, religion or social origin.

2. No derogation from articles 6, 7, 8 (paragraphs 1 and 2), 11, 15, 16 and 18 may be made under this provision.

3. Any State Party to the present Covenant availing itself of the right of derogation shall immediately inform the other States Parties to the present Covenant, through the intermediary of the Secretary-General of the United Nations, of the provisions from which it has derogated and of the reasons by which it was actuated. A further communication shall be made, through the same intermediary, on the date on which it terminates such derogation.

Article 5

1. Nothing in the present Covenant may be interpreted as implying for any State, group or person any right to engage in any activity or perform any act aimed at the destruction of any of the rights and freedoms recognized

herein or at their limitation to a greater extent than is provided for in the present Covenant.

2. There shall be no restriction upon or derogation from any of the fundamental human rights recognized or existing in any State Party to the present Covenant pursuant to law, conventions, regulations or custom on the pretext that the present Covenant does not recognize such rights or that it recognizes them to a lesser extent.

PART III

Article 6

1. Every human being has the inherent right to life. This right shall be protected by law. No one shall be arbitrarily deprived of his life.

2. In countries which have not abolished the death penalty, sentence of death may be imposed only for the most serious crimes in accordance with the law in force at the time of the commission of the crime and not contrary to the provisions of the present Covenant and to the Convention on the Prevention and Punishment of the Crime of Genocide. This penalty can only be carried out pursuant to a final judgement rendered by a competent court.

3. When deprivation of life constitutes the crime of genocide, it is understood that nothing in this article shall authorize any State Party to the present Covenant to derogate in any way from any obligation assumed under the provisions of the Convention on the Prevention and Punishment of the Crime of Genocide.

4. Anyone sentenced to death shall have the right to seek pardon or commutation of the sentence. Amnesty, pardon or commutation of the sentence of death may be granted in all cases.

5. Sentence of death shall not be imposed for crimes committed by persons below eighteen years of age and shall not be carried out on pregnant women.

6. Nothing in this article shall be invoked to delay or to prevent the abolition of capital punishment by any State Party to the present Covenant.

Article 7

No one shall be subjected to torture or to cruel, inhuman or degrading treatment or punishment. In particular, no one shall be subjected without his free consent to medical or scientific experimentation.

Article 8

1. No one shall be held in slavery; slavery and the slave-trade in all their forms shall be prohibited.

2. No one shall be held in servitude.

3. (*a*) No one shall be required to perform forced or compulsory labour;

(*b*) Paragraph 3 (*a*) shall not be held to preclude, in countries where imprisonment with hard labour may be imposed as a punishment for a crime, the performance of hard labour in pursuance of a sentence to such punishment by a competent court;

(*c*) For the purpose of this paragraph the term "forced or compulsory labour" shall not include:

(i) Any work or service, not referred to in subparagraph (b), normally required of a person who is under detention in consequence of a lawful order of a court, or of a person during conditional release from such detention;

(ii) Any service of a military character and, in countries where conscientious objection is recognized, any national service required by law of conscientious objectors;

(iii) Any service exacted in cases of emergency or calamity threatening the life or well-being of the community;

(iv) Any work or service which forms part of normal civil obligations.

Article 9

1. Everyone has the right to liberty and security of person. No one shall be subjected to arbitrary arrest or detention. No one shall be deprived of his liberty except on such grounds and in accordance with such procedure as are established by law.

2. Anyone who is arrested shall be informed, at the time of arrest, of the reasons for his arrest and shall be promptly informed of any charges against him.

3. Anyone arrested or detained on a criminal charge shall be brought

promptly before a judge or other officer authorized by law to exercise judicial power and shall be entitled to trial within a reasonable time or to release. It shall not be the general rule that persons awaiting trial shall be detained in custody, but release may be subject to guarantees to appear for trial, at any other stage of the judicial proceedings, and, should occasion arise, for execution of the judgement.

4. Anyone who is deprived of his liberty by arrest or detention shall be entitled to take proceedings before a court, in order that that court may decide without delay on the lawfulness of his detention and order his release if the detention is not lawful.

5. Anyone who has been the victim of unlawful arrest or detention shall have an enforceable right to compensation.

Article 10

1. All persons deprived of their liberty shall be treated with humanity and with respect for the inherent dignity of the human person.

2. (*a*) Accused persons shall, save in exceptional circumstances, be segregated from convicted persons and shall be subject to separate treatment appropriate to their status as unconvicted persons;

(*b*) Accused juvenile persons shall be separated from adults and brought as speedily as possible for adjudication.

3. The penitentiary system shall comprise treatment of prisoners the essential aim of which shall be their reformation and social rehabilitation. Juvenile offenders shall be segregated from adults and be accorded treatment appropriate to their age and legal status.

Article 11

No one shall be imprisoned merely on the ground of inability to fulfil a contractual obligation.

Article 12

1. Everyone lawfully within the territory of a State shall, within that territory, have the right to liberty of movement and freedom to choose his residence.

2. Everyone shall be free to leave any country, including his own.

3. The above-mentioned rights shall not be subject to any restrictions except those which are provided by law, are necessary to protect national security, public order (*ordre public*), public health or morals or the rights and freedoms of others, and are consistent with the other rights recognized in the present Covenant.

4. No one shall be arbitrarily deprived of the right to enter his own country.

Article 13

An alien lawfully in the territory of a State Party to the present Covenant may be expelled therefrom only in pursuance of a decision reached in accordance with law and shall, except where compelling reasons of national security otherwise require, be allowed to submit the reasons against his expulsion and to have his case reviewed by, and be represented for the purpose before, the competent authority or a person or persons especially designated by the competent authority.

Article 14

1. All persons shall be equal before the courts and tribunals. In the determination of any criminal charge against him, or of his rights and obligations in a suit at law, everyone shall be entitled to a fair and public hearing by a competent, independent and impartial tribunal established by law. The press and the public may be excluded from all or part of a trial for reasons of morals, public order (*ordre public*) or national security in a democratic society, or when the interest of the private lives of the parties so requires, or to the extent strictly necessary in the opinion of the court in special circumstances where publicity would prejudice the interests of justice; but any judgement rendered in a criminal case or in a suit at law shall be made public except where the interest of juvenile persons otherwise requires or the proceedings concern matrimonial disputes or the guardianship of children.

2. Everyone charged with a criminal offence shall have the right to be presumed innocent until proved guilty according to law.

3. In the determination of any criminal charge against him, everyone shall be entitled to the following minimum guarantees, in full equality:

(*a*) To be informed promptly and in detail in a language which he understands of the nature and cause of the charge against him;

(*b*) To have adequate time and facilities for the preparation of his defence and to communicate with counsel of his own choosing;

(*c*) To be tried without undue delay;

(*d*) To be tried in his presence, and to defend himself in person or through legal assistance of his own choosing; to be informed, if he does not have legal assistance, of this right; and to have legal assistance assigned to him, in any case where the interests of justice so require, and without payment by him in any such case if he does not have sufficient means to pay for it;

(*e*) To examine, or have examined, the witnesses against him and to obtain the attendance and examination of witnesses on his behalf under the same conditions as witnesses against him;

(*f*) To have the free assistance of an interpreter if he cannot understand or speak the language used in court;

(*g*) Not to be compelled to testify against himself or to confess guilt.

4. In the case of juvenile persons, the procedure shall be such as will take account of their age and the desirability of promoting their rehabilitation.

5. Everyone convicted of a crime shall have the right to his conviction and sentence being reviewed by a higher tribunal according to law.

6. When a person has by a final decision been convicted of a criminal offence and when subsequently his conviction has been reversed or he has been pardoned on the ground that a new or newly discovered fact shows conclusively that there has been a miscarriage of justice, the person who has suffered punishment as a result of such conviction shall be compensated according to law, unless it is proved that the non-disclosure of the unknown fact in time is wholly or partly attributable to him.

7. No one shall be liable to be tried or punished again for an offence for which he has already been finally convicted or acquitted in accordance with the law and penal procedure of each country.

Article 15

1. No one shall be held guilty of any criminal offence on account of

any act or omission which did not constitute a criminal offence, under national or international law, at the time when it was committed. Nor shall a heavier penalty be imposed than the one that was applicable at the time when the criminal offence was committed. If, subsequent to the commission of the offence, provision is made by law for the imposition of the lighter penalty, the offender shall benefit thereby.

2. Nothing in this article shall prejudice the trial and punishment of any person for any act or omission which, at the time when it was committed, was criminal according to the general principles of law recognized by the community of nations.

Article 16

Everyone shall have the right to recognition everywhere as a person before the law.

Article 17

1. No one shall be subjected to arbitrary or unlawful interference with his privacy, family, home or correspondence, nor to unlawful attacks on his honour and reputation.

2. Everyone has the right to the protection of the law against such interference or attacks.

Article 18

1. Everyone shall have the right to freedom of thought, conscience and religion. This right shall include freedom to have or to adopt a religion or belief of his choice, and freedom, either individually or in community with others and in public or private, to manifest his religion or belief in worship, observance, practice and teaching.

2. No one shall be subject to coercion which would impair his freedom to have or to adopt a religion or belief of his choice.

3. Freedom to manifest one's religion or beliefs may be subject only to such limitations as are prescribed by law and are necessary to protect public safety, order, health, or morals or the fundamental rights and freedoms of others.

4. The States Parties to the present Covenant undertake to have respect

for the liberty of parents and, when applicable, legal guardians to ensure the religious and moral education of their children in conformity with their own convictions.

Article 19

1. Everyone shall have the right to hold opinions without interference.

2. Everyone shall have the right to freedom of expression; this right shall include freedom to seek, receive and impart information and ideas of all kinds, regardless of frontiers, either orally, in writing or in print, in the form of art, or through any other media of his choice.

3. The exercise of the rights provided for in paragraph 2 of this article carries with it special duties and responsibilities. It may therefore be subject to certain restrictions, but these shall only be such as are provided by law and are necessary:

(*a*) For respect of the rights or reputations of others;

(*b*) For the protection of national security or of public order, or of public health or morals.

Article 20

1. Any propaganda for war shall be prohibited by law.

2. Any advocacy of national, racial or religious hatred that constitutes incitement to discrimination, hostility or violence shall be prohibited by law.

Article 21

The right of peaceful assembly shall be recognized. No restrictions may be placed on the exercise of this right other than those imposed in conformity with the law and which are necessary in a democratic society in the interests of national security or public safety, public order (*ordre public*), the protection of public health or morals or the protection of the rights and freedoms of others.

Article 22

1. Everyone shall have the right to freedom of association with others, including the right to form and join trade unions for the protection of his interests.

2. No restrictions may be placed on the exercise of this right other than those which are prescribed by law and which are necessary in a democratic society in the interests of national security or public safety, public order (*ordre public*), the protection of public health or morals or the protection of the rights and freedoms of others. This article shall not prevent the imposition of lawful restrictions on members of the armed forces and of the police in their exercise of this right.

3. Nothing in this article shall authorize States Parties to the International Labour Organisation Convention of 1948 concerning Freedom of Association and Protection of the Right to Organise to take legislative measures which would prejudice, or to apply the law in such a manner as to prejudice, the guarantees provided for in that Convention.

Article 23

1. The family is the natural and fundamental group unit of society and is entitled to protection by society and the State.

2. The right of men and women of marriageable age to marry and to found a family shall be recognized.

3. No marriage shall be entered into without the free and full consent of the intending spouses.

4. States Parties to the present Covenant shall take appropriate steps to ensure equality of rights and responsibilities of spouses as to marriage, during marriage and at its dissolution. In the case of dissolution, provision shall be made for the necessary protection of any children.

Article 24

1. Every child shall have, without any discrimination as to race, colour, sex, language, religion, national or social origin, property or birth, the right to such measures of protection as are required by his status as a minor, on the part of his family, society and the State.

2. Every child shall be registered immediately after birth and shall have a name.

3. Every child has the right to acquire a nationality.

Article 25

Every citizen shall have the right and the opportunity, without any of the distinctions mentioned in article 2 and without unreasonable restrictions:

(*a*) To take part in the conduct of public affairs, directly or through freely chosen representatives;

(*b*) To vote and to be elected at genuine periodic elections which shall be by universal and equal suffrage and shall be held by secret ballot, guaranteeing the free expression of the will of the electors;

(*c*) To have access, on general terms of equality, to public service in his country.

Article 26

All persons are equal before the law and are entitled without any discrimination to the equal protection of the law. In this respect, the law shall prohibit any discrimination and guarantee to all persons equal and effective protection against discrimination on any ground such as race, colour, sex, language, religion, political or other opinion, national or social origin, property, birth or other status.

Article 27

In those States in which ethnic, religious or linguistic minorities exist, persons belonging to such minorities shall not be denied the right, in community with the other members of their group, to enjoy their own culture, to profess and practice their own religion, or to use their own language.

PART IV

Article 28

1. There shall be established a Human Rights Committee (hereafter referred to in the present Covenant as the Committee). It shall consist of eighteen members and shall carry out the functions hereinafter provided.

2. The Committee shall be composed of nationals of the States Parties to the present Covenant who shall be persons of high moral character and recognized competence in the field of human rights, consideration being given to the usefulness of the participation of some persons having legal experience.

3. The members of the Committee shall be elected and shall serve in their personal capacity.

Article 29

1 . The members of the Committee shall be elected by secret ballot from a list of persons possessing the qualifications prescribed in article 28 and nominated for the purpose by the States Parties to the present Covenant.

2. Each State Party to the present Covenant may nominate not more than two persons. These persons shall be nationals of the nominating State.

3. A person shall be eligible for renomination.

Article 30

1. The initial election shall be held no later than six months after the date of the entry into force of the present Covenant.

2. At least four months before the date of each election to the Committee, other than an election to fill a vacancy declared in accordance with article 34, the Secretary-General of the United Nations shall address a written invitation to the States Parties to the present Covenant to submit their nominations for membership of the Committee within three months.

3. The Secretary-General of the United Nations shall prepare a list in alphabetical order of all the persons thus nominated, with an indication of the States Parties which have nominated them, and shall submit it to the States Parties to the present Covenant no later than one month before the date of each election.

4. Elections of the members of the Committee shall be held at a meeting of the States Parties to the present Covenant convened by the Secretary-General of the United Nations at the Headquarters of the United Nations. At that meeting, for which two thirds of the States Parties to the present Covenant shall constitute a quorum, the persons elected to the Committee shall be those nominees who obtain the largest number of votes and an absolute majority of the votes of the representatives of States Parties present and voting.

Article 31

1. The Committee may not include more than one national of the same State.

2. In the election of the Committee, consideration shall be given to equitable geographical distribution of membership and to the representation of the different forms of civilization and of the principal legal systems.

Article 32

1. The members of the Committee shall be elected for a term of four years. They shall be eligible for re-election if renominated. However, the terms of nine of the members elected at the first election shall expire at the end of two years; immediately after the first election, the names of these nine members shall be chosen by lot by the Chairman of the meeting referred to in article 30, paragraph 4.

2. Elections at the expiry of office shall be held in accordance with the preceding articles of this part of the present Covenant.

Article 33

1. If, in the unanimous opinion of the other members, a member of the Committee has ceased to carry out his functions for any cause other than absence of a temporary character, the Chairman of the Committee shall notify the Secretary-General of the United Nations, who shall then declare the seat of that member to be vacant.

2. In the event of the death or the resignation of a member of the Committee, the Chairman shall immediately notify the Secretary-General of the United Nations, who shall declare the seat vacant from the date of death or the date on which the resignation takes effect.

Article 34

1. When a vacancy is declared in accordance with article 33 and if the term of office of the member to be replaced does not expire within six months of the declaration of the vacancy, the Secretary-General of the United Nations shall notify each of the States Parties to the present Covenant, which may within two months submit nominations in accordance with article 29 for the purpose of filling the vacancy.

2. The Secretary-General of the United Nations shall prepare a list in alphabetical order of the persons thus nominated and shall submit it to the States Parties to the present Covenant. The election to fill the vacancy

shall then take place in accordance with the relevant provisions of this part of the present Covenant.

3. A member of the Committee elected to fill a vacancy declared in accordance with article 33 shall hold office for the remainder of the term of the member who vacated the seat on the Committee under the provisions of that article.

Article 35

The members of the Committee shall, with the approval of the General Assembly of the United Nations, receive emoluments from United Nations resources on such terms and conditions as the General Assembly may decide, having regard to the importance of the Committee's responsibilities.

Article 36

The Secretary-General of the United Nations shall provide the necessary staff and facilities for the effective performance of the functions of the Committee under the present Covenant.

Article 37

1. The Secretary-General of the United Nations shall convene the initial meeting of the Committee at the Headquarters of the United Nations.

2. After its initial meeting, the Committee shall meet at such times as shall be provided in its rules of procedure.

3. The Committee shall normally meet at the Headquarters of the United Nations or at the United Nations Office at Geneva.

Article 38

Every member of the Committee shall, before taking up his duties, make a solemn declaration in open committee that he will perform his functions impartially and conscientiously.

Article 39

1. The Committee shall elect its officers for a term of two years. They may be re-elected.

2. The Committee shall establish its own rules of procedure, but these rules shall provide, *inter alia*, that:

(*a*) Twelve members shall constitute a quorum;

(*b*) Decisions of the Committee shall be made by a majority vote of the members present.

Article 40

1. The States Parties to the present Covenant undertake to submit reports on the measures they have adopted which give effect to the rights recognized herein and on the progress made in the enjoyment of those rights:

(*a*) Within one year of the entry into force of the present Covenant for the States Parties concerned;

(*b*) Thereafter whenever the Committee so requests.

2. All reports shall be submitted to the Secretary-General of the United Nations, who shall transmit them to the Committee for consideration. Reports shall indicate the factors and difficulties, if any, affecting the implementation of the present Covenant.

3. The Secretary-General of the United Nations may, after consultation with the Committee, transmit to the specialized agencies concerned copies of such parts of the reports as may fall within their field of competence.

4. The Committee shall study the reports submitted by the States Parties to the present Covenant. It shall transmit its reports, and such general comments as it may consider appropriate, to the States Parties. The Committee may also transmit to the Economic and Social Council these comments along with the copies of the reports it has received from States Parties to the present Covenant.

5. The States Parties to the present Covenant may submit to the Committee observations on any comments that may be made in accordance with paragraph 4 of this article.

Article 41

1. A State Party to the present Covenant may at any time declare under this article that it recognizes the competence of the Committee to receive

and consider communications to the effect that a State Party claims that another State Party is not fulfilling its obligations under the present Covenant. Communications under this article may be received and considered only if submitted by a State Party which has made a declaration recognizing in regard to itself the competence of the Committee. No communication shall be received by the Committee if it concerns a State Party which has not made such a declaration. Communications received under this article shall be dealt with in accordance with the following procedure:

(*a*) If a State Party to the present Covenant considers that another State Party is not giving effect to the provisions of the present Covenant, it may, by written communication, bring the matter to the attention of that State Party. Within three months after the receipt of the communication the receiving State shall afford the State which sent the communication an explanation, or any other statement in writing clarifying the matter which should include, to the extent possible and pertinent, reference to domestic procedures and remedies taken, pending, or available in the matter;

(*b*) If the matter is not adjusted to the satisfaction of both States Parties concerned within six months after the receipt by the receiving State of the initial communication, either State shall have the right to refer the matter to the Committee, by notice given to the Committee and to the other State;

(*c*) The Committee shall deal with a matter referred to it only after it has ascertained that all available domestic remedies have been invoked and exhausted in the matter, in conformity with the generally recognized principles of international law. This shall not be the rule where the application of the remedies is unreasonably prolonged;

(*d*) The Committee shall hold closed meetings when examining communications under this article;

(*e*) Subject to the provisions of subparagraph (*c*), the Committee shall make available its good offices to the States Parties concerned with a view to a friendly solution of the matter on the basis of respect for human rights and fundamental freedoms as recognized in the present Covenant;

(*f*) In any matter referred to it, the Committee may call upon the States Parties concerned, referred to in subparagraph (*b*), to supply any relevant information;

(*g*) The States Parties concerned, referred to in subparagraph (*b*), shall have the right to be represented when the matter is being considered in the Committee and to make submissions orally and/or in writing;

(*h*) The Committee shall, within twelve months after the date of receipt of notice under subparagraph (*b*), submit a report:

(*i*) (i) If a solution within the terms of subparagraph (*e*) is reached, the Committee shall confine its report to a brief statement of the facts and of the solution reached;

(ii) If a solution within the terms of subparagraph (*e*) is not reached, the Committee shall confine its report to a brief statement of the facts; the written submissions and record of the oral submissions made by the States Parties concerned shall be attached to the report.

In every matter, the report shall be communicated to the States Parties concerned.

2. The provisions of this article shall come into force when ten States Parties to the present Covenant have made declarations under paragraph 1 of this article. Such declarations shall be deposited by the States Parties with the Secretary-General of the United Nations, who shall transmit copies thereof to the other States Parties. A declaration may be withdrawn at any time by notification to the Secretary-

General. Such a withdrawal shall not prejudice the consideration of any matter which is the subject of a communication already transmitted under this article; no further communication by any State Party shall be received after the notification of withdrawal of the declaration has been received by the Secretary-General, unless the State Party concerned has made a new declaration.

Article 42

1. (*a*) If a matter referred to the Committee in accordance with article 41 is not resolved to the satisfaction of the States Parties concerned, the Committee may, with the prior consent of the States Parties concerned,

appoint an *ad hoc* Conciliation Commission (hereinafter referred to as the Commission). The good offices of the Commission shall be made available to the States Parties concerned with a view to an amicable solution of the matter on the basis of respect for the present Covenant;

(*b*) The Commission shall consist of five persons acceptable to the States Parties concerned. If the States Parties concerned fail to reach agreement within three months on all or part of the composition of the Commission, the members of the Commission concerning whom no agreement has been reached shall be elected by secret ballot by a two-thirds majority vote of the Committee from among its members.

2. The members of the Commission shall serve in their personal capacity. They shall not be nationals of the States Parties concerned, or of a State not Party to the present Covenant, or of a State Party which has not made a declaration under article 41.

3. The Commission shall elect its own Chairman and adopt its own rules of procedure.

4. The meetings of the Commission shall normally be held at the Headquarters of the United Nations or at the United Nations Office at Geneva. However, they may be held at such other convenient places as the Commission may determine in consultation with the Secretary-General of the United Nations and the States Parties concerned.

5. The secretariat provided in accordance with article 36 shall also service the commissions appointed under this article.

6. The information received and collated by the Committee shall be made available to the Commission and the Commission may call upon the States Parties concerned to supply any other relevant information.

7. When the Commission has fully considered the matter, but in any event not later than twelve months after having been seized of the matter, it shall submit to the Chairman of the Committee a report for communication to the States Parties concerned:

(*a*) If the Commission is unable to complete its consideration of the matter within twelve months, it shall confine its report to a brief statement of the status of its consideration of the matter;

(*b*) If an amicable solution to the matter on tie basis of respect for human rights as recognized in the present Covenant is reached, the Commission shall confine its report to a brief statement of the facts and of the solution reached;

(*c*) If a solution within the terms of subparagraph (*b*) is not reached, the Commission's report shall embody its findings on all questions of fact relevant to the issues between the States Parties concerned, and its views on the possibilities of an amicable solution of the matter. This report shall also contain the written submissions and a record of the oral submissions made by the States Parties concerned;

(*d*) If the Commission's report is submitted under subparagraph (*c*), the States Parties concerned shall, within three months of the receipt of the report, notify the Chairman of the Committee whether or not they accept the contents of the report of the Commission.

8. The provisions of this article are without prejudice to the responsibilities of the Committee under article 41.

9. The States Parties concerned shall share equally all the expenses of the members of the Commission in accordance with estimates to be provided by the Secretary-General of the United Nations.

10. The Secretary-General of the United Nations shall be empowered to pay the expenses of the members of the Commission, if necessary, before reimbursement by the States Parties concerned, in accordance with paragraph 9 of this article.

Article 43

The members of the Committee, and of the *ad hoc* conciliation commissions which may be appointed under article 42, shall be entitled to the facilities, privileges and immunities of experts on mission for the United Nations as laid down in the relevant sections of the Convention on the Privileges and Immunities of the United Nations.

Article 44

The provisions for the implementation of the present Covenant shall apply without prejudice to the procedures prescribed in the field of human rights by or under the constituent instruments and the conventions of the United Nations and of the specialized agencies and shall not prevent the States Parties to the present Covenant from having recourse to other procedures for settling a dispute in accordance with general or special international agreements in force between them.

Article 45

The Committee shall submit to the General Assembly of the United Nations, through the Economic and Social Council, an annual report on its activities.

PART V

Article 46

Nothing in the present Covenant shall be interpreted as impairing the provisions of the Charter of the United Nations and of the constitutions of the specialized agencies which define the respective responsibilities of the various organs of the United Nations and of the specialized agencies in regard to the matters dealt with in the present Covenant.

Article 47

Nothing in the present Covenant shall be interpreted as impairing the inherent right of all peoples to enjoy and utilize fully and freely their natural wealth and resources.

PART VI

Article 48

1. The present Covenant is open for signature by any State Member of the United Nations or member of any of its specialized agencies, by any State Party to the Statute of the International Court of Justice, and by any other State which has been invited by the General Assembly of the United Nations to become a Party to the present Covenant.

2. The present Covenant is subject to ratification. Instruments of ratification shall be deposited with the Secretary-General of the United Nations.

3. The present Covenant shall be open to accession by any State referred to in paragraph 1 of this article.

4. Accession shall be effected by the deposit of an instrument of accession with the Secretary-General of the United Nations.

5. The Secretary-General of the United Nations shall inform all States which have signed this Covenant or acceded to it of the deposit of each instrument of ratification or accession.

Article 49

1. The present Covenant shall enter into force three months after the date of the deposit with the Secretary-General of the United Nations of the thirty-fifth instrument of ratification or instrument of accession.

2. For each State ratifying the present Covenant or acceding to it after the deposit of the thirty-fifth instrument of ratification or instrument of accession, the present Covenant shall enter into force three months after the date of the deposit of its own instrument of ratification or instrument of accession.

Article 50

The provisions of the present Covenant shall extend to all parts of federal States without any limitations or exceptions.

Article 51

1. Any State Party to the present Covenant may propose an amendment and file it with the Secretary-General of the United Nations. The Secretary-General of the United Nations shall thereupon communicate any proposed amendments to the States Parties to the present Covenant with a request that they notify him whether they favour a conference of States Parties for the purpose of considering and voting upon the proposals. In the event that at least one third of the States Parties favours such a conference, the Secretary-General shall convene the conference under the auspices of the United Nations. Any amendment adopted by a majority of the States Parties present and voting at the conference shall be submitted to the General Assembly of the United Nations for approval.

2. Amendments shall come into force when they have been approved

by the General Assembly of the United Nations and accepted by a two-thirds majority of the States Parties to the present Covenant in accordance with their respective constitutional processes.

3. When amendments come into force, they shall be binding on those States Parties which have accepted them, other States Parties still being bound by the provisions of the present Covenant and any earlier amendment which they have accepted.

Article 52

Irrespective of the notifications made under article 48, paragraph 5, the Secretary-General of the United Nations shall inform all States referred to in paragraph 1 of the same article of the following particulars:

(*a*) Signatures, ratifications and accessions under article 48;

(*b*) The date of the entry into force of the present Covenant under article 49 and the date of the entry into force of any amendments under article 51.

Article 53

1. The present Covenant, of which the Chinese, English, French, Russian and Spanish texts are equally authentic, shall be deposited in the archives of the United Nations.

2. The Secretary-General of the United Nations shall transmit certified copies of the present Covenant to all States referred to in article 48.

Bibliography

Ackerman, Bruce, 1980. *Social Justice in the Liberal State*. New Haven: Yale University Press.

Al-Ahsan, Abdullah, 2009. "Law, Religion and Human Dignity in the Muslim World Today: An Examination of OIC's Cairo Declaration of Human Rights", *Journal of Law and Religion*, 24: 569-597.

Alston, P. and Crawford, J. (eds.), 2000. *The Future of UN Human Rights Treaty Monitoring*. Cambridge: Cambridge University Press.

Alston, P. and Goodman, R. (eds.), 2013. *International Human Rights*. Oxford: Oxford University Press.

Alston, P., 1999. *Promoting Human Rights through Bills of Rights*. Oxford: Oxford University Press.

Anaya, S., 2004. *Indigenous Peoples in International Law*. Oxford: Oxford University Press.

Aristotle, 1893. *The Nichomachean Ethics*, trans. F.H. Peters. London: Kegan Paul, Trench, Truebner & Co.

Bailey, S., 1994. *The UN Security Council and Human Rights*. New York: St. Martin's Press.

Baker, J., 1994. *Group Rights*. Toronto: University of Toronto Press.

Barber, Benjamin 2003 [1984]. *Strong Democracy: Participatory Politics for a New Age*. California: University of California Press.

Baxi, Upendra, 2007. *Human Rights in a Posthuman World: Critical Essays*. New Delhi: Oxford University Press.

Baxi, Upendra, 2008 [2002]. *The Future of Human Rights*, Third Edition. New Delhi: Oxford University Press.

Bayefsky, Anne, 2001. *The UN Human Rights Treaty System: Universality at the Crossroads*, Ardsley, NY: Transnational.

BBC, 2011. "Four in Five Regard Internet Access as a Fundamental Right: Global Poll" (PDF), BBC News. Retrieved December 15.

Beetham, D., 1995. "What Future for Economic and Social Rights?", *Political Studies*, 43: 41-60.

Beitz, C., 2009. *The Idea of Human Rights*. Oxford: Oxford University Press.

Bentham, Jeremy, 1843. Anarchical Fallacies. Edinburgh.

Bentham, *Jeremy,* 1987. "Anarchical Fallacies", in Jeremy Waldron (ed.), *Nonsense upon Stilts: Bentham, Burke and Marx on the Rights of Man*. London: Methuen.

Beyleveld, D., 1991. *Dialectical Necessity of Morality: An Analysis and Defense of Alan Gewirth's Argument to the Principle of Generic Consistency*. Chicago: University of Chicago Press.

Boerefijn, I., 1999. *The Reporting Procedure under the Covenant on Civil and Political Rights: Practice and Procedures of the Human Rights Committee*. Antwerp: Intersea; Oxford: Hart Pub.

Boylan, M. (ed.), 1999. *Gewirth: Critical Essays on Action, Rationality, and Community.* Lanham, MD: Rowman and Littlefield.

Branco, Manuel Couret, 2009. *Economics versus Human Rights.* London: Routledge

Brandt, R. B., 1983. "The Concept of a Moral Right," *Journal of Philosophy*, 80: 29–45.

Brems, E., 2009. "Human Rights: Minimum and Maximum Perspectives," *Human Rights Law Review*, 9: 343–372.

Broomhall, B., 2003. *International Justice and the International Criminal Court.* Oxford: Oxford University Press.

Brownlee, K., 2013. "A Human Right against Social Deprivation," *Philosophical Quarterly*, 63: 251, 199–222.

Buchanan, A., 2010. *Human Rights, Legitimacy, and the Use of Force*. Oxford: Oxford University Press.

Buchanan, A., 2013. *The Heart of Human Rights*. Oxford: Oxford University Press.

Bunch, C., 2006. "Women's Rights as Human Rights, " in B. Lockwood (ed.), *Women's Rights: A Human Rights Quarterly Reader*. Baltimore: Johns Hopkins University Press.

Cameron, I., 2004. "Jurisdiction and Admissibility Issues under the ICC Statute," in D. McGoldrick *et al*, (eds.) *The Permanent International Criminal Court.* Oxford: Hart Publishing.

Campbell, T., 1983. *The Left and Rights*. London: Routledge & Kegan Paul.

Carlyle, A. J., 1903. *A History of Medieval Political Theory in the West*. 1. Edinburgh.

Carlyle, R. W. and A. J. Carlyle, 1903. *A History of Medieval Political Theory in the West*. Edinburgh and London: W. Blackwood and Sons.

Carroll, Lewis, 1871. *Through the Looking-Glass, and What Alice Found There*. London: Macmillan.

Cassirer, Ernst. 1963. *The Myth of the State*. New Haven: Yale University Press.

Claude, R. and Weston, B. (eds.), 2006. *Human Rights in the World Community*, 3rd edn. Philadelphia: University of Pennsylvania Press.

Cohen, Jean, 2012. *Globalization and Sovereignty*. Cambridge: Cambridge University Press.

Cohen, Joshua, 2004."Minimalism about Human Rights: The Most We Can Hope For?", *Journal of Political Philosophy*, 12: 90–213.

Corradetti, C. (ed.), 2012. *Philosophical Dimensions of Human Rights.* New York: Springer.

Corradetti, C. 2009. *Relativism and Human Rights*, New York: Springer.

Cranston, Maurice, 1962. *Human Rights Today*. London: Ampersand.

Cranston, Maurice, 1967. "Human Rights, Real and Supposed," in D. D. Raphael (ed.), *Political Theory and the Rights of Man*. London: Macmillan.

Cranston, Maurice, 1973. *What Are Human Rights?*, London: Bodley Head.

Cruft, R., 2012. "Human Rights as Rights," in Ernst, G. and Heilinger, J. (eds.), 2011. *The Philosophy of Human Rights: Contemporary Controversies*. Berlin: Walter de Gruyter.

Cruft. R., Liao, S., and Renzo, M. (eds.), 2015. *Philosophical Foundations of Human Rights.* Oxford: Oxford University Press.

Davidson, S., 1997. *The Inter-American Human Rights System*. Aldershot: Dartmouth.

Dershowitz, A., 2004. *Rights from Wrongs: A Secular Theory of the Origins of Rights*. New York: Basic Books.

Donnelly, J., 2012. *International Human Rights*, 4th edn., Philadelphia: Westview Press.

Donnelly, J., 2013. *Universal Human Rights in Theory and Practice*, 3rd edn. Ithaca, NY and London: Cornell University Press.

Dworkin, R., 1978. *Taking Rights Seriously*. Harvard: Harvard Univ. Press.

Dworkin, R., 2011. *Justice for Hedgehogs*. Harvard: Harvard University Press.

Dworkin, Ronald, 1981. "What Is Equality?", *Philosophy and Public Affairs*, 10 (3):185-246.

Eide, A. *et al.* (eds.), 1992. *The Universal Declaration of Human Rights: A Commentary*. Norway: Scandanavian University Press.

Ernst, G. and Heilinger, J. (eds.), 2011. *The Philosophy of Human Rights: Contemporary Controversies*. Berlin: De Gruyter.

Etinson, A. (ed.), 2015. *Human Rights: Moral or Political?*. Oxford: Oxford University Press.

Evans, G., 2008. *The Responsibility to Protect*. Washington, DC: Brookings Institution.

Evans, M. and Murray, R. (eds.), 2011. *The African Charter on Human and People's Rights*, 2nd edn. Cambridge: Cambridge University Press.

Farer, T., 1997. "The Rise of the Inter-American Human Rights Regime", *Human Rights Quarterly*, 19: 510–546.

Feinberg, J., 1973. *Social Philosophy*. Englewood Cliffs, NJ: Prentice-Hall.

Finnis, John, 2011. *Natural Law & Natural Rights*. Oxford: Oxford University Press.

Freeman, Michael, 2002. *Human rights: An interdisciplinary approach*. Cambridge: Polity Press.

Fromm, Erich, 1973. *The Revolution of Hope: Toward a Humanized Technology*. New York: Bantam.

Gardiner, S., 2013. "Human Rights in a Hostile Climate," in Holder C, and Reidy, D. (eds.), 2013. *Human Rights: The Hard Questions*, pp. 211–230. Cambridge: Cambridge University Press.

Garry Wills, 1979. *Inventing America*. New York: Vintage Books.

Gewirth, A., 1978. *Reason and Morality*, Chicago: University of Chicago Press.

Gewirth, A., 1982. *Human Rights*. Chicago: University of Chicago Press.

Gewirth, A., 1982. *Human Rights: Essays on Justification and Applications*. Chicago: University of Chicago Press.

Gewirth, A., 1996. *The Community of Rights*. Chicago: University of Chicago Press.

Gilabert, P. 2011. "Humanist and Political Perspectives on Human Rights," *Political Theory*, 39: 439–467.

Glendon, M., 2001. *A World Made New: Eleanor Roosevelt and the Universal Declaration of Human Rights*. New York: Random House.

Glendon, Mary Ann, 2004. "The Rule of Law in the Universal Declaration of Human Rights", *Northwestern University Journal of International Human Rights. 2: 5.*

Gould, C., 2004. *Globalizing Democracy and Human Rights.* Cambridge: Cambridge University Press.

Green, Thomas Hill, 1895. *Lectures on the Principles of Political Obligation*. New Jersey: The Lawbook Exchange.

Griffin, J., 2008. *On Human Rights*. Oxford: Oxford University Press.

Gutmann, Amy, 1993. "The challenge of multiculturalism in political ethics", *Philosophy and Public Affairs*, 22 (3): 171-206.

Hampshire, Stuart 1989. *Innocence and Experience*. St Ives: Penguin.

Hart, H.L.A., 1995. "Are There Any Natural Rights?", *Philosophical Review* 64: 175-91.

Harvey, Ray Forrest (1937). *Jean Jacques Burlamaqui: A Liberal Tradition in American Constitutionalism*. Chapel Hill, N.C.

Hathaway, O., 2005. "The Promise and Limits of the International Law of Torture," in O. Hathaway and H. Koh (eds.), *Foundations of International Law and Politics*. New York: Foundation Press.

Hayden, P. (ed.), 2001. *The Philosophy of Human Rights*. St. Paul, MN: Paragon Press.

Hayward, T., 2005. *Constitutional Environmental Rights.* Oxford: Oxford University Press.

Hegel, Georg W. F., 1967 [1821]. *Hegel's Philosophy of Right*. T.M. Knox, trans., New York: Oxford University Press.

Henkin, L. 1978. *The Rights of Man Today*. Boulder, CO: Westview Press.

Henkin, L., Neuman, G., Orentlicher, D. and Leebron, D. (eds.), 2009. *Human Rights*, 2nd end. New York: Foundation Press.

Henrard, K., 2000. *Devising an Adequate System of Minority Protection*. The Hague: Martinus Nijhoff.

Hobhouse, L.T., 1922. *The Elements of Social Justice*. London: Allen & Unwin. pp. 62-63.

Hodgson, D., 1998. *The Human Right to Education*. Aldershot, England: Ashgate Publishing.

Hoffmann, Stefan-Ludwig 2010. *Human Rights in the Twentieth Century*. Cambridge University Press.

Holder C, and Reidy, D. (eds.), 2013. *Human Rights: The Hard Questions*. Cambridge: Cambridge University Press.

Holmes, S. and Sunstein, C., 1999. *The Cost of Rights: Why Liberty Depends on Taxes*. New York: Norton.

Horwitz, Morton, 1979. *The Transformation of American Law*. Cambridge, MA: Harvard University Press.

Howard, R., 1987. "The Full-Belly Thesis: Should Economic Rights Take Priority over Civil and Political Rights?" *Human Rights Quarterly*, 5: 467–90.

Hutcheson, Francis. 2004 [1725]. *An Inquiry into the Original of Our Ideas of Beauty and Virtue*. Ann Arbor: University of Michigan.

Hutcheson, Francis. 1755. *A System of Moral Philosophy*. Indianapolis: Indiana University.

Ignatieff, M., 2004. *The Lesser Evil*. Princeton: Princeton University Press.

Jacobs, F. and White, R., 2010. *The European Convention on Human Rights*, 5th edn., Oxford: Clarendon Press.

Janis, M., Kay, R., and Bradley, A. (eds.), 2008. *European Human Rights Law: Texts and Materials*. Oxford: Oxford University Press.

Jones, Peter, 1994. *Rights*. Palgrave Macmillan.

Joseph, S., Schultz, J.,and Castan, M. (eds.), 2013. *The International Covenant on Civil and Political Rights: Cases, Materials, and Commentary*, 3rd edn. New York: Oxford University Press.

Kamminga, M., 1992. *Inter-State Accountability for Violations of Human Rights*. Philadelphia: University of Pennsylvania Press.

Kateb, G., 2011. *Human Dignity*. Cambridge, MA: Harvard University Press

Kennedy, D., 2004. *The Dark Sides of Virtue: Reassessing International Humanitarianism*. Princeton: Princeton University Press.

King, J., 2012. *Judging Social Rights*. Cambridge: Cambridge University Press.

Kinley, David, 2009. *Civilising Globalisation: Human Rights and the Global Economy*. Cambridge: Cambridge University Press.

Korey, W., 1998. *NGOs and the Universal Declaration of Human Rights*. New York: St. Martin's.

Kundera, Milan, 1991. *Immorality*. London: Faber.

Kymlicka, W., (ed.), 1995. *The Rights of Minority Cultures*. Oxford: Oxford University Press.

Kymlicka, W., 1989. *Liberalism, Community, and Culture*. Oxford: Clarendon Press.

Langford, M. et.al. (eds.), 2013. *The Millenium Development Goals and Human Rights*. Cambridge: Cambridge University Press.

Lauren, P., 2003. *The Evolution of International Human Rights*, 2nd end.. Philadelphia: University of Pennsylvania Press.

Liao, M. and Etinson, A., 2012. "Political and Naturalistic Conceptions of Human Rights: A False Polemic?", *Journal of Moral Philosophy*, 9: 327–352.

Locke, J., 1689. *The Second Treatise on Civil Government*. New York: Prometheus Books, 1986.

Lockwood, B. (ed.), 2006. *Women's Rights: A Human Rights Quarterly Reader*. Baltimore: Johns Hopkins University Press

Lukes, S., 1993. "Five fables about human rights", in S. Shute and S. Hurley (eds.), *On Human Rights: The Oxford Amnesty Lectures*. New York: Basic.

Luther, Martin, 1523. *On Secular Authority*. Cambridge: Cambridge University Press

Lynd, Staughton, 1969. *Intellectual Origins of American Radicalism*. New York: Vintage Books.

Maclntyre, A., 1981. *After Virtue*. London: Duckworth.

Maier, Pauline, 1993. *American Scripture: Making the Declaration of Independence*. New York: Alfred A. Knopf.

Mandela, Nelson, 1994. *Long Walk to Freedom*. Boston: Little Brown & Co

Marx, Karl, 1987. "On the Jewish Question", in Jeremy Waldron (ed.),

Nonsense upon Stilts: Bentham, Burke and Marx on the Rights of Man. London: Methuen.

McGoldrick, D. *et al.* (eds.), 2004. *The Permanent International Criminal Court*. Oxford: Hart Publishing.

McIlwain, Charles H., 1932. *The Growth of Political Thought in the West: From the Greeks to the End of the Middle Ages*. New York: University of Michigan.

Morsink, J., 1999. *Universal Declaration of Human Rights: Origins, Drafting, and Intent*. Philadelphia: University of Pennsylvania Press.

Moyn, S., 2010. *The Last Utopia: Human Rights in History*. Cambridge, MA: Harvard University Press.

Moyn, Samuel, 2010. "Human Rights in History: Human rights emerged not in the 1940s but the 1970s, and on the ruins of prior dreams", *The Nation*, August 30/September 6, Retrieved 8 July 2017.

Nickel, J. 2007. *Making Sense of Human Rights*, 2nd edn. Malden, MA: Blackwell Publishing.

Nickel, J. 2008. "Rethinking Indivisibility: Towards a Theory of Supporting Relations between Human Rights," *Human Rights Quarterly*, 30: 984–1001 .

Nickel, J. 2013. "Goals and Rights—Working Together?", in M. Langford, et al., *The MDGs and Human Rights: Past, Present, and Future*. Cambridge: Cambridge University Press.

Nickel, J., 1993. "The Human Right to a Safe Environment," *Yale Journal of International Law*, 18: 281–295.

Nozick, R., 1974. *Anarchy, State, and Utopia*. New York: Basic Books.

Nussbaum, M., 2000. *Women and Human Development: The Capabilities Approach*. Cambridge, MA: Harvard University Press.

Nussbaum, M., 2007. *Frontiers of Justice*. Cambridge, MA: Harvard University Press.

O'Neill, Onora, 1989. "Children's rights and children's lives" in Onora O'Neill, *Constructions of Reason*. Cambridge: Cambridge University Press.

OHCHR 1951. *"Convention relating to the Status of Refugees",* Available at: http://www.ohchr.org/EN/ProfessionalInterest/Pages/StatusOfRefugees.aspx, Retrieved September 29, 2015.

Okin, S., 1998. "Feminism, Women's Human Rights, and Cultural Differences," *Hypatia*, 13: 32–52.

O'Neill, O, 2005. "The Dark Side of Human Rights", *International Affairs*, 81: 427-439.

O'Neill, O., 1986. *Faces of Hunger: An Essay on Poverty, Development and* Justice. London: Allen and Unwin.

Orend, B., 2002. *Human Rights: Concept and Context*, Peterborough, Ont.: Broadview Press.

Pangle, Thomas L., (1988). *The Spirit of Modern Republicanism: The Moral Vision of the American Founders and the Philosophy of John Locke.* Chicago: University of Chicago Press.

Parekh, Serena, 2008. *Hannah Arendt and the Challenges of Modernity: Phenomenology and Human Rights*. New York and London: Routledge.

Plant, R., 1988. "Needs, Agency, and Welfare Rights", in Donald Moon (ed.) *Responsibility, Rights and Welfare*. Boulder, Colo: Westview.

Plant, Raymond, 1991. *Modern Political Thought*. Oxford: Blackwell.

Pogge, T., 2000. "The International Significance of Human Rights,"*Journal of Ethics*, 4: 45–69.

Pogge, T., 2002. *World Poverty and Human Rights: Cosmopolitan Responsibilities and Reforms*. Cambridge: Polity Press.

Price, Richard, 1979 [1776]. *Observations on the Nature of Civil Liberty.* Part I. Reprinted in: Peach, Bernard, (Ed.) *Richard Price and the Ethical Foundations of the American Revolution*. Duke University Press.

Ramcharan, B., (ed.) 2005. *The Protection Role of National Human Rights Institutions*. Leiden: Martinus Nijhoff.

Ramcharan, B., 2002. *The Security Council and the Protection of Human Rights*. The Hague: Martinus Nijhoff.

Rawls, J., 1971. *A Theory of Justice*. Cambridge, MA: Harvard University Press.

Rawls, J., 1999. *The Law of Peoples*. Cambridge, MA: Harvard University Press.

Raz, J., 2010. "Human Rights without Foundations" in Besson, S., and Tasioulas, J. (eds.), *The Philosophy of International Law*. Oxford: Oxford University Press.

Reid, John Phillip, 1987. *Constitutional History of the American Revolution: The Authority to Tax*. Madison, Wisconsin: University of Wisconsin Press.

Sandel, Michael, 1982. *Liberalism and the Limits of Justice*. New York: Cambridge University Press.

Schabas, W., 2011. *An Introduction to the International Criminal Court*, 4th edn. Cambridge: Cambridge University Press.

Shapiro, Ian, 1986. *The Evolution of Rights in Liberal Theory*. Cambridge: Cambridge University Press.

Shue, H., 1996. *Basic Rights*, Second edition. Princeton: Princeton University Press.

Sigler, J., 1983. *Minority Rights*. Westport, CT: Greenwood Press.

Sumner, L., 1987. *The Moral Foundation of Rights*. Oxford: Clarendon Press.

Sumner, W., 1906. *Folkways: A Study of the Sociological Importance of Usages, Manners, Customs, Mores, and Morals*. Boston: Ginn and Co.

Talbott, W., 2005. *Which Rights Should be Universal?*. Oxford: Oxford University Press.

Tannehill, Linda and Morris Tannehill, 1993 [1970]. *The Market for Liberty: Is Government Really Necessary?*, Third Edition. San Francisco, California: Fox & Wilkes.

Tasioulas, John, 2011. "On the Nature of Human Rights," in Ernst, G. and Heilinger, J. (eds.), *The Philosophy of Human Rights: Contemporary Controversies*. Berlin: Walter de Gruyter.

Tasioulas, John, 2013. "Human Rights, Legitimacy, and International Law," *American Journal of Jurisprudence* 58: 1–25.

Tasioulas, John, 2009. "Are Human Rights Essentially Triggers for Intervention?', *Philosophy Compass*, 4(6): 938-50.

Teson, F., 2005. *Humanitarian Intervention: An Inquiry into Law and Morality*. Ardsley, NY: Transnational.

Thomson, J., 1990. *The Realm of Rights*, Cambridge. MA: Harvard University Press.

Tierney, B., 1997. *The Idea of Natural Rights*, Grand Rapids. MI: Wm. B. Erdmans Publishing Co.

Tuck, W., 1979. *Natural Rights Theories: Their Origin and Development*. Cambridge: Cambridge University Press.

Tucker, Benjamin Ricketson, 1897. *Instead of a Book*. New York: B.R. Tucker.

Turnbull, George, 1742. *Observations Upon Liberal Education, In All Its Branches: In Three Parts*. Indiana: Indiana University.

Tushnet, Mark, 1981. *The American Law of Slavery*. Princeton: Princeton University Press.

Unger, Roberto, 1975. *Knowledge and Politics*. New York: Macmillan.

Van Dervort, T., (ed.), 1987. *Nonsense Upon Stilts: Bentham, Burke and Marx on the Rights of Man*. London: Methuen.

Van Dervort, T., 1993. *Liberal Rights*. Cambridge: Cambridge University Press.

Van Dervort, T., 1997. *International Law and Organization*. Thousand Oaks, CA: Sage Publications.

Van Dervort, T., 2002. *God, Locke, and Equality: Christian Foundations in Locke's Political Thought*. Cambridge: Cambridge University Press.

Waldron, Jeremy (ed.), 1987. *Nonsense upon Stilts: Bentham, Burke and Marx on the Rights of Man*. London: Methuen.

Wellman, C., 1982. *Welfare Rights*. Totowa. N.J: Rowman & Allanheld.

Wellman, C., 1995. *Real Rights*. New York: Oxford University Press.

Wellman, C., 1998. *The Proliferation of Rights: Moral Progress or Empty Rhetoric?*. Boulder, CO: Westview Press.

Wellman, C., 2010. *The Moral Dimensions of Human Rights*. Oxford: Oxford University Press

Wills, Garry, 1979. *Inventing America*. New York: Vintage Books.

Wilson, James, 2007. *The Collected Works of James Wilson*. Cambridge: Harvard University Press.

Wolterstorff, N., 2008. *Justice: Rights and Wrongs*. Princeton: Princeton University Press.

Zuckert, Michael P., 1996. *The Natural Rights Republic: Studies in the Foundation of the American Political Tradition*. South Bend, Ind.: University of Notre Dame Press.

Zuckert, Michael P., 1998. *Natural Rights and the New Republicanism*. Princeton: Princeton University Press.

Zuckert, Michael P., 2002. *Launching Liberalism: On Lockean Political Philosophy*. Lawrence: University Press of Kansas.

Index